ISHMAEL MY B

ISHMAEL MY BROTHER

A Biblical Course on Islam

Anne Cooper, *Course compiler*

MARC Europe
MARC International
STL Books
Evangelical Missionary Alliance

STL Books are published by Send The Light (Operation Mobilisation), PO Box 48, Bromley, Kent, England.

The Evangelical Missionary Alliance is a fellowship of evangelical missionary societies, agencies and training colleges that are committed to world mission. Its aims are to encourage cooperation and provide coordination between member societies and colleges, and to assist local churches to fulfil their role in world mission. The EMA offices are at Whitefield House, 186 Kennington Park Road, London SE11 4BT.

MARC Europe is an integral part of World Vision, an international Christian humanitarian organisation. MARC's object is to assist Christian leaders with factual information, surveys, management skills, strategic planning and other tools for evangelism. We also publish and distribute related books on mission, church growth, management, spiritual maturity and other topics.

MARC International, a ministry of World Vision International, is based at 919 W. Huntingdon Drive, Monrovia, California 91016, USA.

US Library of Congress No 85-52294

British Library Cataloguing in Publication Data
Ishmael my brother : a Biblical course on Islam.
  1. Islam—Relations—Christianity
  2. Christianity and other religions—Islam
  I. Cooper, Anne
  297   BP172

ISBN 0–947697–12–8 MARC Europe
ISBN 0–912552–47–6 MARC International
ISBN 0–947697–17-9 EMA
ISBN 1–85078–004–8 STL

COURSE OUTLINE

INTRODUCTION

The title of this book is a reminder that both Christians and Muslims look back to Abraham as father. In Genesis chapter 17, we read of the covenant God made with Abraham, to be passed on to his son Isaac. We read (verse 18) of how Abraham prayed, 'If only Ishmael might live under your blessing!' God answered that prayer by saying,

> And as for Ishmael, I have heard you: I will surely bless him; I will make him fruitful and greatly increase his numbers. He will be the father of twelve rulers, and I will make him into a great nation.
> But my covenant I will establish with Isaac...
> (Genesis 17:20–21).

So Islam and Christianity have common roots. The aim of this course book is to bridge some of the rifts which have increased over time and to prepare Christians to be able to explain their understanding of the covenant promise. As Badru Kateregga and David Shenk write in their book *Islam and Christianity*, 'We both recognise the faith of Abraham and seek to understand and live in accordance with the faith which he exercised.'[1]

The children of Ishmael have certainly been fruitful and their numbers have greatly increased, and are still increasing. Islam has some 850 million adherents. This means that out of every 11 people in the world, two are Muslim. In the past, Muslims have lived almost exclusively in Muslim countries. Now, through migrations, there are more than six million in western Europe, more than one million in Britain, and two and a half million in the United States, where Islam is now the third largest religious group. Even more significant, perhaps, are the millions living in eastern Europe and central Asia, where there is practically no

Christian witness to Muslims at all.

Over the last 20 years oil has been found in many Muslim areas. This has given Islam new confidence and new power as Islamic countries produce, control, and price much of the world's oil supply. This economic power has gone hand in hand with the resurgence of a more militant, fundamentalist expression of Islam.

Although Muhammad seems to have known and learnt from both Jews and Christians, hostility began when they did not accept his teaching or his prophethood. Since then, exacerbated by historical events like the Crusades and later European colonial rule, the rifts have grown deeper. Today, the fear, misunderstanding, and hostility between the two religions is described by Bishop Kenneth Cragg, using a Nigerian term, as 'avoidance relations'.

This course in no way minimises the deep doctrinal differences between Christianity and Islam. It does, however, try to dispel some of the barriers and prejudices which negate the fostering of personal relationships and exclude a real understanding of each other's faith.

Christian witness to the Muslim world has been weak both numerically and theologically, with the few outstanding missionaries lacking the support that they needed for a significant breakthrough. Few Muslims have a clear idea of the teaching of Christ, or of the good news of salvation through him. It is our prayer that this book will be used to help those of us who are in contact with Muslims to present a biblical view and to share our faith with them.

As we look out on the Muslim world and get to know Muslims personally, we cannot but feel the need for increased prayer. This must be our first priority. we are reminded how Abraham prayed for Ishmael, and we know that there have been Christians praying faithfully down through the years. One such group is the Fellowship of Faith for the Muslims, a prayer fellowship which, for the last 70 years, has linked those with a burden to pray for Muslims and has tried to increase Christian understanding of Islam.

To end this introduction and to start the course appropriately here is a prayer of Samuel Zwemer, adapted by Ronald Waine, one of our course team and the present Chairman of FFM. You may like to use this prayer as you study the course.

A prayer for the Muslim world today:

> *Almighty God, our heavenly Father, you have made of*

one blood all nations, and promised that many shall come to sit down with Abraham in your kingdom. We pray for your more than eight hundred million people in Muslim lands who are still far off, that they might be brought near by the blood of Christ. Look upon them in pity because they are without understanding of your truth. Take away blindness of heart, and reveal to them the surpassing beauty and power of your Son Jesus Christ. Convince them of their sin and pride in rejecting the sacrifice of the only Saviour. Give courage to those who love you that they may boldly confess your name. Equip your messengers in Muslim lands with the power of the Holy Spirit that they may demonstrate the loveliness and tenderness of the Lord Jesus Christ. Make bare your arm O God and show your power.

Father, the hour has come; glorify your Son in the Muslim world, and fulfil through him the prayer of Abraham your friend, 'Oh that Ishmael might live before you.' For Jesus' sake, Amen.

Note

1 KATEREGGA, Badru, and SHENK, David. *Islam and Christianity: A Dialogue*, Eerdmans, Grand Rapids, Michigan, 1980, p169.

COURSE STUDY GUIDE

Welcome to this home study course! Although we may never meet, we hope that a helpful relationship will be built up between you, as you study, and our course team. This book is essentially a team effort. We have met many times to discuss the material and to pray about it. We have shared together and have contributed to one another's chapters. For this reason you will find that the names of the writers are mentioned in the course study guides, but not elsewhere. I do want, however, to mention the name of the Revd Colin Chapman at this point. For much of the time the work has been in progress he has been our consultant and has done a great deal to improve the material in the course. His book, *You Go and Do the Same*, is one of the key books for the course. It is the recommended book for Chapter 7 and is quoted in a number of the other chapters. I also want to thank Sharon Wylie, who put the first draft on to a word processor, and Sara Townsend, who has done an enormous amount of work in putting the revisions and additions on to a word processor and in editing them. Elsie Maxwell has compiled the Arabic glossary, and we are grateful to her for this and for her advice and correction of the Arabic in the text.

This distance learning type of study may be new to you. Obviously it has limitations but it has advantages as well. You can study in your own time, at your own rate and can choose sections which are especially relevant in your situation for more thought and study. The course will be more valuable if you are able to meet with fellow students from time to time while you are doing it. It will be better still if experienced leadership is available; perhaps your church, or your Christian organisation will be able to arrange this.

The Evangelical Missionary Alliance (EMA) has produced an educational pack containing audio cassettes, leader's notes, and discussion material which can either be used in individual study, or for a group. This pack has ben compiled by the course team, with church groups particularly in mind. It takes up the main themes of the course, giving further information and drawing out other aspects related to a biblical view of Islam. The pack can be obtained from EMA, Whitefield House, 186 Kennington Park Road, London SE11 4BT.

The course is arranged in chapters of varying length, but each is designed to take three to four hours' study time. Although they are of the same, non-specialist, educational level, the style of writing varies to some extent. This is deliberate. We hope that it will add to the interest of your study, as well as giving each writer more scope in developing his material. At the same time, each chapter has a similar framework, which should prevent unhelpful diversity and should enable students to see the course as a whole.

The chapters are arranged in parts under main subject headings. We look first at Christian attitudes in relating to those of other faiths and the practical implications of meeting with Muslims (Chapters 1 and 2). Part 2 considers the beliefs and practices of Islam (Chapters 3, 4, 5 and 6). The historical development of Islam is set out in Part 3 (Chapters 8, 9, 10 and 11). Part 4 takes up the cultural dimension in studying Islam and Christian church growth (Chapters 13, 14 and 15). There are two bridging chapters; Chapter 7, on the life of Muhammad, looks at both theological and historical perspectives, while Chapter 12, in discussing Islam in the modern world, takes in political and cultural aspects.

You will see that there are activities to complete while you are reading and studying. It would be perfectly possible to ignore these and press on with the course. This would, however, be a pity! Participation is an important part of distance learning and completing the various types of activity will help you to understand and to remember the material, as well as giving you a sense of achievement. Most of the activities do not have a simple question-answer format. They are designed to draw out principles and to help you to apply them. Do not worry if you cannot always find satisfactory answers: the text will give you guidelines. This is all part of the learning process!

You will get more out of the course if you are prepared to do some background reading. At the end of each chapter there is a list of books; some of these are referred to in the text, others are also relevant to the subject being studied. The lists are divided into two categories, 'Recommended Reading' and 'Additional Reading'. While no book is essential for the study of the course, those listed as recommended will definitely add to your understanding and, we hope, enjoyment of the material. It may be helpful to have the recommended book for the chapter beside you to refer to from time to time as you study.

The additional books are listed in case some particular subject especially interests you, or is relevant to your situation and you wish to study it in more depth. When other books are referred to in the text, details concerning their publication are usually included in the general bibliography. The chapter book lists vary considerably in length. This is because some chapters lead to more background reading than others. We have tried to take this into consideration in arranging the length of the chapters. A full bibliography is included at the end of the course. The recommended books can be obtained from EMA Books, Whitefield House, 186 Kennington Park Road, London SE11 4BT.

As indicated in Chapter 1, there are differing views on a number of issues which are taken up in the course. The aim of the team has been to present some different perspectives, but all within a biblical view of Islam. We want to make clear that we do not necessarily agree with all the material in the course. We believe, however, that it does present ideas which are worthy of consideration and that you, the student, will want to decide what is valid for you. Our objective is to present facts and theories within a biblical framework.

Unless otherwise stated biblical references are from the New International Bible and those from the Qur'an are taken from A J Arberry's, *The Koran Interpreted*.[1] Both Qur'an and Koran are acceptable anglicised spellings. The course uses Qur'an as being more phonetically correct. Koran occurs in a number of quotations.

So now, let's get going!

Note

1   ARBERRY, Arthur J. *The Koran Interpreted*, OUP, 1983.

Chapter 1

THE CHRISTIAN AND OTHER FAITHS

1 Study Guide

This chapter is designed to help you consider prayerfully how Christians should relate to those of other faiths. It will be helpful to think about some of the issues involved before plunging into a more detailed study of Islam. Anne Cooper has compiled the chapter, aiming to provide a foundation for the more detailed material which is to come.

Learning objectives
When you have completed this chapter you should:

1 Have a foundation on which to develop a Christian attitude to those of other faiths.
2 Understand that there are differing views and interpretations of the subject.
3 Be able to form your own opinion as a basis for meeting and relating to those of other faiths.

Christians may find themselves asking questions which relate to meeting and sharing with those of other faiths. You may have asked such questions yourself, or know committed Christians who are asking them. These are the sort of questions we have in mind:

Is there some truth in other faiths, or does only Christianity have the truth, all others being totally in error?
Should we try to understand the beliefs and practices of those of other faiths?
Are all those who do not believe in Jesus Christ

7

destined for eternal damnation?

Do we want our non-Christian friends to have the same opportunity of presenting their faith to us as we would like to have to present ours?

Are we reticent about discussing the Christian faith in a country where Christian standards are rapidly ceasing to be practised?

Are we disturbed by accusations of intolerance when we are not able to accept what we believe to be compromise?

Are we prepared to spend time in prayer and preparation for what may turn out to be a seemingly useless exercise?

Will we be patient, earning the right to talk about our beliefs after we have established genuine friendship and understanding?

There may be no 'right' or 'wrong' answer to most of these questions, nor can this course guarantee to give wholly satisfactory answers. They are put here to stimulate thought, and perhaps to deepen spiritual perception.

Activity
Please spend time in thinking how you would answer the questions above before reading on.

2 How Should Christians Respond to Those of Other Faiths?

Christians have different ways of answering this question. The recently published report of the Anglican Inter-Faith Counsultative Group of the Board for Mission and Unity, *Towards a Theology for Inter-Faith Dialogue*, defines three different views which people may hold:

> 1 *Exclusivism*. People who hold this view believe that truth is found only in Christianity. Many believe other faiths to be devised by Satan and to be essentially evil. 'They are either wholly in error, or simply inadequate for salvation, and reflect nothing of the real saving grace of God.'[1] It is understandable that those with this persepective concentrate on proclaiming the Gospel and expect to have little, if any, mutual sharing or dialogue.

2   *Inclusivism*. People described in the report as 'holding firmly to the belief that God was supremely manifest in Jesus,' but at the same time believing in the 'universal presence of God's Spirit through the whole of creation.'[1] There are variations within inclusivist theory, but generally inclusivists will find aspects of truth and spiritual insights in other faiths which can be shared fruitfully.

3   *Pluralism*. People who suggest 'that the different religions present different images of God which represent different experiences of the divine life spread abroad in history and culture.'[2] Christians holding this view will not be pushing their own religious message, nor insisting on the central uniqueness of Christ and faith in him.

Pluralism is very near to, perhaps even synonymous with, syncretism. Before further consideration of syncretism it may be helpful to pause and to assess which of these three perspectives is nearest to your own belief. You may not have fully formulated this yet and what follows may help you to do so. You may, however, like to consider the alternatives prayerfully at this point.

3   Syncretism

This is the view that all religions are partial expressions of divine truth and that each contributes in part to a universal religion. Most evangelicals are totally opposed to syncretistic views, but they are nevertheless becoming increasingly popular. Sir Norman Anderson writes:

The world today is characterised not only by rampant atheism but also by an almost feverish curiosity about religion and a wistful, sometimes frantic, quest for something which transcends mere materialism; and this longing for reality must not be fobbed off with a synthetic and misleading solution.[3]

The Evangelical Alliance booklet *Christianity and Other Faiths* states that in the light of the Christian claim that Jesus Christ is supreme over all, 'no solution which makes Jesus one of many "lords" or which acknowledges many paths to God can possibly be accepted. If this may seem narrow-minded or intolerant, we must remember that truth in its very nature is intolerant!'[4] The accusation of intolerance is often levelled at evangelical Christians who cannot accept syncretistic ideas.

This brings us to the first basic principle by which we operate: that *our attitudes and relationships must be firmly based on biblical truth*.

4 What Does the Bible Say About Other Faiths?

Does the Bible add light on the subject? The Bible as a whole clearly differentiates between the Jews — and later the Christians — who have a special relationship with God, and those who are outside. There is no suggestion of other groups which have different beliefs and practices, but are equally acceptable to God and have a genuine revelation from him.

It may be helpful to look in more detail at a specific passage in the Bible. John chapter 4 has been chosen as it is an account of a conversation between Jesus himself and someone from another faith, a Samaritan woman.

Activity
Please read John 4:4–26. It will be helpful to jot down the points you think might help you in meeting those belonging to other faiths.

You will probably have included the following:
1 Jesus makes it quite clear that it is the water he gives which permanently quenches thirst and which 'will become (for the person who drinks it) a spring of water welling up to eternal life' (v10).
2 Although the water is available for everyone, it is only those who actually drink it who will benefit from it (v14).
3 There is a right way and a wrong way to worship God. The Jews have knowledge which is linked to salvation. The time has now come when 'true worshippers' will worship 'in spirit and in truth.'

It is interesting to note, too, that Jesus uses different levels of conversation in this dialogue. He moves from the physical, 'Will you give me a drink' (v7), through the moral, 'Go, call your husband and come back' (v16), to the spiritual, 'God is spirit, and his worshippers must worship in spirit and in truth' (v24). This will be taken up again when different levels of dialogue are considered.

It seems that not only this woman but also her fellow Samaritans accepted the unique message which Jesus brought (v39–42).

5 Attitudes to Other Faiths

Vivienne Stacey is an experienced teacher and writer working in the Muslim world. She has contributed to a booklet which enlarges on some of the points that have been considered and introduces others:

> Some Afghan friends report that woven into a carpet in the United Nations building in New York are words from the famous Persian poet Saadi who was one of the poets of that lovely city of Shiraz. The English translation of the Persian verse is:
>
> 'All men are members of the same body,
> Created from one essence.
> If fate brings suffering to one member
> The others cannot stay at rest.
> You who remain indifferent to the burden of
> pain of others
> Do not deserve to be called human ...'
>
> God has created of one blood all nations of the earth (Acts 17:26). We are all created in the image of God. The Lord Jesus Christ became man. These facts remind us of our common humanity. We approach men and women of other faiths not so much as Hindus, Muslims, Buddhists, Jains, Sikhs, Parsees, Jews and Communists, but as fellow human beings. We are not to be so engrossed with their religious systems that we forget that they, like us, are human and deserve the respect that must surely be given to those who are created in God's image and beloved by God himself. Our recognition of the love and purposes of God for mankind will shape our attitudes to those who have not yet come to see the glory of God in the face of our Lord Jesus Christ. When we become too absorbed by religious systems we begin to see our own faith as a system, rather than seeing it in terms of relationships. In seeking to share the Gospel in appropriate ways, Christians necessarily try to understand the world-views and belief systems of people of other faiths. In our effort to understand, several things will shape our attitudes.

1 *The sovereignty of God and our humility*. Sometimes we forget that God is Lord over all. A heathen king like Nebuchadnezzar is described by the prophet Jeremiah as God's servant (Jeremiah 43:10). It follows that God is master not only of Nebuchadnezzar, but also of his gods. Cyrus, King of Persia, is called by the prophet Isaiah God's shepherd and God's anointed (Isaiah 44:28 and 45:1). God is Lord of these rulers and of the systems, both religious and political, that they represent. If we share the view of the prophets we will not regard as totally evil and irredeemable all that is involved in other world-views and faiths. God can and does use them for his own purposes. In our arrogance we sometimes see things as black or white, forgetting that God is master of all.

2 *The work of the Holy Spirit and our faith*. Do we lack faith in the power of God the Holy Spirit to convince men of sin and to bring them to himself? Many have laboured in unresponsive and difficult fields and have lost confidence in the power of the Spirit of God. Preaching correct doctrine is not enough. He who sows must sow in faith that a harvest will come. What then of those devout neighbours around us who pray so regularly to a God whom they do not know through Jesus Christ? Cornelius is a biblical character who both encourages and warns us. He is very like a sincere Muslim, 'a devout man who feared God with all his household, gave alms liberally to the people, and prayed constantly to God.' The angel of God told him that his prayers and his alms had ascended as a memorial before God. God answered the prayers of this man. He and his household came to faith in Christ and were baptised (Acts 10:2, 4, 44, and 48). In the light of Scripture, should we not believe that when a person is devoutly seeking God he shall find him? I have a Muslim friend whom I have known for over 30 years. She follows her faith as keenly as I do mine. I do not know her heart, but I believe that if she is truly seeking God she shall yet find Jesus who alone cleanses the heart and satisfies its hunger.

3 *The uniqueness of the Lord Jesus Christ and our assurance.* Muslims generally regard a declaration of assurance of the forgiveness of sins as presumption. They hope and work for acceptance with God, but cannot ever be sure of it. This is partly because they have not understood that it is God's intention in redeeming man to forgive his sins and to give him the assurance of forgiveness. They have not understood the uniqueness and authority of the Christ who says, 'My son, your sins are forgiven' (Mark 2:5 RSV). They have also not understood the function of law in Christ's scheme of things. 'The law of Moses was in fact given to a redeemed people as a way of life not to an unredeemed people as a means of redemption.'[5]

To the Muslim, God reveals his will in a book — the Qur'an. The Christian claims that God reveals himself in a Person, and therefore holds to the unique revelation of God in the unique person of his Son, the Lord Jesus Christ, the eternal Word. As Sir M Monier-Williams said in 1887 at a Church Missionary Society meeting, speaking of the Bible: 'First, where else do we read of a sinless Man who was "made sin"? Secondly, where else do we read of a dead and buried Man who is "Life"?' Many Hindus seek the one God through the many or through philosophy. Among Hindus we may feel like Paul at Athens: 'I perceive that in every way you are very religious. For as I passed along, and observed the objects of your worship, I found also an altar with this inscription, "To an unknown god." What therefore you worship as unknown, this I proclaim to you' (Acts 17:22–23 RSV). Paul proclaimed the risen Christ — the unique Christ — in whom he had assurance of forgiveness of sins and of the gift of eternal life.

4 *The power of the Word of God and our use of it.* If we believe in the unique Lord Jesus Christ as revealed in the Bible, we will present him through the words of the inspired writings even though we may adapt our method of presentation so that our hearers appreciate and understand the message. We are committed to the eternal Word — the Bible. In our time there is a tendency to underesti-

mate the power of Scripture. We do not memorize it as we ought. We do not quote it as we might. We sometimes think that if we have given some personal testimony to Jesus our Saviour, we have preached the Gospel. However, we may have omitted the objective testimony of Scripture. We should seek to sit down with our Hindu or Buddhist or Muslim friend and study Scripture.

5 *The need of our fellow men and our compassion.* What should motivate us as we live among people of other faiths? Should not the love of Christ constrain us, as it did Paul? What of hell and damnation? Knowing that our God is a consuming fire (Hebrews 12:29) we should plead with people to be reconciled to God and to flee from the wrath to come. When I have wept for the salvation of others, I have seen the Lord work and bring some to himself. We must seek this balance between love and compassion, and the knowledge of judgement. How often Jesus was moved with compassion. How little I am moved with compassion or moved to tears for the lost. Or are they lost? Is there any hope of salvation for a godly person of any religion who does not know or follow the Lord Jesus Christ?

Paul in his letter to the Romans shows that God will judge men by what they have known of the truth and how they have responded to it (Romans 1:20–21). Certainly there is a mystery here. There is no salvation except by virtue of what Christ has wrought. Like Abraham we can bring our questions to God and still declare in faith: 'Shall not the judge of all the earth do right?' (Genesis 18:25 RSV).[6]

6 Clarifying the Questions

It will be worthwhile pausing to consider the material studied so far. Perhaps it has helped to clarify at least some of the questions in your mind. Do you have a better biblical basis on which to go out and meet friends of other faiths? You may well think that we have only just scratched the surface. You may have quite different questions in your mind from those mentioned here. Whatever your reaction is, a lifetime of learning and exploring is ahead of you. Consideration must be backed up with prayer and with the belief that God has much more to reveal to all of us. We must be open and sensitive to his revelation. In Vivienne Stacey's paper the reader is encouraged to look at and study his own faith, memorising and quoting from the Bible. This leads to the next basic principle: that *any activity of reaching out to others should look for the deepening of our own spiritual understanding.*

7 Witnessing to those of other Faiths

We turn now to consider ways of witnessing to those of other faiths. The Evangelical Alliance booklet *Christianity and Other Faiths* describes four aspects of Christian attitude and action.[7] The following types of witness are included:

1 Presence
This involves identifying with the particular group or community.

> So the Christian will seek to understand the feelings of the community, to involve himself in its joys and sorrows and to get to know its leaders, and he will be deeply concerned that all its members should be able to live their lives in freedom and dignity, following the cultural pattern they have inherited.[8]

There is no short cut to other forms of witness. Christian presence is of vital importance. So too is the next type of witness.

2 Service
Following the pattern of our Lord himself, 'one who serves' (Luke 22:27) can be a real joy. There is no need for a false dichotomy between 'service' and 'preaching'; both are part of Christ's commission.

> Where people are in social need, are the victims of injustice and discrimination or are facing problems they cannot cope with, this fact itself represents a claim on the Christian's service, irrespective of the evangelistic opportunity that may result.[9]

The other two areas listed in the EA booklet are dialogue and proclamation. It may be helpful to pause here, however, and introduce another of the basic principles of sharing with those of other faiths: that *we relate to a person not to a religion. It is important that evangelism is part of personal communication, interest, friendship, caring, and understanding.*

As Vivienne Stacey wrote in the first section of her paper, 'We approach men and women of other faiths not so much as Hindus, Muslims, Buddhists, Jains, Sikhs, Parsees, Jews and Communists, but as fellow human beings.' They are people with all the potential for good or evil that we have ourselves. They are people with their own background, interests, emotions, and cultural norms. They are people created in the image of God. It is necessary to tread carefully in the same way as we would like others to do with us.

3 Dialogue

This is probably the most controversial aspect of our Christian action. The EA booklet defines it as ' ... inter-religious discussion, in which the participant seeks to listen as well as to bear witness, to understand the other's faith at the deepest possible level, as *he* understands it, as well as to share his own faith with the other at a like level.'[10] Some Christians believe that dialogue spells compromise and to engage in it means not to be honest either with oneself or with the other participant.

Dialogue may be intellectual in character, emphasizing human reason and believing that reasoned argument can lead to truth. It may emphasize our common humanity which unites, while doctrine divides. It may be secular dialogue which seeks to reach others through the problems of the world and of society. Interior dialogue emphasises the mystical and the contemplative aspects of religion, the sharing of religious experiences. Dr. Michael Nazir-Ali writes in his book, *Islam: A Christian Perspective*,

> The maintenance and development of an element of 'discursive dialogue' in Christian/Muslim relations seems to me to be necessary if other forms of dialogue are going to succeed. If, for example, there is to be real encounter at the level of 'interior dialogue', each partner will need to understand the ways in which spiritual experiences are interpreted by the other. From the Christian side it will need to be made clear that for the Christian the paradigm of God's revelation to man is the life, death and resurrection of Jesus Christ. All spiritual experiences are to be tested

against this touchstone. Again at the level of 'secular dialogue', if Christians and Muslims are ever to cooperate meaningfully in bringing about a new order in the world, they will have to understand what are each other's views of the world and expectations of the world. [11]

(Discursive dialogue is presenting an argument for one's own belief as well as trying to understand the other person's belief.)

4 Proclamation

Recognising the centrality of sharing the good news about Jesus Christ, the EA booklet states, 'The aim is that people may really grasp the message of God's wonderful love and mercy in Christ not only with the head but with the heart and may respond to it as free persons.'[12] This will not simply be a matter of proclaiming the Gospel, but proclaiming it in such a way that it is communicated, making it possible for the other person to respond. For, as Christopher Lamb writes in the July 1984 edition of *Co-ordinate*,

> So much preaching and writing is preaching and writing past people, meeting neither felt nor real need. We answer questions people are not asking, or have ceased to ask, or have not yet thought of asking. We talk our own jargon in our own tongue and wonder why no-one understands us.[13]

If the Gospel is to be communicated a deep knowledge of the other person's own faith and own system of belief is imperative. This leads to the next basic principle: that *it is essential that we listen to and learn from those of other faiths if a meaningful relationship is to be established. This means that we shall want to meet Muslims, to read their writings, and to hear what they say about their faith.*

This course book encourages friendships to be formed and the religion of Islam to be studied through using books and other material written by both Muslims and Christians and by listening to what both Muslims and Christians have to say. It is very important, if preparation for ministry to Muslims is to be effective, that a practical as well as a theoretical approach be employed.

Activities

1 If you do not already have one or more Muslim friends, now is the time to begin looking for them; married couples can

17

relate to Muslim couples, but others should choose someone of their own sex.

2 The Apostle Paul has a great deal to teach us through his evangelistic methods. Please read Acts 17:16–34. It is interesting to compare Paul's teaching in Athens, where the Athenians have a Greek religious background, with his teaching to Jews; look, for example, at Acts 17:1–9 where he is speaking to a largely Jewish audience. Paul has seen the altar to the 'unknown god' and used this as a starting point. From your present knowledge of Islam, what might be a useful starting point in sharing with Muslims?

3 You may like at this point to obtain a preliminary outline of Muslim beliefs. A useful way of doing this is to read one of the free leaflets written by Muslims to explain Islam to Christians. You can write to either the Islamic Foundation, 232 London Road, Leicester, or the Muslim Educational Trust, 130 Stroud Green Road, London N4 3RZ for a copy of their leaflets, or get one from a mosque or Islamic centre.

Recommended Reading

There is no book in this category for Chapter 1.

Additional Reading

ANDERSON, Sir Norman. *Christianity and World Religions*, IVP, Leicester, 1984.
BOARD OF MISSION AND UNITY. *Towards a Theology for Inter-Faith Dialogue*, Church Information Office, London, 1984.
DOWSETT, Dick. *God, That's Not Fair*, OMF/STL, Sevenoaks/Bromley, Kent, 1982.
EVANGELICAL ALLIANCE. *Christianity and Other Faiths*, Paternoster Press, Exeter, 1983.

Notes

1 ANGLICAN INTER-FAITH CONSULTATIVE GROUP OF THE BOARD OF MISSION AND UNITY. *Towards a Theology for Inter-Faith Dialogue*, Church Information Office, London, 1984, p8.

2 Ibid, p9.

3 ANDERSON, Sir Norman. *Christianity and World Religions*, IVP, Leicester, 1984, p16.
4 EVANGELICAL ALLIANCE. *Christianity and Other Faiths*, Paternoster Press, Exeter, 1983, p21.
5 ANDERSON, Sir Norman. *God's Law and God's Love: An Essay in Comparative Religion*, Collins, Glasgow, 1981, p45.
6 STACEY Vivienne. In *Perspectives on Mission*, Mariano Di Gangi, ed., BMMF International, Toronto, 1985, pp28–30.
7 EVANGELICAL ALLIANCE. *Christianity and Other Faiths*, Paternoster Press, Exeter, 1983, pp25–34.
8 Ibid, p26.
9 Ibid, p27.
10 Ibid, p29.
11 NAZIR-ALI, Michael. *Islam: A Christian Perspective*, Paternoster Press, Exeter, 1983, pp148–149.
12 EVANGELICAL ALLIANCE. *Christianity and Other Faiths*, Paternoster Press, Exeter, 1983, pp148–149.
13 LAMB, Christopher. *Co-ordinate*, July 1984, p3.

Chapter 2

MAKING MUSLIM FRIENDS

1 Study Guide

This chapter presents some of the practical aspects of meeting and sharing with Muslim friends. It looks first at our own attitudes, then goes on to consider what might be emphasised and what should be avoided. It gives some basic information, particularly about family life. It is essentially a practical chapter; the thoughts and ideas will need to be put into practice. We hope you find it useful. Most people feel dissatisfied with their efforts, especially at first. A more experienced Christian friend with whom you can discuss the activities will be invaluable. Roger Malstead has written this chapter.

Learning objectives
When you have completed this chapter you should:

1 Have focused on your own attitudes and methods of sharing your faith.
2 Be ready to start your study of Islam and how to relate to Muslims.

2 Introduction

Professor J N D Anderson once said, 'You don't need to know a lot about Islam to be able to talk to Muslims. The more you know the better, but you don't need to know a lot to tell them that Jesus loves them.' I think this is a balanced view regarding our reaching out to Muslims. We in the Christian church in this repect are found in two groups. The one, the experts, know quite a bit about Islam and are learning more. But then there is the large majority of people in our churches who do not know so much about Islam, but are the ones who are often in contact with Muslim peoples, especially in the UK and Europe. They, as much as the experts, can reach out in love and concern. This is not to say we do not continue to read, to study, and to learn more of Islam and the peoples to whom we go, but we do need to begin now to witness, in love, of the One who has redeemed us.

I recently spoke with a Turkish man who had come to know Christ from a Muslim background. He is a graduate of a university. I asked him what it was that influenced him. He told me simply that it was someone in Turkey who had shown love to him. This man was not a professional 'missionary', but he simply showed his Turkish friend the love of Christ. We must grasp the fact that the need today is for Christian people who will show genuine love and concern for Muslim men and women as they witness, whether in the West, or in the cities or villages where they live in a Muslim country.

In approaching anyone, including a Muslim, we must realise the truth of the words, 'God said, "Let us make man in our image, in our likeness"' (Genesis 1:27). We need to remind ourselves at the very beginning that at the heart of Muslim evangelism there exists the principle that Christians must deal with Muslims in the same way as they would any other next door neighbour. Dr Francis Schaeffer, a Christian writer and thinker, has reminded us very strongly that, even though the image may be marred, each person still deserves to be treated as someone who has been created very specially by God himself.

3   What Should Be Our Attitudes?

One important attitude is that of compassion. We see very clearly from the New Testament that Jesus was often 'moved with compassion' and a deep concern for others. This involves a sincere caring attitude that must result in deeds, and also includes a concern for people's eternal destiny. If we have genuine compassion for those with whom we seek to share the Gospel, then it will be evident to those concerned that we really do care for them. It will show!

Showing practical love with courtesy and politeness should be high on the list of priorities. This is not just behaving in a polite way towards others which can often be a facade, but involves a genuine attitude of the heart. It recognises that people are very important and valuable in God's sight. There is an American Indian saying which says: 'Walk a mile in someone's moccasins before you criticise him.' Bishop Kenneth Cragg writes, 'Our first task in approaching another people, another culture, another religion, is to take off our shoes, for the place we are approaching is holy'.[1]

Activity
Look back on your own experience. What made you first listen to the Gospel? Does this help you know how to witness to others?

A very useful book on evangelism in general is Rebecca Manly Pippert's *Out of the Salt Shaker*. On one occasion she was in conversation with a non-Christian friend when she began to realise she was 'turning her off': 'Suddenly I realised how ridiculous all this was, so I said, "Look, I feel really bad. I am very excited about who God is and what he's done in my life. But I hate it when people push 'religion' on me. So if I'm coming on too strong, will you just tell me?"'

Her friend was amazed, as she had never previously met Christians who would speak to her in this way. She responded: '"I never knew Christians were aware that we hate being recipients of a running monologue." (So much for my evangelistic skill!)'

Rebecca informed her that, in fact, 'most Christians ... are very hesitant to share their faith precisely because they're afraid they'll offend.'

'"As long as you let people know that you're aware of where they're coming from, you can say anything you want!" she responded immediately. "And you just tell Christians that I said so".'[2]

4   Finding Muslim Friends

We have read a bit now about the need to show love to people. Your assignment is to visit the home of a Muslim you may know personally or have some contact with at work. If you need help in finding such a person, contact your pastor, or another pastor in an area of your city who may know of people who are working with Muslims, or a student organisation at a nearby college or university which may be in contact with Muslims. What to do when you meet? One way of starting a friendship will be to talk about the country from which your friend originates. It is genuinely interesting to find out about different ways of life. Don't forget to share your experiences as well. Sometimes, as the friendship develops and you both share more deeply, you will be surprised at how much you have in common. You will probably find that your Muslim friend is much more ready to start sharing spiritual experiences than a neighbour from the West would be. Don't rush it, though. Westerners have the reputation of being too 'pushy' and impatient.

There are, of course, a number of other ways that one may meet Muslim peoples. For example, one may go to the local social services offices and ask if there is a need for volunteer help. There no doubt would be opportunities to help in housing, child care, and other areas where social services are involved in the lives of the people of the area.

There are other ways in which you may search out points of contact for yourself. There may be day care centres in your area where working mothers bring their children. Possibly they need volunteers and in this way you would be able to meet the mothers or fathers or both. In many Muslim areas there are coffee-houses or tea-houses where Muslim men come together to sit and talk. They probably would be speaking their own language, but you would no doubt be able to meet some and begin to converse and develop an acquaintance.

It is important to remember that both friendship and voluntary help are valuable in themselves, not just as evangelistic tools. We must also be aware of two possible dangers in looking for Muslim friends:

1 It would be easy while doing this course to use your friend merely as a kind of 'guinea pig' to help you in your study of Islam. This must be a genuine friendship; your friend will not be happy if he feels he is essentially a target of evangelism. It may be that you will not find deep friendship developing with the first Muslim you meet. We do not automatically 'click' with a person. If this is so, look for someone else. However, give time for a friendship to develop first; there are enormous barriers of language and culture to overcome.

2 The second factor to keep in mind is that your friend may not know very much about his or her religion. Did you know much about the Christian religion before you found faith in Christ and the guidance of the Holy Spirit? If you are an average Christian you will probably still find it quite difficult to explain your beliefs. It may be that your friend knows a lot and sincerely practises his faith, but he or she is not able to express himself easily in

English. He may well be grateful for help with this, particularly if you are interested in learning some of his language at the same time.

These are some of the difficulties. Here is something on the positive side. Your Muslim friend will be much more ready to accept references to the Bible without questioning their validity than your British neighbour would be.

Now you are ready for this assignment!

Here is a quote from *Islam and Christian Witness*, by Martin Goldsmith. It will be helpful to have a copy of this book beside you as you study the next section.

> Since the realities and complexities of actual encounter with living Muslims do not allow for any neat pre-packaged evangelism, few of us will be in a position to engage in a witness closely related to Muslim backgrounds. But all of us can share what Jesus Christ means to us with joy and enthusiasm... While we may sometimes confess that we do not know all the theological answers or understand the deep mysteries of the Christian faith, our joyful testimony to what God has done for us in Christ and by his Spirit will remain real and attractive.[3]

5 Guidelines for Initial Contact with Muslims

These are some 'do's and don'ts' to keep in mind as we go out to make friends with Muslims and to share the Gospel with them.

1 Always show respect for your Bible, never placing it on the floor, nor in any other way showing disrespect. In fact, it might be good to have one New Testament or Bible which you have not marked to take along with you as you speak to Muslims. They would never write in a Qur'an, and therefore, to show respect for God's Word, it might be best not to take one with any markings in it. However, if they see your Bible in which you have marked, you can share with them that although we respect God's Word, we really do want to honour him by studying it and to mark it helps us to keep in mind some of God's teaching. Also, we can share that we believe the real Word of God is manifested in the Lord Jesus Christ.

2   When entertaining Muslims, never serve them food containing pork or bacon, nor offer them any alcoholic beverages. This is a very good opportunity to show your creativity and willingness to learn the foods and spices that they use in cooking when they entertain. In a very natural way you can share your delight and interest in the foods that they serve.
3   Don't give or take food with your left hand. This is the 'dirty hand' in most Muslim countries, if not all, and it is *not* used in taking or receiving food.

Points 4–8 introduce some of the theological aspects of sharing with Muslims. They will be discussed in more detail in Chapter 6.

4   Learn to use phrases such as 'the Word of God' rather than 'Jesus, the Son of God,' as this phrase is highly emotive and miscommunicates to Muslims. It is true that we believe Jesus is the Son of God, but we do not believe in any way that implies any kind of physical relationship. That is, we do not believe, as some Muslims mistakenly think we do, that God had relations with Mary and their son is Jesus. We believe that, amongst many other things, the term 'Son of God' refers to a very special spiritual relationship. Other phrases describing Jesus that would be familiar and which are acceptable to Muslims are 'the Breath of God' or 'the Spirit of God.' Others that may be used in Muslim countries are 'the Saviour, Jesus' or 'the Lamb of God.'
5   As mentioned earlier, be completely natural and genuine in the sharing of your faith as well as in your questioning Muslims about their own beliefs and religious practices. Somehow easterners have very keen insight into people who are not being honest and open and real with them.
6   Do not let yourself be drawn into heated arguments. There is a place, of course, for open and frank discussion, about our similarities and differences, but as the Bible says, 'The Lord's servant must not quarrel' (2 Timothy 2:20). That is, we do not want to win an argument which might alienate our friends. If we see clearly that there are things with which we disagree, it is best to say something like, 'It's obvious that we don't agree on this point, so let's not argue over God or his truths, but let's learn to respect each other.' In this way, you are showing Muslims that you do respect them as people, as individuals, but you do not necessarily agree with their doctrines or teachings.
    Remember not to speak ill of, or to degrade Muhammad, nor the Qur'an. I am sure you realise that this is not the way to win friends and witness to people. In the gospels, following

an incident where Jesus was slighted, the disciples asked if they could call down fire upon that town. Jesus rebuked them sternly for their judgemental and hostile attitudes (Luke 9:51–56). We must resist the tendency towards petty hostility and anger within us, that wants to condemn others for their religion. May we be the servants of Jesus, who are filled with graciousness and a winning and loving attitude towards those to whom we wish to witness. We never want, however, to say anything which will compromise the truth.

7   Muslims' belief that the Old and New Testaments have been changed often arises in discussion. We can prepare ourselves for this by reading books that give good ways of responding to this misunderstanding. (See book list at the end of the chapter.) There are many good books which demonstrate that there is absolutely no proof that any change has been made in the biblical texts, other than a few insignificant errors due to copying. In no way do these small discrepancies influence any major, or minor, doctrine.

One way in which some people handle this objection is to ask Muslim friends, 'Do you think the all-powerful God would ever allow little *man* to change his Word?' The fact is, that even the Qur'an itself says, 'No man can change the words of God.' (6:34) So we as Christians simply believe that since God is all-powerful and since his Word is eternal, he would not allow it to be changed by puny man. (There is more discussion on the subject in Chapter 6, **The Testimony of the Qur'an to the Bible**.)

8   Another objection that may arise is that we are thought to believe in three Gods. Of course, it is true that ultimately the doctrine of the Trinity is something that is very mysterious. I like to ask Muslims if they understand all about God themselves. It seems to me that if we understand every single thing about God, he must be very small. However, someone so great must be incomprehensible to our finite minds. We *can* understand all that he has revealed to us; that is why it is necessary to study the Bible, which is God's self-revelation. But some things we will not understand in this life. If you would like to read further on this subject, Professor Sir Norman Anderson has an excellent section on this in his book *The Mystery of the Incarnation*.[4] (There is further discussion on this subject in Chapter 6, section 2, **Islamic Objections to the Doctrine of the Trinity**.)

9   Martin Goldsmith, in his book *Islam and Christian Witness*, writes:

In many cultures today we need to move away from teaching only through abstract concepts and begin to use vivid stories as a didactic means. The story should not be just an illustration which is subordinate to the actual point. The story is in itself the teaching.[5]

Mr Goldsmith has many good suggestions on how to witness. He mentions that just as Jesus told stories or taught in parables, this may be a very useful way to present the gospel to Middle Eastern and Asian peoples. Muslims love stories, as do many other peoples, and especially in working with village people and children it might be helpful to learn how to tell a good story. Secondly, he reminds us to be pictorial in our witness to Muslims, that is, to use illustrations and draw pictures with our words just as Jesus did. He says that we should avoid abstract reasoning, except perhaps with students and others who think more in those terms. He mentions the need to present the Gospel in a 'tangential' form, so that we can take off from idea to idea rather than in some logical, set, and prescribed manner.

10 Jesus often asked questions. Many times a well-placed question can stimulate people to think and to draw inferences that will lead them to a truth of Scripture, or of the Lord Jesus Christ. Here is an opportunity for the person witnessing to be very creative, and as Jesus said, to bring out of his store new things and old. Many people who have worked with Muslims encourage us to use Old Testament stories, especially the story of Abraham ready to sacrifice his son. Perhaps we can ask what this sacrifice means to our friend. We may then have the opportunity to say what we believe.

11 In the book of Acts we see that the disciples took every opportunity to proclaim the resurrection of Jesus from the dead. We should continue to proclaim his death and resurrection with boldness. I believe we should, as Peter says, 'Always be prepared to give an answer to everyone who asks you to give reason for the hope that you have' (1 Peter 3:15). The hope that we have is in Jesus, who is alive. (In Chapter 6, section 3, **The Witness of the Qur'an to Jesus**, there is discussion on Muslim beliefs about Jesus.)

12 One of the most important things to remember as we witness is the need to be constantly in prayer. Many, many people who have witnessed to Muslims testify to the fact that as they prayed for their Muslim friends, God gave them specific answers to questions, or specific things they could do for their friends. So may we be, as Jesus and Paul were, constant in

prayer, always remembering to pray for our Muslim friends.

6   Muslim Family Life

Most Muslims do not come from western, industrialised societies, so do not have a western cultural background. Many of the differences which we note are due to this, rather than to specifically Muslim differences. At the same time, it is important to realise at this point that Islam is a complete way of life, not simply a religion. Cultural differences are of religious significance in Islam.

Some of these differences have already been noted in the 'do's and don'ts' we have just been looking at. Because family life is important and your Muslim friend will be a member of a family, we will consider family life briefly now.

6:1 *Nuclear and extended families*

Although families may have been split up due to migration of some members, the extended family is the norm in Islam. As sons marry they bring their wives into their parents' home, where their children are born and grow up. Daughters, on the other hand, marry into another extended family and only return to their parents for occasional visits. The extended family is the unit. All important decisions are made by the head of the family, in consultation with other members. Muslims living in other countries may live as nuclear families, parents and their children living separately, but there is still a strong bond between those who have migrated and members of the extended family remaining in the country of origin. Children who have professional careers, even responsible positions in society, may refer back to their father, or elder brother, before making decisions which affect the family. Sometimes, one after another, a whole extended family may have uprooted itself and now be settled in another country.

6:2 *Arranged marriages*

Most of us in the West are horrified at the thought of parents choosing whom we should marry! This is, however, the normal procedure in some other cultures. It is not only accepted, it is expected, and on the whole it works well. In Muslim families the bride and groom may not have met before the marriage ceremony. Marriage, like the rest of living, is a family matter and great efforts are made by the family to find the right partners for their children. The contract is between the families, not between

28

the individuals.

6:3 *Children*

Large families are usual and children are welcomed and enjoyed. Childlessness is a shame and a tragedy. The gender of children is of considerable cultural significance. Boys will grow up to carry on the family and to work to support their parents in old age. They are greatly preferred to girls who will leave the family on marriage and for whom expensive marriage arrangements will have to be made. From early childhood the children are taught their differing roles. Boys are encouraged to make decisions and to take initiative, girls to stay in the background, looking after the younger children and helping with work in the home.

6:4 *Women in Islam*

Speaking on the subject of divorce the Qur'an says, 'Women have such honourable rights as obligations, but their men have a degree above them. God is All-mighty, All-wise' (2:228).

Many see Islam as giving an inferior status to women. Muslims point out that it is a difference of role rather than status. *Surah* 2:282 of the Qur'an says, 'And call in to witness two witnesses, men; or if two be not men, then one man and two women, such witnesses as you approve of, that if one of the two women errs the other will remind her...' The financial dealings being discussed in this *surah* were not considered to be the sphere of women. This may have been why two were required in place of one man! The Muslim writer Ghulam Sarwar, in *Islam: Beliefs and Teachings*, says this:

> Islam is a religion of common sense and is in line with human nature. It recognises the realities of life. This does not mean it has recognised equality of man and woman in every respect. Rather, it has defined their duties in keeping with their different biological make-up (2:228). Allah has not made man and woman identical, so it would be against nature to have total equality between a man and a woman.[6]

This subject is taken up again in Chapter 10, section 5, **The Sources of Authority for Islamic Law.**

It is very important that Christian men and women understand the Muslim concept of the man as the head of the household, the decision-maker and the woman as the home-maker, the bearer and nurturer of children. This is particularly important when living and working in a Muslim country when we are called upon not only to understand, but also to practise these roles.

6:5 *Purdah*

This is the practice of women concealing themselves, from the age of puberty, except from near relatives and women friends. *Purdah* is the Persian word for a curtain or veil. *Surah* 24:31–33 says, 'And say to the believing women, that they cast down their eyes and guard their private parts, and reveal not their adornment save such as is outward; and let them cast their veils over their bosoms, and not reveal their adornment save to their husbands....'

Most Muslim women do not appear to regard *purdah* as a bondage, but as a protection. A family's decision as to whether its girls keep *purdah* does not depend so much on whether they are educated as on whether they hold traditional beliefs. In Muslim countries many highly educated women have professional careers while remaining in *purdah*. In the West *purdah* may be practised not by women wearing veils, but by their never going out in public, which is more restricting for them.

It is important to recognise that the freedom of women in the West is a traumatic issue for Muslims and that it raises questions such as the provision of single-sex schools. For the purposes of this course it should be noted that extreme sensitivity is needed in relating to Muslims of the other sex. The advice given in Chapter 1, Activity 1, about choosing friends of your own sex, should now make more sense. Men visiting in Muslim homes should be careful not to shake hands with women or girls, nor should they sit next to them on settees or sofas. Muslim men may sometimes seem unacceptably familiar with western women, even when they hardly know them. This is because they have had little experience of coping with the freer relationship between the sexes of the West. Islam has strict standards of sexual morality for both men and women.

Activities
1 This chapter only gives an outline of some of the issues involved in meeting Muslims. It will need filling out by discussion with your Muslim friends. Do not be afraid to ask whether something is culturally acceptable. Show that you really want to understand how to behave.
2 Look back at the basic principles mentioned in Chapter 1. Consider how these can be worked out practically in the light of the discussion in Chapter 2.

Recommended Reading

GOLDSMITH, Martin. *Islam and Christian Witness*, Hodder and Stoughton, London, and STL Books, Bromley, 1982.

Additional Reading

ANDERSON, Sir Norman. *The Mystery of the Incarnation*, IVP, Madison, Wisconsin, 1978. Hodder and Stoughton, London, 1978.
MILLER, William. *A Christian Response to Islam*, STL, Bromley, Kent, 1981.
PIPPERT, Rebecca Manley. *Out of the Saltshaker*, IVP, Leicester, 1979.
STACEY, Vivienne. *Practical Lessons for Evangelism among Muslims*. Orientdienst, eV. Wiesbaden, West Germany (undated).

Notes

1 CRAGG, Bishop Kenneth. *Sandals at the Mosque*, SCM Press, London, 1959, p9.
2 PIPPERT, Rebecca Manley. *Out of the Saltshaker*, IVP, Leicester, 1979, p25.
3 GOLDSMITH, Martin. *Islam and Christian Witness*, Hodder and Stoughton, London, 1982, p114.
4 ANDERSON, Sir Norman. *The Mystery of the Incarnation*, IVP, Madison, Wisconsin, 1978. Hodder and Stoughton, London, 1978, pp141–150.
5 GOLDSMITH, Martin. *Islam and Christian Witness*, Hodder and Stoughton, London, 1982, pp130–131.
6 SARWAR, Ghulam. *Islam: Beliefs and Teachings*, Muslim Educational Trust, London, 3rd ed., 1984, pp167–168.

Chapter 3/4

MUSLIM BELIEFS AND PRACTICES

1   Study Guide

We move on now to the start of our study of Islam. This double chapter gives an outline of the beliefs and practices. It was initially put together by Torbjorn Brorson. When he left London, Sarah James continued the work on it. Torbjorn was anxious that it should be more than a factual account and that readers should obtain some understanding of the impact of the religion on its followers. For this reason, the references are either from the Qur'an, or from the works of Muslim writers. Later, in Chapter 6, there will be opportunity to consider what Christian writers say and how the two compare. We urge you to spend time on this material; it is basic for obtaining a grasp of what follows after.

Learning objectives
After completing this chapter you should:

1 Be able to give an account of the fundamental beliefs of Islam.
2 Understand something of how they are popularly taught by one of the most outstanding Islamic thinkers in this century.

2   Introduction

When we are concerned to know about a particular faith, we must have the courage to collect information with a view to examining it critically for authenticity and correctness. However, we must go beyond a mere description of the facts and proceed towards a deeper understanding and appreciation of that faith which is able to incorporate the 'inside' views of one who professes and practises that faith.

For this reason discussion with Muslim friends will be valuable; but first we suggest you look back at Chapter 2, section 4, **Finding Muslim Friends**.

In the following chapters you will find that a few Muslim writers will be allowed to 'state their case' or 'give witness to Islam.' Our task is to hear what they have to say and to comment on it. I will share my comments with you throughout these chapters and you should think through the issues for yourself.

3   What is the Meaning of Islam?

The word 'Islam' actually means 'submission' or 'surrender'. Islam is not seen as a religion but as a complete way of life. Muslims consider that Islam is concerned with the guidance provided by God for all mankind, which guides and governs all aspects of individual and corporate living. Islam also means peace, because it has surrendered to the Law of God: peace is the result of obedience to God's will. Islam claims that anyone who lives in complete obedience and submission to God's will, whatever race, colour, community, or country he belongs to, is a Muslim.

For a Muslim, faith (*iman*) includes the following:

The confession of faith (the *shahada*).

Obedience to the prophet Muhammad.

Belief in God's angels.

Belief in God's books.

Belief in God's prophets and messengers.

Belief in life after death and the day of judgement.

Faith and worship (*ibadat*), which is the practical outworking of faith through submission to God in all areas of life, constitute the central core of Islam. *Qadr*, which can be translated power or fate, is a fundamental attribute of God. It shows his power and his will in contrast to man's weakness and helplessness. It is one of the articles in the basic Muslim statement of belief.

Although there is a glossary at the end of the course, it may be helpful to start making a list of Arabic words. You will find there are quite a number of them in the course and it is important to understand and use them as Arabic is the language of Islam. The glossary gives meanings and some guidance about pronunciation.

The four bases from which the doctrines and precepts of Islam

are derived are:
1 *The Qur'an*, God's word as revealed through Muhammad.
2 *The sunnah*, the customs, habits and approvals of Muhammad, which are next in importance to the Qur'an.
3 *Ijma*, the unanimous agreement of the Muslim nation, or rather of its learned scholars.
4 *Qias*, 'measuring', by which is meant analogical reasoning of the scholars with regard to difficult, doubtful, or new questions of doctrine and practice. The scholars compare the cases before them with similar ones already settled by the authority of the Qur'an, *sunnah*, or *ijma* and thus arrive at an answer.

4 A Muslim's faith is firmly rooted in the belief that the source of Islam is God and that Muhammad is 'only' the last and final spokesman for this universal faith. Before going any further, we suggest you pause to consider what you already know about the origin and development of Islam. How would you answer the following questions?
1 When did the religion of Islam arise?
2 Where did it arise?
3 Who founded the religion?
4 How did Islam spread and develop?

As a Christian your answers may have been:
1 In the seventh century AD.
2 In what is today Saudi Arabia.
3 Muhammad.
4 By preaching and conquest.

A Muslim would probably have answered:
1 It has always existed.
2 With God in heaven.
3 God.
4 By divine revelation and intervention.

No wonder Christians and Muslims have had a hard time communicating with each other!

Muslims hold that 'Islam' is not one religion among many, but *the* religion, (or better still, the Religion of Nature or natural religion, in Arabic, *'din-al-fitrah'*.) Islam is the religion of God. The Qur'an states: 'The true religion with God is Islam' (3:17).

Adam is considered to be the first Muslim. Muslims believe that the core message of the prophets and messengers from Adam to Muhammad is the same: obedience to Allah alone and submission to his law. Previous messages were for certain peoples only, and with time they were distorted. Islam, as revealed through the Qur'an and the exemplary role of Muhammad's life, is seen as the universal and final religion, because it is

34

the perfection of what God originally meant religion to be.

Under the heading, 'Islam — what does it mean?', Mawlana Mawdudi, in his book *Towards Understanding Islam*, writes:

> ... ours is a law-governed universe and everything in it is following the course that has been ordained for it... As the whole of creation obeys the law of God, the whole universe, therefore, literally follows the religion of Islam — for Islam signifies nothing but obedience and submission to Allah, the Lord of the universe... Everything in the universe is 'Muslim' for it obeys God by submission to his laws. Even a man who refuses to believe in God, or offers his worship to someone other than Allah, has necessarily to be a 'Muslim' as far as his existence is concerned.[1]

However, Mawdudi states that although man 'is completely caught in the grip of the law of nature and is bound to follow it,' he has also been given the gift of free will and can determine his own behaviour. As a result, although man's body is bound to submit to God's natural law, man can, in the area of his will, decide for himself whether or not to be a Muslim. How this freedom of choice is exercised determines whether one is a believer or an unbeliever. Of one who chooses to submit to God's law it can be said that:

> [He has] achieved completeness in his Islam by consciously deciding to obey God in the domain in which he was endowed with freedom of choice. He is a perfect Muslim. Now his entire life has become one of submission to God and there is no conflict in his personality.[2]

On the other hand, the unbeliever, having made a conscious decision to deny God commits '*kufr*' (literally this means 'to cover' or 'to conceal'. The unbeliever conceals what is inherent in his own nature by his unbelief and is a '*kafir*' — an unbeliever). The one who commits *kufr* is in total rebellion to God. Mawdudi describes the unbeliever in the following way:

> Such a man destroys the calm and poise of life on earth. And in the life hereafter he will be held guilty for the crimes he committed against his nature. Every organ of his body — his very brain, eyes, nose, hands, and feet — will complain against the injustice and

cruelty he has done unto them. Every tissue of his being will decry him before God who, as the very fountain of justice, will punish him as he deserves. This is the inglorious consequence of *kufr*. It leads to the blind alleys of utter failure, both here and hereafter. [3]

By stark contrast: 'The life of a Muslim will always be filled with godliness, piety, righteousness and truthfulness...'[4]

Because the Muslim knows that God is ever present, he will be fair and just in everything he does. In eternity, the believer will be showered with God's choicest blessings, 'for he will have discharged his duty ably, fulfilled his mission successfully, and emerged from his trial triumphantly.'[5] The Muslim 'is successful in life in this world and in the hereafter will live in eternal peace, joy and bliss.'[5]

Mawdudi paints a rather naive, idealistic, and optimistic picture of actual human behaviour. We probably all share Mawdudi's longings towards the kind of utopian society he outlines, but the way towards its realisation is described in the Bible in a radically different way.

Activity
How could you explain these differences to a Muslim friend?

One way to explain might be to say that the Bible tells us that we have all sinned (Romans 3:23) and that spiritual death is the consequence (Romans 6:23). If we look around us in the world today there is plenty of evidence of this. The Bible also tells us that only through faith in Jesus Christ can we have eternal life (John 1:12). This is a gift of God (Romans 6:23); it is not attainable by living a good life (Ephesians 2:8–9). We are not promised worldly success (Mark 9:35). Again, if we look around us, we can see that riches and influence do not necessarily lead to peace and happiness.

5   The Articles of Faith in Islam

The Oneness of God or the unity of Allah
In these chapters I shall use 'God' (with a capital G) and 'Allah' as synonymous terms. We do both Muslims and Arabic-speaking Christians grave disservice if we regard 'Allah' as the 'God of the Muslims'. 'Allah' is the word for God used by Muslims and it is used by Arab Christians as well. While there is the important question as to whether 'Allah' is the God of the Bible or not, it is

not our intention to enter into that debate at this point.

The doctrine of the unity and oneness (*tawhid*) of the godhead is the most fundamental and the most important part of *iman* (faith). The first duty of a Muslim is to declare his faith in the words, 'There is no God (or deity) but Allah' (*La ilaha illallah*) and 'Muhammad is Allah's messenger'. This expression of *tawhid* — 'There is no God but Allah' — is known as the primary creed (*kalima*) of Islam.

But as Mawdudi states:

> If the kalima is repeated without any understanding, it cannot work the revolution which it is meant to bring about. This can occur if a person grasps the full meaning of the doctrine, realises its significance, reposes true belief in it, and accepts and follows it in letter and spirit.[6]

Tawhid implies that God is:

1 One in his essence; he is not composed of parts.
2 One in his attributes; not having a multiplicity of powers or wills.
3 One in his works; no other being besides God has any influence on God at all.

Surah (chapter) 112 in the Qur'an (Surat-al-Ikhlas) expresses the idea of *tawhid* in this way:

> In the name of God, the Merciful, the Compassionate
> Say: 'He is God, One,
> God, the Everlasting Refuge,
> who has not begotten, and has not been begotten,
> and equal to Him is not any one.'

For Mawdudi, belief in the unity of God will give the believer a generous and broad-minded outlook on life and will enhance his self-respect, produce modesty and humility, and make him virtuous and upright in all his dealings. Furthermore, understanding and belief in this primary *kalima* will enable the Muslim to be optimistic, satisfied with life, patient, persevering and determined, as well as brave. But, Mawdudi considers that the most important influence of *tawhid* is that it will ensure that the believer will obey the laws of God: '... He will shun what God has forbidden and he will carry out his behests even in solitude and in darkness, because he knows that God's "police" never leaves him alone, and he dreads the court whose warrant he can never avoid.'[7] And Ghulam Sarwar, in *Islam: Beliefs and Teachings*, writes: 'A believer in Tawhid seeks the pleasure of Allah by making his belief and action go together. Belief without practice has no place in Islam.'[8]

Having considered the essential importance of *tawhid* in Islam, let us examine why Islam accuses Christians of committing the grave sin of '*shirk*' — associating others with God in his divinity, in particular Jesus Christ.

Firstly, Muslims suggest that because Christians believe in the incarnation of God in Christ, they fail to differentiate clearly between the divine and the natural (see previous section 3, **What is The Meaning of Islam?**).

It is important to remember that we cannot talk about God without talking about man, about how man acquires knowledge of God. Both Christianity and Islam affirm that reality is a dualism — that the transcendental realm, the Creator and the natural realm of creation co-exist. They also agree that in this respect we can know something of God only because God has chosen to reveal something of himself. Revelation is a free and deliberate act of God. Both religions agree that God has not revealed all that he is, so that the questions which arise concerning God's revelation turn on *how* and *what* God reveals. As a result, Christianity and Islam make different statements about God.

Islam would suggest that God does not reveal himself; he only reveals his will. This is because it is not considered possible to reconcile complete transcendence and self-revelation.

On the other hand, Christians believe that God in Christ not only revealed something of his will, but also something of himself as God. He even promised to dwell in every believer so that they become 'God's temples' and 'living stones' (I Corinthians 3:17, I Peter 2:5).

Activity

Can you think of some of the claims of Jesus found in the Bible which, in the eyes of Muslims, mean he and his followers are guilty of *shirk*?

Here are some: Matthew 8:27; Matthew 10:32; John 14:23; John 15:16; Mark 13:31.

5:2 *God's angels*

Angels are a special creation of God. They are beings endued with bodies created from divine light. They neither eat nor drink. There is no distinction of sexes among them.

Angels do not have free will, their chief chacacteristic being complete obedience to the will of God. Their time is spent praising God day and night and carrying out their given duties.

There has been a theological discussion in the history of Islam as to whether angels are to be regarded as superior in rank to human beings, in particular the prophets, because they do not deviate from God's law. However, the Qur'an says:

> And when thy Lord said to the angels, 'See, I am creating a mortal of a clay of mud moulded. When I have shaped him, and breathed My spirit in him, fall you down, bowing before him!' Then the angels bowed themselves all together, save Iblis (the devil); he refused to be among those bowing (15:34–35).

Prominent among the angels are the four archangels: *Jibra'il* (Gabriel), God's messenger and the Angel of Revelation, because he brought God's revelation to Muhammad; *Mika'il* (Michael), who is said to have been the friend and protector of the Jews (Daniel 12:1); *Izra'il*, who is considered the angel of death; and *Israfil*, who will blow the trumpet at the day of resurrection and judgement.

In addition to these archangels there are guardian angels, who protect man from dangers and calamities which are not decreed by God. Two recording angels attend every man. The one on his right records his good deeds and words; the one on his left records all his sins. There are also the *throne-bearers* and the *cherubim*. Angels will receive the obedient believer in heaven and will throw the disobedient wrong-doer into hell.

Two other angels are *Munkar* and *Nakir*. They are two huge, fierce-looking angels who visit every man in his grave immediately after the funeral is over to examine him as to his beliefs in God and in Muhammad, and to torture him if he cannot answer satisfactorily.

5:3 *The Books of God*

Every Muslim is to believe in the divinely inspired books which God has sent down from time to time, to various peoples, through his apostles or prophets. Ghulam Sarwar writes: 'Allah's greatest favour to mankind is his guidance contained in the books of revelation.'[9]

The number of books sent down is believed to be 104. Of these, *only five* are named in the Qur'an. They are:

The *Scrolls of Abraham* (now lost).

The *Tawrat* (the Torah) given to the prophet Musa (Moses).

The *Zabur* (the Psalms) given to the prophet Dawud (David).

The *Injil* (the Gospel) given to the prophet Isa (Jesus).

The *Qur'an* revealed to the prophet Muhammad.

Some Muslims suggest that all other books except the Qur'an have been changed, altered and corrupted, in both language and content.

Mawdudi lists two 'very pertinent differences' between the Qur'an and the other books:

> 1   The original texts of most of the former Divine Books were lost altogether, and only their translations exist today. The Qur'an, on the other hand, exists exactly as it was revealed to the Prophet; not a word — nay, not a syllable of it — has been changed. It is available in its original text and the Word of God has been preserved for all time.
>
> 2   In the former Divine Books man mixed his words with God's, but in the Qur'an we find only the words of God — and in their pristine purity. This is admitted even by the opponents of Islam.[10]

The Qur'an is a book that was revealed in the Arabic tongue and is seen to be an exact copy of a book that exists in heaven on a tablet. It was brought down to Muhammad by the angel Gabriel, who instructed him to recite it.

Chapter 5 gives a more detailed account of the Qur'an and Chapter 6 discusses the question of corruption of the other books.

5:4 *The prophets of God*
Ghulam Sarwar writes:

> Since the beginning of creation, Allah has sent his guidance for mankind through his selected people. These chosen people are called prophets or messengers. They asked the people of their time to obey and worship Allah alone. They taught, guided and trained the people to follow the way of Allah.[11]

Like the holy books which God revealed to man, the sending of the prophets is also to be considered as an act of free grace on the part of God. According to a saying of Muhammad, God has sent 124,000 prophets. The Arabic and Hebrew word for prophet is *nabi* but Muhammad is also a *rasul* or Apostle and Messenger. He is also described as a *nadhir* or warner and a *monvir* or announcer.

The Qur'an mentions only the 25 most prominent prophets by name. Twenty-one of them are biblical figures (they are not necessarily prophets in the biblical sense). Out of the 124,000, 313 are said to have been special 'messengers', sent with Books, while the others were merely 'prophets', that is divinely guided men with a general message but without a Book.

The central core of the messages of all the prophets and messengers was the same, *la ilaha illalla* (there is no God but Allah). According to the Qur'an, God has sent prophets to every nation and people throughout history, to direct them; so that on the day of judgement no one will be able to say he never knew the right path.

Muslims are to affirm and believe in all God's prophets, from Adam to Muhammad. Anyone who does not believe in a particular prophet is an unbeliever, even if he believes in all the others. Faith in God's prophets rests on the assumption that they all taught the same straight path, that is, Islam.

Muslims believe in Jesus as a bringer of Islam like Muhammad. This is why Muslims often, with sadness, ask Christians, 'We believe in Jesus, why do you not believe in Muhammad?'

5:5 *Belief in life after death*
The Qur'an says, 'What, does man reckon We shall not gather his bones? Yes indeed; We are able to shape again his fingers' (75:3–4).

Allah is the one who gives life and has appointed the hour for man to die. Belief in life after death (*akhirah*) is one of the three most important beliefs in Islam. Ghulam Sarwar writes:

> Belief in *Akhirah* is very important and is vital for all Muslims. Our life on this earth is temporary and is meant to be a preparation for *Akhirah* which is *never ending*. Life on this earth becomes meaningless if good actions are not rewarded and bad conduct punished.[12]

Mawdudi also stresses its importance, writing, 'The Prophet Muhammad (blessings of Allah and peace be upon him) has directed us to believe in resurrection after death and in the Day of Judgement.'[13] He lists the 'essential ingredients of this belief' as follows:

1 There will be a last day, when life on earth will end and everything be annihilated.
2 God will sit in judgement on that day. All human beings who have ever lived, will be presented to him.
3 The full record of everyone's good and bad deeds will be presented to him.
4 Each person will either be rewarded if his good deeds outweigh his bad ones, or punished if his bad outweigh his good.
5 Those who are rewarded will go to Paradise; those who are punished will go to Hell.

There are popular stories about death and the end of the world, of which the following is an example. Immediately after the funeral is over, the two angels, Munkar and Nakir, visit the dead man in his grave, whether or not he is a Muslim. They examine the dead person as to his belief in *tawhid* and the divine mission of Muhammad. In response to the questions, 'Who is your Lord?', 'What is your religion?', and 'Who is your prophet?' a true believer will answer, 'Allah is my Lord, Islam is my religion and Muhammad is my prophet.' Following such a satisfactory answer, the obedient believer is assured of the mercy of God and the delights of Paradise. His grave is made wide and comfortable and a window is put in, so that he can look into Paradise and behold what is in store for him.

There are also signs which it is thought will inaugurate the last day. These are:
1 The appearance of the *mahdi*, a mighty conqueror, who will cause the Muslims to become a great nation.
2 The appearance of Antichrist from between Iraq and Syria. He will roam the world for 40 days, laying it waste, before he is slain by Jesus.
3 The return of Jesus, Ibn Maryam, who will take a wife and have children. He will call everyone to accept Islam. During his 40 years on earth there will be peace such as has never existed before (as described in Isaiah 11:6). Then he will die and be buried alongside Muhammad in Medina.
4 The sun will rise from the west.
5 The destruction of the Ka'ba and the removal of written copies of the Qur'an and its words from people's memories.

The Qur'an describes life after death and the day of judgement in some detail, for example:

Surely for the godfearing awaits a place of security,
gardens and vineyards
and maidens with swelling breasts, like of age,
and a cup overflowing.
Therein they shall hear not idle talk, no cry of lies,
for a recompense from thy Lord, a gift, a reckoning,
Lord of the heavens and earth, and all that between them is,
the All-merciful
of whom they have no power to speak (78:34–35).

Truly the godfearing shall dwell amid shades and fountains,
and such fruits as their hearts desire (77:41).

There are also warnings concerning the fate of unbelievers:

Lo, we have warned you of a nigh chastisement,
upon the day when a man shall behold what his hands
have forwarded,
and the unbeliever shall say, 'O would that I were
dust!' (78:40).

Activities
1 Please look back over the six articles of faith, considering the Christian teaching relating to them. For each article note, firstly, the things which, as a Christian, you agree with, secondly, the things you disagree with and, thirdly, the things you would like to add.
2 Discuss the beliefs of Islam with your Muslim friends. Remember the hints given in Chapter 2, about finding Muslim friends, before you do this.

THE FIVE PRACTICAL DUTIES OF ISLAM

6 Introduction

This part concentrates on the practical duties of Islam. It is important that you take time to find out what they mean in the lives of practising Muslims.

There are five practical duties and they are often referred to as the 'Five Pillars'. They are:

1	The Declaration of Faith	(*Shahada*)
2	Five compulsory daily prayers	(*Salat*)
3	Welfare contribution	(*Zakat*)
4	Pilgrimage to Mecca	(*Hajj*)
5	Fasting during the month of Ramadan	(*Sawn*)

Shiite Muslims would add *jihad*, 'striving in the cause of God' to this list.

All the practical duties are important. Allah has put them together as a training programme for all mankind, designed to control evil desires and passions. Mawdudi says, 'The more assiduously we follow the training, the better equipped we are to harmonise ideals and practices.'[14] Ghulam Sarwar says that if we perform the five basic duties regularly and correctly, we come closer to Allah.[15]

However, the five compulsory daily prayers (*salat*) are considered the most fundamental of these obligations.

7:1 *The declaration of As-Shahada*

The first duty of a Muslim is to declare his faith that 'there is no God (or deity) but Allah' and 'Muhammad is Allah's messenger (apostle).' To say this declaration in Arabic in front of a judge, or two witnesses, and to believe it, are all that are required of a person to become a member of the community of believers (*ummah*).

7:2 *The five compulsory daily prayers (Salat)*

Before any prayers, ritual washing is performed by washing in a prescribed way. The name for this is *wudu*.

Muslims always pray facing the direction of Mecca. This direction is the *qiblah*.

The five prescribed prayers consist of a set cycle of words and ritual gestures (bowings/*raka'hs*). At the early stages Muhammad and his followers performed only two prayers, the morning prayer before sunrise and the evening prayer after sunset. Besides these they used to spend a great part of the night in prayer. After the famous night journey of Muhammad, five daily prayers were prescribed (*Surah* 17:80).

Additional *raka'hs* are recommended according to the *sunnah* (sayings and deeds of Muhammad). These are called *sunnah* prayers.

The words which accompany the gestures must be learnt by heart and uttered in the Arabic tongue, regardless of the language of the person praying. *Salat* is seen as a collective and social act. The common use of Arabic by all worshippers emphasises the universality of Islam. This sense of solidarity is also reinforced by the knowledge that Muslims everywhere, each day, are repeating the same words and gestures, while facing the city of Mecca, the birthplace of the prophet and the scene of his first revelations and of his triumph over the Meccans. Muslims may pray in mosques at other times, but Muslim men are expected to attend a mosque on Friday afternoons to pray and to hear a sermon. At the main festivals, the large mosques are filled with hundreds of Muslims. This, too, helps to give a sense of unity in worship and of brotherhood.

Personal prayers (*du'a*), whether praise, thanksgiving, or supplication may be added afterwards. These may be uttered in one's own language, but it is considered better to memorise some in Arabic.

7:3 *Welfare contributions (Zakat)*

Zakat is the third pillar of Islam. It is not almsgiving or charity because it is a compulsory payment. On the other hand it is not a general tax because it is to be spent under fixed headings. Muhammad emphasized *zakat* as a religious duty. He was an orphan himself and so was concerned for the destitute, poor, and needy. The Qur'an also mentions a voluntary type of giving which is called *sadaqah* (charity).

7:4 *Fasting (Sawm) in the month of Ramadan*

Sawm is the fourth pillar of Islam. All adult Muslims (male and female who have reached the age of puberty) must abstain from all food, drink, and conjugal relations from sunrise to sunset. Travellers and sick persons as well as menstruating women can defer *sawm* during Ramadan and make up for it later. Young children and old people, insane persons, pregnant and nursing women are exempted from observing *sawm*.

The month of Ramadan is the ninth month in the Islamic calendar. This means that Ramadan moves slowly around our calendar, beginning eleven days earlier each year and needing about 33 years to complete the cycle. Even though *sawm* cannot be considered a complete fast over 30 days, as Muslims are allowed to eat, drink, and have conjugal relations between sunset and sunrise, it does require a considerable degree of self-discipline from everyone observing the fast. Fasting is seen as an important part in building one's spiritual character.

On the subject of fasting Mawdudi writes:

> Rigour and discipline during this month bring us face to face with the realities of life and help us make our life, during the rest of the year, a life of true subservi-

ence to his Will.

… Fasting has an immense impact on society, for all the Muslims irrespective of their status must fast during the same month. This emphasises the essential equality of men and thus goes a long way towards creating in them sentiments of love and brotherhood.[16]

Activity

Ask a Muslim to tell you about fasting. He or she will undoubtedy first of all give you a textbook answer, but if he or she has become your friend you may also ask about his personal experiences with fasting. As you talk together think about what the Bible says about fasting. Here are some verses which may help you: Matthew 6:16–18; Luke 5:33–35; Acts 13:2–3.

7:5 *Pilgrimage (Hajj) to Mecca*

Now we come to the fifth and last of the pillars of Islam.

Muslims believe that the first Al-Ka'ba was built by Adam. This stone building was damaged and rebuilt many times throughout history. The Ka'ba was a centre for worship among the Arabs before the time of Muhammad. Inside the building is a big room. This room is now empty. In pre-Islamic times the room was full of statues of idols. When Muhammad and his followers entered Mecca in 630 AD, the pinnacle of Islam's triumph, they destroyed the idols. Muslims all over the world pray in the direction of this building.

'The Black Stone' is a meteorite stone located in the northeastern corner of the Ka'ba. It is believed to have been white at the time of Adam, but man's iniquities are supposed to have given it its present colour.

A man who has performed the *hajj* may dye his beard yellow or orange and may wear a small white skull cap. These marks then become a visible sign of his spirituality. In many areas this gives him higher status. He is known as a '*hajji*'.

The traditions of Muhammad say that every step taken by the pilgrim in the direction of the Ka'ba blots out a sin and the person who dies on his pilgrimage is enrolled among the martyrs.

Activity

Try to find a Muslim friend who has been on *hajj* and ask him to tell you about it.

7:6 *Jihad*

Jihad does not belong to the five practical pillars of Islam, but is repeatedly emphasised in the Qur'an and the Traditions. The word has been interpreted and understood in various ways since the time of Muhammad. It is an Arabic word which means 'to struggle to the utmost of one's capacity.'[17] It has varying interpretations: A 'holy war' and defence of Islam; raiding and conquest druing the early spread of Islam; a modern call to propagate Islam; and personal self discipline.

Jihad has been fought with swords and modern weapons, with speech, and pen and paper, with a call to moral, intellectual and spiritual renewal. *Jihad* is continually being fought within the believer and, at times, between believers and non-believers. *Jihad* has many sides. Some writers have played down the war aspect and underlined the ethical and moral aspects instead. Most writers mention the word as propagation of and call to Islam.

Activities

1 You may like to ask your Muslim friend how he views the concept of *jihad* and how it is to be interpreted in today's world.
2 From your discussions with Muslims, what percentage of Muslims would you say keep all five pillars of the faith?
3 Do Muslims who keep the pillars feel more assured of a place in heaven?

Recommended Reading

MAWDUDI, Abul A'la. *Towards Understanding Islam*, Islamic Foundation, Leicester, 1981.

Additional Reading

ARBERRY, Arthur J. *The Koran Interpreted*, OUP, 1983. Recommended reading for Chapter 5.
SARWAR, Ghulam. *Islam: Beliefs and Teachings*, Muslim Educational Trust, London, 3rd ed., 1984.

Notes

1 MAWDUDI, Abul A'la. *Towards Understanding Islam*, Islamic Foundation, Leicester, 1981, p18.
2 Ibid, p19.
3 Ibid, pp21–22.
4 Ibid, p25.
5 Ibid, p26.
6 Ibid, p62.
7 Ibid, p72.
8 SARWAR, Ghulam. *Islam: Beliefs and Teachings*, Muslim Educational Trust, London, 3rd ed., 1984, p23.
9 Ibid, p29.
10 MAWDUDI, Abul A'la. *Towards Understanding Islam*, Islamic Foundation, Leicester, 1981, p75.
11 SARWAR, Ghulam. *Islam: Beliefs and Teachings*, Muslim Educational Trust, London, 3rd ed., 1984, p26.
12 Ibid, p37.
13 MAWDUDI, Abul A'la. *Towards Understanding Islam*, Islamic Foundation, Leicester, 1981, p79.
14 Ibid, p88.
15 SARWAR, Ghulam. *Islam: Beliefs and Teachings*, Muslim Educational Trust, London, 3rd ed., 1984, p74.
16 MAWDUDI, Abul A'la. *Towards Understanding Islam*, Islamic Foundation, Leicester, 1981, p91.
17 Ibid, p94.

Chapter 5

THE QUR'AN

1 Study Guide

You will have seen the central place the Qur'an has in Islam from studying Chapter 3/4. Ronald Waine has written this introduction to further study of the book to help you as you read and try to understand it. When you have completed the chapter you will not be able to understand the Qur'an fully but will have looked at the way it is constructed and at some of the main subjects of its teaching.

Learning objectives
When you have completed this chapter you should:

1 Understand why Muslims hold the Qur'an in such high esteem.
2 Have seen why in Muslim eyes the Qur'an was necessary.
3 Be able to relate the development of the Qur'an to events in the life of Muhammad and know how the text of the book was collected.
4 Begin to understand the place the Qur'an has in formulating Muslim beliefs.
5 Understand Muslim objections to translating the Arabic text.

2 Introduction

Thomas Carlyle in *Heroes and Hero Worship* said, 'Nothing but a sense of duty could carry a European through the Qur'an.'

Yet the Qur'an is the book accepted by more than 850 million human beings as God's final message to mankind. Its influence on the course of history has been, and will continue to be, immense. It has been the inspiration of an amazing culture. It is the basis of religious belief. It is the basis of Islamic law. It moulds Muslim thought and is the blueprint for Islamic society.

But above all, for the orthodox Muslim it is 'a scripture to be confessed', 'a sacrament of mind and voice'. The actual recitation of the Qur'an brings blessing and merit, so Muslims are encouraged to learn it by heart.

3   Unless you read Arabic you will have to be content with an 'interpretation', for the first important fact to recognise is that it is an *Arabic* Qur'an. The Arabic words are considered to be God's words, so the language itself is an intrinsic part of the revelation.

> We have made it an Arabic Koran; haply you will understand it (43:2).

> An Arabic Koran for people having knowledge (41:2).

> Had we revealed the Koran in a foreign tongue they would have said 'If only its verses were expounded! Why in a foreign tongue when the prophet is Arabian?' (41:44, Dawood).

These and other *surahs* have led almost all Muslim commentators to agree that God willed the revelation to Muhammad to be an Arabic Qur'an. This doctrine applies both to its *form* and to its *substance*. If God willed it to be an Arabic Qur'an it is no part of 'submission' to translate it. In fact Muslims assert that it is untranslatable. So Pickthall (an English Muslim) calls his English translation *The Meaning of the Glorious Qur'an* and A J Arberry calls our recommended book *The Koran Interpreted*.

Activity
A question to think about is: If Muhammad had had access to the Bible in Arabic during his lifetime, would there have been a Qur'an?

In fact the Bible had not at that time been translated into Arabic and all that Muhammad learnt of the history of the Jews and the life and teachings of Christ was from the Jews and Christians he had met.

4   The Origin and Transmission, Compilation and Preservation of the Qur'an

Origin
Muslim theologians all agree that the Qur'an is the words of Allah and declare that the text is on a 'guarded tablet' kept in the presence of Allah.

> Nay, but it is a glorious Koran in a guarded tablet (85:21).

> It is a transcript of Our Eternal Book (Arabic = 'Mother of the Book') sublime, full of wisdom (43:3, Dawood).

Muslims believe that the Qur'an is the miracle which authenticates Muhammad's claim to be a prophet. It enhances the miracle when, as is widely believed, Muhammad could neither read nor write.

Transmission
How did the Qur'an come to Muhammad and what does Qur'an mean?

We have already noted (Chapter 3/4, section 5:3, *The Books of God*) the circumstances of Muhammad's 'vision' of the angel Gabriel and the instruction then received to 'recite'. See *surah* 96, which is generally believed to be the first of the oracles brought to Muhammad.

This word 'recite' (*iqra*) is the word from which Qur'an is derived. So the Qur'an is a recitation, or thing to be recited, or a reading or word to be read. Following the first vision in 611 AD, there was a gap of two years and only after the encouragement of his wife Khadija did the visions recommence and continue intermittently throughout his life until his death in 632 AD. The whole of the Qur'an was 'received' in 23 years.

5   The Qur'an around the Life of Muhammad

It is convenient in this introductory study to consider the Qur'an around the life of Muhammad. (We shall be studying the life of Muhammad in more detail in Chapter 7. His ministry started in the city of Mecca. Later, in 622, he moved with his followers to Medina.) It is customary to divide the 'revelations' as coming in three periods; The First Meccan period (611–615 AD), the Second Meccan period (616–622 AD); and the Medinan period (623–632 AD).

5:1 *The First Meccan Period*
During the first period Muhammad is mainly a 'warner' (see 87:9). Those who accept the warnings will be blessed, but those who turn aside will 'burn forever in the great fire' (98:6). *Surahs* received during this period contain many of the leading ideas of the Qur'an.

The recitation of the oracles has a twofold purpose: It is a teaching method; and it enables men, by the use of the very words of Allah, to perform acceptable worship. The oracles declare God's goodness in creation. The oracles are a written revelation of Allah's will. The oracles call for man to turn from the worship of idols and false gods to worship the one true God, ALLAH. (You will remember the name is the Arabic word meaning 'The God').

The *surahs* from this period are mostly short. The first revelation is *surah* 96. Read this and some of the others of this period such as 112 for a clear statement on the Muslim concept of the unity of God. Other *surahs* which touch on this theme are 81, 83, 74, 111, and 87.

5:2 *The Second Meccan Period*
The first period ends with growing opposition to the new teaching which caused some Muslims to emigrate to Abyssinia. Muhammad seems to have thought that his movement would be free to develop under the patronage of the Christian emperor there. His hope was disappointed. Now the *surahs* get longer. There is more discussion and more doctrine. Biblical material creeps in. Some *surahs* are given the names of Bible characters as titles, eg Noah, Mary, Joseph, Abraham. Islam is now declared to be the one true religion. 'Your religion is but one religion, and I am your only Lord' (21:92, Dawood).

The miraculous nature of the Qur'an is now affirmed and previous 'revelations' in the early *surahs* are reiterated and confirmed. *Surahs* from this period include 53, 43, 38, 39, 17, 23, 46, and 72.

5:3 *The Medinan Period*

The period from the *hijra*, 622 AD, to his death was when Muhammad was the leader of the new community based in Medina. The main thrust of the messages is now the divine approval and blessing of Muhammad's leadership. There are numerous references to historic events which emphasise his growing political authority.

Students have noted two leading features in the *surahs* of this period. Firstly, Muhammad changed from preacher to prince. He begins to legislate in order to control the development of the new community. The times for prayer are fixed in more detail and the fast is changed from the Day of Atonement to the month of Ramadan. Secondly, Muhammad also changed his attitude to the Jews and Christians who had refused to accept his claim to be the apostle of Allah and his prophet. See *surah* 33:40, where he is stated to be: '... the Messenger of God and the seal of the Prophets.' The style of the earlier periods remains but the subject matter changes.

During this period some of the oracles seem to be included to justify his own family life. For example, he had married the divorced wife of his adopted son, Zaid, contrary to traditional custom. *Surah* 33:2,23,33, and 37 refer to this with approval.

6 *'The Cow'*

Perhaps the best known *surah* of this period is that with the strange title 'The Cow'. This *surah* sets forth in a kind of sequence some fundamental principles of Islam.

Extracts from 'The Cow' (Surah 2)	*Some of the Concepts of Islam*
The book wherein is no doubt (v2).	The authority and divine origin of the Qur'an.
A guidance to the godfearing (v2).	
He (Allah) Who created for you all that is in the earth (v26).	God is creator of heaven and earth.
And We said, 'Adam draw not nigh to this tree! Then Satan caused them to slip....' (v33).	Satan caused Adam to sin.

And We gave to Moses the Book, and after him sent succeeding messengers (v81).

God has given precious scriptures which the Qur'an confirms.

We gave Jesus the son of Mary the clear signs and confirmed him with the Holy Spirit (v82).

He (Gabriel) it was that brought it (the Qur'an) down upon thy heart by the leave of God, confirming what was before it, and for a guidance and good tidings to the believers (v92).

And for whatever verse We abrogate or cast into oblivion We bring a better or the like of it (v100).

Later scriptures abrogate former where there is a difference. Even later verses of the Qur'an can replace earlier ones.

They (the Christians) say, God has taken to Him a son' ... Nay (Dawood, 'God forbid')....' (v110).

Allah could not beget a son.

Take to yourselves Abraham's station for a place of prayer (v118). (Refers to Ka'ba; see Chapter 3/4, section 7:5)

Islam is the true faith of Abraham.

Who therefore shrinks from the religion of Abraham, except he be foolish-minded (v123).

Activity

Read through *surah* 2, 'The Cow', and find other themes which are also included in the Bible. Note how these are presented and compare the differences in the two books.

A useful aid to the study of the Qur'an is *Topical Concordance to Qur'an*, translated by Aubrey Whitehouse from Muhammad al Araby al Azuzy.

7 Notes on the Surahs

The Qur'an is divided into 114 *surahs* of unequal length. The word *'surah'* derives, so most think, from a Hebrew word meaning a 'row' (of bricks in a wall or of vines in a vineyard). The *surahs* are not numbered in oriental editions but have the titles which were originally given in the collection made by Uthman, the Third Caliph. In preparing the Qur'an for book form the editors arranged the *surahs* generally in order of length. Each *surah*, except No 9, 'Repentance', begins with the phrase 'In the name of Allah, the compassionate, the merciful'. The verses, or *ayat*, were not marked in the original manuscripts. Numbers given in English translations may vary by as many as four or five verses, so if those you look up do not seem right, look at the adjacent verses as well. No adequate explanation has ever been given for the mysterious letters which appear after the inscription 'in the name of Allah ...' in 29 of the *surahs*.

8 How the Text was Collected and Preserved

Muslim tradition asserts that the first collection of the Qur'an was made under Abu Bakr, Muhammad's successor and First Caliph. Umar, the Second Caliph, had become disturbed that many of the 'reciters' of the Qur'an who had committed the oracles to memory were being killed, and it was feared that the Qur'an would become irretrievably lost. So Abu Bakr commissioned Zayd-ibn-Thabit, who had been one of Muhammad's secretaries, to collect the Qur'an. He carried out his task with great care. One tradition records that he collected 'not only from the hearts of men, but also from pieces of parchment or papyrus, flat stones, palm leaves, shoulder blades, ribs of animals, pieces of leather and wooden boards.' It is said that he wrote all he collected on sheets of equal size which after the death of Umar passed into the care of Hafsa, a widow of Muhammad.

This collection by Zayd was almost certainly the basis of a completion of the text ordered by Uthman. There is little doubt that the book we have today is the Uthmanic Qur'an. When disputes arose as to the different readings the dialect of the Quraysh (Muhammad's tribe) was preferred. Four standard copies were placed at Medina, Kufa, Basra, and Damascus. Variant readings were destroyed. Muslim theologians always assume the authenticity of the text as we have it now and have never questioned the divine origin and inspiration and authority of the Qur'an.

9 What Does the Qur'an Mean to a Muslim?

Colin Chapman in his book, *You Go and Do the Same*, presents four answers to this question:

> It is essential to realise that the Qur'an is to the Muslim what Jesus is to the Christian. It is a mistake to make a direct comparison between the role of Jesus in Christianity and the role of Muhammad in Islam, or between the place of the Bible in Christianity and the place of the Qur'an in Islam.

He then points out, 'Muslims believe that the revelation of the Qur'an was itself a miracle, since Muhammad himself was not able to read or write.'[1]
The third point he mentions is:

> In order to appreciate what the Qur'an means to a Muslim we ought to hear it recited. Since the Qur'an was revealed in Arabic, the Arabic of the Qur'an is an essential part of the message and part of the appeal of the Qur'an for the Muslim lies in the beauty of the Arabic.[2]

The final point is that, for the Muslim, the Qur'an is 'a message which calls him to worship and surrender.' This means that he is not worried by its lack of chronological order, it is not a historical account.

10 The Crucial Question

Perhaps the crucial question Christians have to ask is, 'Is the Qur'an the word of God or isn't it?'
Some phrase the question differently and ask, is it 'a word from God' or does it contain 'part of God's word'? Most modern scholars prefer not to answer this question.
For example Montgomery Watt in his work, *Muhammad and Mecca* writes:

> In order to avoid deciding whether the Qur'an is, or is not, the word of God I have refrained from using the expressions 'God says' and 'Muhammad says' when referring to the Qur'an and have simply said, 'The Qur'an says'.[3]

Older writers, almost without exception, were more ready to assert categorically that it was not the word of God. Some were ready to label it 'the devil's supreme counterfeit'. Many would still take this view.

The orthodox Muslim has no doubt whatsoever. 'Every pious Muslim holds that the Qur'an is, in the simplest and fullest possible sense, The word of God. There is no human element in it.'[4]

Several points must be made:

1   The Qur'an and the New Testament contradict each other.

2   The Qur'an's 'One God' and the New Testament 'Triune God' are different, yet similar.

3   Qur'anic law cannot be reconciled with the grace of God.

4   The Qur'an categorically denies that Christ died on the cross and rose again on the third day, facts of crucial significance for the Christian and which are affirmed to be historical events in the New Testament.

The answer we give to the question, 'Is the Qur'an the word of God, or not?' will undoubtedly be influenced by our attitude to the Bible. For those who hold the Bible to be the inspired, infallible Word of God the answer is clear. The Qur'an cannot be. It can only be, at best, the record of a sincere, but misguided man seeking to express his convictions about the relation of man (the slave) to God (the master).

Some Christians, whilst holding firmly to the belief that the Bible is the divinely inspired and infallible Word of God, would be prepared to concede that parts of the Qur'an, where it agrees with the Bible, or where it points to a biblical truth, are true, and may therefore be used as a starting point in reaching out to Muslims. We accept that the Qur'an is true, in part, without necessarily according to it divine inspiration.

If one goes further and accepts the present-day pluralist view that there are many revelations of the godhead, each one designed for a particular time and culture, then both the Qur'an and the Bible are but two of many religious books, seemingly different, but basically all pointing to an ultimate in which all will eventually be found to unite.

Look back at Chapter 1, section 2 *'How Should Christians Respond to Those of Other Faiths?'* to remind yourself about the pluralist view.

The concept of revelation in the New Testament is quite different from that in the Qur'an. It should never be forgotten that

57

whereas the Qur'an claims to be the revelation of the law and will of God, the New Testament claims to be the historic, divinely inspired and accurate record of the life and teachings of Jesus Christ. It also claims that he himself is the Word of God. 'The Word became flesh and lived for a while among us' (John 1:14). 'For God was pleased to have all his fulness dwell in him (Jesus)' (Colossians 1:19).

Christians believe that the writers of the Bible were inspired by God to write the truth in their own language, rather than to receive and pass on God's actual words. 'All scripture is God-breathed ('inspired by God', RSV) ...' (2 Timothy 3:16).

John Stott, commenting on this phrase, writes:

> The meaning, then, is not that God breathed into the writers, nor that he somehow breathed into the writings to give them their special character, but that what was written by men was breathed out by God. He spoke through them. They were his spokesmen.[5]

Activity
Something to think about: How far is it correct to talk about 'a battle of the books'?

This catch phrase is used by Bishop Jens Christenson in his lectures on *The Practical Approach to Muslims*. He says:

> ...There is a sense in which Christianity's contact with Islam is definitely a battle of the books, yet in the final analysis it is utterly wrong to speak of a battle of books as though the New Testament in Christianity had the same position as the Qur'an in Islam.[6]

Look back over the last two sections to make sure you are clear about this.

Recommended Reading

ARBERRY, Arthur J. *The Koran Interpreted*, OUP, 1983.

Additional Reading

AL-AZUZY, Muhammad. *Topical Concordance to Qur'an*, BCV Press, Lilydale, Australia, 2nd ed., 1981. Translated by Aubrey Whitehouse.

DAWOOD, N J. *The Koran Translated with Notes*, Penguin, Harmondsworth, Middlesex, 4th ed., 1974.

Notes

1 CHAPMAN, Colin. *You Go and Do the Same*, CMS, BMMF Int. IFES, London, 1983, p31.
2 Ibid, p32.
3 WATT, W Montgomery. *Mohammed and Mecca*, OUP, 1953, p x.
4 NEILL, Bishop Stephen. *Crises of Belief*, Hodder & Stoughton, London, 1984, p69.
5 STOTT, John R W, *Understanding the Bible*, Scripture Union, London, 1972, p183.
6 CHRISTENSON, Bishop Jens. *The Practical Approach to Muslims*, NAM, Marseilles, 1977, p316.

Chapter 6

CHRISTIANS AND MUSLIMS DEBATING TOGETHER

1 Study Guide and Introduction

This chapter, as its title suggests, moves into the sphere of apologetics, or defence of our beliefs against opposing views. Christians and Muslims have a long history of debating together; indeed, one of the books used in obtaining this material is based on a debate which took place as recently as August 1981. Generally speaking, such debates are rare nowadays. It is, however, important that we should be clear on the issues which divide us. Unless we have grasped what the Bible and the Qur'an say on some of the basic questions of our faith, we cannot explain our point of view. It has been said that we may win an argument, but lose a friend; we must learn to be humble, gentle, and sensitive in our approach to this subject.

Ron George, Sarah James and Roger Malstead have written this chapter. It looks at some of the main doctrines which divide Christians and Muslims. This seemed to be better than attempting to cover all the controversial beliefs. There is no specific book recommended in the reading list at the end of the chapter. All are useful in studying apologetics.

As the chapter is rather longer than the others, no activities are included. If you have time, we suggest that you study the biblical and qur'anic references and their contexts in detail. You could also make notes on how you might answer some of the questions your Muslim friends might ask.

Learning objectives
When you have completed this chapter you should:

1   Begin to understand the main differences in teaching between Christianity and Islam as they relate to the divinity, crucifixion and resurrection of Jesus.
2   Have developed some insights into the ways of counteracting Muslim objections to Christian teaching.

2   The Testimony of the Qur'an to the Bible

2:1 *Qur'anic references to the Bible*
It is important to see what the Qur'an actually says about the Bible.

With reference to the Torah, which is the books of the law (the Pentateuch), the Qur'an states:

> Indeed, We gave Moses the Book; so be not in doubt concerning the encounter with Him; and We appointed it for a guidance to the Children of Israel (32:24).

> Surely We sent down the Torah, wherein is guidance and light; thereby the Prophets who had surrendered themselves gave judgement ... following such portion of God's Book as they were given to keep and were witnesses to (5:47).

Referring to the *Injil*, which is the New Testament:

> And We sent, following in their footsteps, Jesus son of Mary, confirming the Torah before him; and We gave to him the Gospel wherein is guidance and light, and confirming the Torah before it, as a guidance and an admonition unto the godfearing (5:50).

Referring to the whole Bible, the Qur'an says: 'And We have sent down to thee the Book with the truth, confirming the Book that was before it, and assuring it' (5:52).

There does not seem to be any doubt that the Qur'an teaches that the Bible is from God and must be believed.

2:2 *Corruption of the Bible*
Most Muslims claim that the Bible has been changed or corrupted. In answer to this we can point to many manuscripts in the

original Hebrew and Greek that make that claim invalid; even the Qur'an itself makes no such statement. In fact, it says:

> Perfect are the words of thy Lord in truthfulness and justice; no man can change His words; He is the All-hearing, the All-knowing (6:45).

> No man can change the words of God... (6:34).

> There is no changing the words of God; that is the mighty triumph (10:65).

It appears then, that any Muslim who says that the Bible has been changed is contradicting the Qur'an!

Possibly Muslims base their assertion on the following *surah*: 'Hast thou not regarded those who were given a share of the Book purchasing error, and desiring that you should also err from the way?' (4:47).

But it is clear from the context that Muhammad was speaking only of some of the Jews who opposed his teaching and who verbally, by mispronouncing words, twisted the meaning of the message. No such charge is ever made against Christians in the Qur'an (4:48–49).

It is interesting, at this point, to see what one Muslim writer says about corruption of the Bible:

> The Bible, as it is available today, has many incorrect things in it. Its authenticity and divinity are doubtful. It contains misleading and false stories about the Prophets. The message of Allah sent through them was either lost or distorted through neglect and folly of their followers. As against this, the Qur'an contains Allah's guidance for mankind in its original language, unchanged and undistorted. It restates in clear and unambiguous language the message of Allah which the followers of ealier prophets have lost. The message of the Qur'an is valid for all times and conditions.[1]

The Logic of Faith by Dale Rhoton discusses the reliability of the biblical text:

> There is far more evidence for the reliability of the New Testament text than for that of many classical writings which are accepted without question.

Strangely enough, historians are often more ready to accept the authority of the New Testament than are many theologians.[2]

Archaeological findings continue to confirm the reliability of the biblical text. Sceptics have often laughed at incredulous events recorded in the Bible. Their laughter has repeatedly been silenced by new archaeological discoveries substantiating the biblical account.[3]

Both historical and archaeological evidence against the corruption of the Bible is strong. In *Sharing Your Faith with a Muslim*, Abdiyah Akbar Abdul-Haqq makes other points which show that the claim of Muslims concerning the corruption is so unlikely as to be virtually impossible. Dr. Abdul-Haqq points out that, as we have seen from *surah* 4:14, the Qur'an speaks only of the Jews. Muslims believe, however, that both Jews and Christians corrupted their scriptures. If so, they must have been working together, otherwise there would be two different corrupted versions in circulation. Considering the very poor relationship between Jews and Christians at the time, it is difficult to believe that they entered into a conspiracy together.

On the whole idea of the Bible being corrupted, Dr. Abdul-Haqq writes:

Again, how could all available manuscripts of the Bible have been corrupted so completely and worldwide that not a single copy survived? Such a preposterous vandalism could never have gone undetected in history recorded both by the friend and the foe.[4]

Dr. Abdul-Haqq also suggests why the idea of corruption of the Bible arose in the first place. As Muslims began to have opportunities to read it and to discuss it with more knowledgeable Christians and Jews, they saw the divergences between it and the Qur'an; it became important to explain these in some way.

The Arabic word used for corruption of the Bible is *'tahrif'*. Muslims recognise two types, *tahrif-i-lafzi* (corruption of words) and *tahrif-i-manawi* (corruption of meaning). Dr. Abdul-Haqq continues:

In the face of all the imposing evidence against a belief in actual corruption of the Bible, there are many Muslims who have chosen to allege *tahrif-i-lafzi*. This impossible position is not only an attempt to account for the divergence of the Koran from the Bible in material common to both of them, but is also a calculated explanation for the apparent lack of references which, according to the Koran, the Bible makes to Muhammad. Thus for example, they allege that Christians have expunged the word 'Ahamd' from the New Testament and inserted the expression 'Son of God' in different places in their Scripture. The narrative of the crucifixion, death and resurrection of Jesus Christ is also considered by these Muslims as an example of corruption of the Injil.[5]

3   The Witness of the Qur'an to Jesus

In the conclusion of his book *Jesus in the Qur'an*, Geoffrey Parrinder writes:

> Jesus is mentioned in 15 suras of the Qur'an, but not in the other 99. 93 verses speak of him, but there are 6,226 (or 6,211) verses in the whole Qur'an. He receives many honourable names but he is placed in the succession of the prophets and teaching about the prophets is only one element in the Qur'an.[6]

The Qur'an does, however, use some very significant words and phrases to describe Jesus. He is referred to as the Word of God, the Messiah, the Apostle of God, and his Spirit.

> ...The angels said, 'Mary, God gives thee good tidings of a *Word from Him whose name is Messiah*, Jesus, son of Mary; ... (3:40).

> The Messiah Jesus Christ Son of Mary was only the *messenger of God* and *His Word* that He committed unto Mary, and a *Spirit from Him*! (4:168).

(Note that the italics are the present writer's.) See *surahs* 19:19 and 3:45 for further reference to Jesus — 'most pure', 'honoured'.

One of the most remarkable references to Jesus in the Qur'an is: 'Peace be upon me, the day I was born, and the day I die, and the day I am raised up alive!' (19:34).

Muslims interpret this verse in different ways. We look at it again a little further on, where Muslim beliefs about the crucifixion are discussed. One former Muslim *hafiz*, that is, someone who has memorised and is able to recite the whole Qur'an, uses this verse in his loving witness, to show that Jesus predicted his own death and resurrection.

A booklet entitled *Have You Ever Read The Seven Muslim Christian Principles?* gives further helpful thought about Jesus as the Word of God:

> Someone asked a friend of his the following puzzling question: 'Who do you think existed first: God, His Spirit, or His Word?' The friend answered immediately, 'Certainly God, as nothing could have existed before Him.'
>
> The man then said, 'If God was at any time without Spirit or Word, which means a dead or a dumb God, hence an imperfect God, how can He be God at all? The friend thought for a long time about what he had heard and then said, 'You are right, my friend; God cannot be dead, without Spirit, or dumb, without Word, at any time, for in Him, life and perfection are personified.... God's Spirit and Word,' he added, 'were with Him from the very beginning, and will remain, without interruption, till the very end. God, I can see now, cannot be partitioned into God, Word and Spirit. He is ONE God.'

4 Islamic Objections to the Doctrine of the Trinity

To begin this section, here is another excerpt from Ghulam Sarwar's book:

> We believe in *Isa* as a prophet and a servant of Allah (43:59). We don't believe in him as son of Allah. Allah can have no son or daughter. He is above any such notion. Allah is One and Indivisible. There is no idea of unity in *Trinity* in Islam (4:171). *Trinity* is clear partnership (*Shirk*). It is a big sin to say anyone is the son of Allah (5:17, 19:35).[7]

Note: Isa is the Muslim name for Jesus.

Muslims, as is well known, hold the doctrine of the unity of

God in the most absolute and uncompromising form. The Qur'an and traditions, as well as the whole of Muslim literature, are pervaded with this belief. Three pasages in the Qur'an state the unity of God in opposition to the Christian concept of the Trinity:

> So believe in God and His Mesengers, and say not, 'Three.' Refrain: better is it for you. God is only One god (4:169).

> They are unbelievers who say, 'God is the Messiah, Mary's son' (5:77).

> And when God said, 'O Jesus son of Mary, didst thou say unto men, take me and my mother as gods, apart from God?' He said, 'To Thee be glory! It is not mine to say what I have not right to' (5:116).

The same doctrine is more plainly asserted in the gospel of Barnabas (which we examine later on). For example: 'He (God) hath no father nor mother; he hath no sons, nor brethren, nor companions.'

But what is it that the Muslim condemns as the Christian doctrine of the Trinity? There is a remarkable passage in the Qur'an in which the People of the Book (that is, Christians) are told: '... Go not beyond the bounds in your religion, and say not as to God but the truth. The Messiah, Jesus son of Mary, was only the Messenger of God, and His Word that He committed to Mary, and a Spirit from Him' (4:169).

Keeping in mind the fact that the Christians Muhammad met had no clear idea of their faith, being bound up with heretical teaching, it is not, humanly speaking, surprising that Muhammad had a mistaken idea of the Trinity. He, however, claimed to be a prophet, to receive messages directly from God, so, if his claims were genuine, he could be expected to have more complete knowledge than his informers.

The questions Muslims ask about the Trinity are difficult to answer satisfactorily. The Trinity is based on revealed truth, and transcends the power of human reason. We must therefore be careful not to give the impression that we can explain the inexplicable. The sense of mystery and the unfathomable nature of God should, however, be discussed. Our Muslim friend should be invited to study Scripture, particularly the personage of Christ.

First of all, we must emphasise the Christian teaching on the oneness of God. (Exodus 20:3; Deuteronomy 6:4; Mark 12:32;

I Corinthians 8:4, etc.) Some illustrations can be used but they usually fall far short of totally satisfying the human intellect. For example, time is expressed in past, present, and future, three things all complete in themselves and yet one cannot exist without the others. Secondly, Einstein's theory of relativity states that an object travelling at the speed of light has absolute mass and time stands still. God is everywhere and timeless. Thirdly, most Orthodox Muslims are taught that the Qur'an is the eternal Word of God. If the Qur'an has always existed, then God existed with the Qur'an in eternity and, therefore, something is being associated with God. Believing this is thus committing the sin of 'shirk', which is associating something else with God. When pressed to explain such a position most Muslims begin to realise that there are inexplicable doctrines in our different religions and that the fundamental issue is really whether the Book that we read is truly uncorrupted and the revealed Word of God.

Gerhard Nehls says, 'We must get one point quite clear. It is not Christ that became God, no, God became Christ; not to the point, however that God was no where else at that time. That would be a total limitation of God. "God in Christ reconciled the world to Himself"' (II Corinthians 5:19).[8]

One criticism Muslims have of the doctrine of the Trinity is that it is not clearly taught in Scripture. We believe that it is. If we turn to the first page of the Bible we read, 'In the beginning God created the heavens and the earth' (Genesis 1:1).

The word 'God' and, of course, the whole text was written in Hebrew. Since God is an English word we find the Hebrew word *Elohim* in the original. *Elohim* actually means 'Gods' and, in fact, Genesis 1:26 says, 'the *Elohim* said "Let us make man",' and in chapter 11 he says, 'Come let us go down and confuse their language...' (v7). We are left with no doubt as to the unity of God since the Hebrew declaration of faith was, "The Lord our God is one Lord." However, it is not a unit but a unity in the godhead.[9]

Isaiah 7:14 states: 'Therefore the Lord himself will give you a sign: "The virgin will be with child and will give birth to a son and will call him Immanuel".' Immanuel means 'God with us'. And Isaiah 9:6 says: 'For to us a child is born, to us a son is given and the government will be upon his shoulders. And he will be called Wonderful Counsellor, Mighty God, Everlasting Father, Prince of Peace.'

And in John 8:58 we read: '"I tell you the truth," Jesus answered, "before Abraham was born, I am!"' After Jesus had said this they took up stones to kill him. Why? Because 'I am' means '*Jahweh*', which is the word commonly used for God in the Old Testament.

Jesus, himself, commanded his followers: 'Therefore go and make disciples of all nations, baptising them in the name of the Father and of the Son and of the Holy Spirit...' (Matthew 28:19).

5 The Crucifixion and the Resurrection

There is a passage in the Qur'an which Muslims take to mean that Jesus was not crucified. It is referring to the Jews:

> and for their unbelief, and their uttering
> against Mary a mighty calumny,
> and for their saying, 'We slew the Messiah,
> Jesus son of Mary, the Messenger of God' —
> yet they did not slay him, neither crucified him,
> only a likeness of that was shown to them.
> Those who are at variance concerning him surely
> and in doubt regarding him; they have no knowledge
> of him, except the following of surmise;
> and they slew him not of a certainty —
> no indeed; God raised him up to Him; God is
> All-mighty, All-wise (4:155–157).

This passage has formed the basis of Islamic orthodoxy concerning the events of the last few days of Jesus' life on earth.

Ghulam Sarwar writes: 'According to the Qur'an, Prophet *Isa* was not crucified to death rather he was taken up by Allah, the almighty and the Most Wise (4:157–158). Everything is possible for Allah.'[7]

The Gospel narrative agrees with *surah* 4:157 that the Jews 'did not slay him, neither crucified him...' Both Christians and Muslims believe that the method of death was crucifixion. This was the method used by the Romans not by the Jews, who stoned people to death. This was significant. For Jesus to have been stoned to death would have made him a martyr, whereas by being a victim of crucifixion he became cursed according to Jewish law. Deuteronomy 21:23 says, '... anyone who is hung on a tree is under God's curse.'

God could certainly have protected Jesus if he had wished to do so. Both Muslims and Christians believe that he has the power to protect and to allow to die. Referring to the battle of Badr (see Chapter 7, section 3:2 *Main events in the life of Muhammad*) *surah* 8:17 states 'You did not slay them, but God slew them.' God permitted Christ's death by crucifixion, at the hands of Roman soldiers, to ransom humanity. As *surah* 37:107 says, 'We ransomed him with a mighty sacrifice.' As Jesus himself said, '...just as the Son of Man did not come to be served, but to serve, and to give his life as a ransom for many' (Matthew 20:28).

Christ made a number of referencs to his death by crucifixion, for example: 'But I, when I am lifted up from the earth, will draw all men to myself. He said this to show the kind of death he was going to die' (John 12:32–33).

It seems clear that the crowd understood that he was referring to his death. In verse 34 we read that they protested about the idea of Christ dying.

The statement that Jesus was not crucified is followed by 'only a likeness of that was shown to them'. This would seem to suggest that although Jesus was not crucified, God made it appear as if he was. This is interpreted by most Muslims to mean that God made someone else look like Jesus and allowed that person to be crucified instead. 'God raised him up to him' is assumed to mean that God took Jesus into heaven without his having died first.

Although no one would question the power and ability of God to transform the appearance of someone, is it possible to reconcile such an action in relation to the crucifixion, with the concept of a holy, righteous, and just God? To suggest that God would willingly and needlessly cause an innocent bystander to suffer the agony of crucifixion contradicts what we know of the character of God. It is also extremely unlikely that someone would submit to the horror of crucifixion on the grounds that he looked like Jesus, without raising a good deal of resistance.

We must also recognise that in Islam there are reasons why the death of Christ cannot be accepted. All the prophets of Islam are successes and for God to allow a representative of himself to be crucified would mean that God failed his messenger. However, the crucifixion of Jesus brings more glory to God, because more power is manifest in raising a dead man, than in raising a living man from off the cross. The Muslims themselves are in great disarray about who was actually placed on the cross in place of Jesus. Some say it was a disciple; some, quoting Tabari, say it was Sargus; another says a Jew called Tatanus. Josh McDowell in his book, *The Islam Debate*, names others he has found in his research into the subject.

How can we then account for the great repugnance Muhammad has for the crucifixion of Christ? He abhorred the idea of the prophet being left to the mercy of his foes, unaided and unrescued by God. He was ready to compare his own persecutions and rejection by the Quraysh with that of Jesus by the Jews. Could it be that Muhammad saw in his own rejection the possibility of also being defeated and killed? Remember that we are dealing with a series of success stories in the Qur'an, and therefore to have a model of failure is unacceptable for a prophet. So the history of Jesus is brought into harmony with those of other prophets, including his own hoped-for success. Thus God shows his love for the great prophet Jesus by saving him from indignity and a cruel death. Our response to this idea is that Christians regard the crucifixion as a proof of God's love for man (John 3:16). It is also a fact that most of the Jewish prophets were also called upon to suffer for the truth of the Old Testament and many of them even died (Acts 7:52).

The argument is also put forward that Christ had finished his work of teaching and proclaiming the Gospel, therefore there was no need for him to remain any longer to suffer and to die. Muslims miss the point completely since Christ's whole purpose was to come and pay the penalty for sin (Hebrews 9:13,14; Colossians 1:20,22; I Peter 1:18,19).

We can also look at the prophecies in the Old Testament concerning Christ's atoning sacrifice. This purpose of God was made known to his people through the prophetic writings of the Old Testament, and its fulfilment is recorded in the New Testament, sometimes expressly intimating that prophecy is fulfilled (Daniel 9:24; John 19:37; Isaiah 53:7,8).

Crucifixion, so central in the New Testament, has also been mentioned by non-Christian writers and historians, such as the Roman historian Tacitus (*Ann*. 15:44) and by Josephus (*Antiquities* book 18, chapter 3, verse 3).

5:1 *The Swoon Theory*

In more recent years, an alternative theory has emerged concerning the crucifixion of Jesus which suggests that although Jesus was put on the cross, he was taken down before he was dead and in the cool of the tomb revived from his death-like swoon. This swoon theory has been adopted and further embellished by the Ahmadiyyas — an Islamic group which has its origins in nineteenth century India.

This view cannot be substantiated through the Qur'an, but attempts have been made, at least partially, to justify it with reference to the Qur'an.

One such attempt has been made by Maulvi Muhammad Ali (ex-President of the Ahmadiyya-Anjuman-Ishaat-I-Islam of Lahore) who, when discussing the meaning of the term 'crucifixion' in *surah* 4:157, states:

> The word does not negate Jesus being nailed to the
> cross but it negates his having expired on the cross as

a result of being nailed to it... The circumstances relating to the crucifixion, far from showing that Jesus died on the cross, clearly proved that he was taken down alive. [11]

There is no biblical or qur'anic foundation to this theory. Even a cursory investigation of the biblical accounts of Jesus' death and resurrection would show that there is no basis for such a viewpoint.

Firstly, Christ did die on the cross according to the judgement of Joseph, Nicodemus, and the soldiers (who were used to seeing death by crucifixion, and were unlikely to make a mistake — especially considering the importance of Jesus' case and the attention it had aroused).

Secondly, when Jesus appeared to his disciples after his resurrection, it was not in the condition of one reviving from a death-like swoon, of one half-dead from beatings and bleeding, in need of care and attention.

It is also hard to imagine how Jesus, if reviving from a swoon, would have been able to wriggle out of his grave-clothes, move the stone from the entrance of the tomb (without alerting the guards), and escape unnoticed to walk seven miles to Emmaus.

To hold to this theory is also to suggest that Jesus actively helped to propagate a fantastic myth — a 'myth' that has deluded millions of people for two thousand years. How could a prophet of God be involved in such a deliberate deception?

In support of this swoon theory, in recent years the Ahmadiyyas have made much of what they refer to as 'the sign of Jonah' quoting Jesus (Matthew 12:39–40). 'A wicked and adulterous generation asks for a miraculous sign! But none will be given it except the sign of the prophet Jonah. For as Jonah was three days and three nights in the belly of a huge fish, so the Son of Man will be three days and three nights in the heart of the earth.' It is argued that Jesus was put to rest at sunset on Friday and rose early on Sunday morning and that this cannot constitute 'three days and three nights' — or 72 hours.

However, this ignores the existence of a common colloquialism of the period in which the phrase 'a day and a night' referred to at least a portion of that, but not necessarily the entire 24 hours. It was clear that the Jews understood this, for in Matthew 27:63–64 we read that the chief priests and the Pharisees went to Pilate and said: 'Sir ... we remember that while he was still alive that deceiver said, "After three days I will arise again." So give the order for the tomb to be made secure until the third day.'

Because 'the sign of Jonah' was given importance by Jesus, and because it is supposed that the time factor was not fulfilled, then those supporting the swoon theory suggest that the sign of Jonah was concerned with the fact that Jonah went into the fish alive, lived in its belly and came out alive and that this was the parallel which Jesus wished to make. However, this leaves unanswered the question as to what kind of a 'sign' this would be. Jesus had already performed countless miracles which had failed to convince the Pharisees that he was the Messiah. He told them that the only additional sign they would see was the sign of Jonah. But if Jesus had never died how could his reappearance after three days be construed as a miraculous sign?

6 The Gospel of Barnabas

This document which, it is claimed, was written by the Apostle Barnabas (see Acts 4:36), states that Muhammad not Jesus, is the Messiah and that the Apostle Paul, in opposition to Barnabas, introduced corruptions into the original, true teaching of Christianity. It is quite likely that in your discussions with Muslims the subject of the Gospel of Barnabas will be brought up. The Gospel of Barnabas first appeared in Holland in 1709. Muslims claim that the Gospel of Barnabas is an authentic gospel perhaps because it supports many Islamic objections to Christianity. Again, Gerhard Nehls in *Christians Answer Muslims* has an interesting chapter on this gospel (page 119). Nehls quotes 33 mistakes in this gospel and believes it should be regarded as a medieval forgery. This is confirmed by the name of Muhammad appearing in the gospel; he, of course, was born well over 500 years after the gospel was supposed to have been written. Many of the sociological references in this gospel are actually rooted in medieval life; such practices as duels between rival lovers were a creation of medieval society, for example. There are a number of quotations in it from Dante, who lived 1266–1321. Soldiers in the temple rolling wooden casks of wine are mentioned and wooden barrels were invented in Gaul, not used in the East in New Testament times.

Recommended Reading

There is no book in this category for Chapter 6.

Additional Reading

ABDUL-HAQQ, Abdiyah Akbar, *Sharing Your Faith with a Muslim*. Bethany Fellowship, Minneapolis, Minnesota, 1980.
ARBERRY, Arthur J. *The Koran Interpreted*, OUP, 1983.
Have you Ever Read the Seven Muslim Christian Principles? Pamphlet.
KATEREGGA, Badru, and SHENK, David. *Islam and Christianity: A Dialogue*, Eerdmans, Grand Rapids, Michigan, 1980.
McDOWELL, Josh. *Evidence that Demands a Verdict*. Here's Life Publishers, San Bernardino, California, 1979.
—, and GILCHRIST, John. *The Islam Debate*, Here's Life Publishers, San Bernardino, California, 1983.
NEHLS, Gerhard. *Christians Answer Muslims*, 'Life Challenge', Capetown, 1980.
—. *Christians Ask Muslims*. 'Life Challenge', Capetown, 1980.
PARRINDER, Geoffrey. *Jesus in the Qur'an*, Sheldon Press, London, 1965.
SARWAR, Ghulam. *Islam: Beliefs and Teachings*, Muslim Educational Trust, London, 3rd ed., 1984.

Notes

1 SARWAR, Ghulam. *Islam: Beliefs and Teachings*, Muslim Educational Trust, London, 3rd ed., 1984, p30.
2 RHOTON, Dale. *The Logic of Faith*, STL, Bromley, Kent, 1978, p41.
3 Ibid, p42.
4 ABDUL-HAQQ, Abdiyah Akbar. *Sharing Your Faith with a Muslim*, Bethany Fellowship, Minneapolis, Minnesota, 1980, p37.
5 Ibid, p40.
6 PARRINDER, Geoffrey. *Jesus in the Qur'an*, Sheldon Press, London, 1965, p166.
7 SARWAR, Ghulam. *Islam: Beliefs and Teachings*, Muslim Educational Trust, London, 3rd ed., 1984, p158.
8 NEHLS, Gerhard. *Christians Answer Muslims*, 'Life Challenge', Capetown, 1980, p93.
9 Ibid, pp93–94.
10 McDOWELL, Josh and GILCHRIST, John. *The Islam Debate*, Here's Life Publishers, San Bernardino, California, 1983, p157.
11 MAULVI MUHAMMAD ALI, quoted in *The Islam Debate* (see above), p115.

Chapter 7

MUHAMMAD, PROPHET OF ISLAM

1 Study Guide

This is one of the two bridging chapters. It links the first main part of the study (Part 2) with the second (Part 3); the study of beliefs and practices, with the historical and political perspective. The Muslim prophet Muhammad is a key figure in both these areas. This chapter, written by Anne Cooper, asks the questions: what sort of person was Muhammad, how do Muslims view him, and what should our Christian attitude to him be?

Learning objectives
When you have completed this chapter you should:

1   Have looked briefly at the life and times of Muhammad.
2   Understand something of his role in Islam and the attitudes of Muslims towards him.
3   Have begun to think about possible Christian attitudes to Muhammad as a prophet and as a leader.

2 Who Was This Man?

Who was this man whose name is linked with that of God in the saying of the Muslim Creed? Some one in six of the world's population revere and honour him. He is thought by Muslims to be the last and the final prophet. He came from a humble and deprived background, but became a strong and successful leader.

This is how one Muslim describes him: 'In brief, the towering and radiant personality of *this man*, in the midst of such a benighted and dark environment, may be likened to a beacon-light illumining a pitch-dark night or a diamond shining in a heap of dead stones.'[1] 'His is the only example where all the excellencies have been blended into one personality.'[2]

Before we look at some verses from the Qur'an, do you remember the names given to Muhammad in it?

Activity
Try writing the names given to Muhammad in the Qur'an now, using both the English and Arabic words. You will find the answers in Chapter 3/4, section 5:4, *The Prophets of God*.

The name Muhammad is rarely mentioned in the Qur'an. Although Muhammad is usually referred to as a prohpet, the most common name given to him in the Qur'an is *rasul*, that is apostle or messenger.

Here are some examples of the use of these words:

O Prophet, fear God,
and obey not the unblievers
and the hypocrites. God is All-knowing,
All-wise.
And follow what is revealed to thee
From thy Lord; surely God is aware of
the things you do.
And put thy trust in God: God suffices
as a guardian (33:2–3).

Muhammad is not the father of any one
of your men, but the Messenger of God,
and the Seal of the Prophets; God has knowledge
of everything (33:40).

O thou shrouded in thy mantle
arise and warn! (74:2)

To summarise the role of Muhammad, we quote from Tames in *Approaches to Islam*:

Muslims insist that Muhammad was in no sense the author or composer of the Qur'an, which is God's own speech. Rather he was the illiterate vehicle through which God's revelation was conveyed to man. Muslims insist, moreover, that the Prophet was not, and never claimed to be, divine. He was an ordinary human being. But they also hold him to be *al-Insan al-Kamil*, the perfect man, the model to be imitated in all things, as husband or father, as trader or soldier, diplomat, ruler or judge.[3]

3   The Life and Times of Muhammad

3:1 As Colin Chapman points out in *You Go and Do the Same*, chapter 5, it is important to understand something of the background from which Muhammad came. In Arabia before his birth, a number of different factors influenced the life of the area.

Political
The Arabian peninsula was not one unit, but was peopled by a number of separate tribes, some nomadic or semi-nomadic, others settled in small towns. Some of the tribes had made alliances with each other, others had long-standing hostility which led to recurring revenge and blood feuds.

Foreign powers
Arabia was affected by a power struggle which was going on between the two great powers of the time. One of these, the Byzantine Empire, composed of Asia Minor, Syria, Egypt, and southeast Europe, was, '... fiercely "orthodox" (Christian) in doctrine, and strongly opposed to other "heretical" doctrines....'[4] The other was the Persian Empire, which stretched from Iraq to Afghanistan.

Economic and social
Mecca was an important trading centre for the caravans which traded along the trade routes in the area. A number of social evils were practised at that time in Arabia, among them live burial of infants and exploitation of women.

Religious
Mecca was also an important centre for worship. 'Although there is some evidence of belief in one supreme God (Allah)',[5] there were many lesser deities, idol cults, strong belief in fate, sacrifices to spirits, and superstitious rituals. The Arabic language was linked closely with religion through traditional poetry and proverbs.

There were some Jewish communities in the area; also people called *hanif* who were monotheistic in their worship. Some of the nomadic tribes, particularly in the Yemen, had become Christian as early as the fourth century. There were also Syrian monks, living hermit-like existences in desert areas. Most of the Christians, however, were expatriates, such as the dark-skinned Ethiopians.

3:2 *Main events in the life of Muhammad*

Summary of main dates

Birth	570 AD (approximate date)
Marriage to Khadijah	595
First Revelation	610
Hijra	622
Battle of Badr	624
Battle of Uhud	625
Battle of Ahzab	627
Conquest of Mecca	629
Death	632

Muhammad's father died before he was born. His name was Abdullah and he was a member of the Hashim clan of the powerful Quraysh tribe. Muhammad's mother, Amina, also died young, when he was six years old. Muslims often stress the fact that he was an orphan and that he raised himself up from nothing, by his own efforts. After his mother died, Muhammad went to live with his grandfather and a strong bond of love developed between grandfather and grandson. Sadly, two years later the grandfather died. From then onwards Muhammad lived in the house of his uncle, Abu Talib, and was looked after by him. Abu Talib belonged to the poorer branch of the family, so Muhammad became accustomed to living very simply and as soon as he was old enough he began to work for his living. This would account for the Muslim belief that he did not receive any education. He did, however, receive training in weapons of war, which was to stand him in good stead in later years.

When Muhammad grew into manhood, he became a trader. There was insufficient money for him to develop his own trade, nor was it possible to arrange a marriage for him. He went to work for a rich widow, called Khadijah, and she came to trust and to rely on him. Although she was a number of years older than he was, Muhammad married her when he was 25. The marriage was a happy one and they had six children, two boys, who did not live to reach adulthood, and four girls. The youngest girl, Fatima, later married Ali, who became the Fourth Caliph. Muhammad was very fond of her and she became his close companion in later years. During the 25 years Muhammad was married to Khadijah he took no other wife.

It was while he was married to Khadijah, at the age of 40, that Muhammad received his first revelation and message from God. It is said that he was greatly disturbed by it, not knowing whether it was from God, or from the Devil. The revelation took place in a cave in Mount Hira, and the message was that recorded in *surah* 96. Muhammad did not receive another message until some time had elapsed, but after this they were sent down regularly. He began to realise that they were transmitted through the angel Gabriel. As the messages were received by Muhammad he recited them to his growing number of followers. As we have seen in Chapter 6, they were not written down until a number of years later.

It seems clear that Muhammad was already established as an upright, responsible person, able to give others advice and support, before his life was changed by the revelation of God calling him to be his messenger. Gradually those closest to him began to believe in his prophetic role. First Khadijah, then his cousins Ali and Zaid, followed by his great friend Abu Bakr, became his followers. As the group grew larger, they began to experience opposition from disbelieving members of the Quraysh.

This period of growth continued. Muhammad and his band of fellow-believers sought to obey the instructions in the messages he received. Eventually, in 622 AD, the rejection of Muhammad and his message by the leaders of the Quraysh led him to look for some other place where the new religion could be established. The people of Yathrib had expressed interest and openness to Muhammad and his followers, so they secretly left Mecca and established themselves in Yathrib, renamed Medina. This move was of great significance in the development of Islam. Muslims use the date of the migration, the *hijra*, as the start of the Muslim era, putting the letters AH after the numbers in expressing their dates.

Those who welcomed Muhammad and his followers in Medina entered into a covenant to protect them, and themselves became believers. They are known as the *ansar* (helpers) to distinguish them from the *muhajirun* (migrants) who came from Mecca.

Now that Islam was established, Muhammad's ministry underwent changes. We have seen (Chapter 5, section 5:3, *The Medinan Period*) how the teaching in the qur'anic *surahs* changed at this time. In the same way Muhammad's own role changed. As Bell and Watt write in *Introduction to the Qur'an*: 'The changing circumstances of his life — the transition from the preacher of Mecca to the statesman of Medina and then to the ruler of much of Arabia — necessarily affected the use of his time.'[6]

During these early years of estabishing Islam, hostility from the Meccans continued. The course of events was changed by three important battles.

The battle of Badr. A large caravan from Mecca was moving towards Medina and threatening the city. Although smaller in number, the Muslims attacked and defeated the Meccans. This gave the Muslims much confidence not only in their own military ability, but also in the belief that God was on their side.

The battle of Uhud. The Meccans, looking for revenge for their defeat at Badr, attacked the Muslims. At first it looked as if the unbelievers would suffer another defeat. The Muslims proved to be over-confident, however. When they thought that the battle was almost over and the rejoicing had begun, the Meccans counter-attacked. They found the Muslims in disarray and inflicted a heavy defeat on them, resulting in heavy losses of their men. The Muslims were further weakened when, at the height of the counter-attack, a rumour went around that Muhammad had been killed. In fact, he and his followers had escaped to a nearby hill.

The battle of Ahzab. The Meccans formed an alliance with some of the powerful Jewish tribes of the area. They marched together towards Medina, but were foiled by a large trench which the Muslims had built to protect their city. Eventually, after a good deal of intrigue, the Muslims were able to put their army to rout. As a result of this further victory, a treaty was made with the Meccans.

Return to Mecca

When Muhammad decided that the time had come for the Muslims to return to worship in Mecca, they were able to enter the city peacefully. Muhammad soon returned to Medina where he continued to live. He went on establishing the beliefs and practices of Islam. It was at this time that his followers began to collect his sayings and doings; later they were written in the books of traditions, the *hadith*.

Alfred Guillaume writes:

> While the prophet was alive he was the sole guide in all matters whether spiritual or secular. Hadith, or tradition in the technical sense, may be said to have begun at his death, for the extraordinary influence of his personality on his companions and associates created from the beginning a demand that believers should be informed what the prophet had done and taught in various circumstances in order that the life

of the community and the individual might be modelled on that of the revered leader.[7]

At the same time, the Muslims continued to gain supremacy over the remaining non-Muslim tribes, until Muhammad was virtually ruler of the whole of the Arabian peninsula. He visited Mecca again before he died.

3:3 *The Ummah*

While Muhammad was in Medina, he 'welded his believers into a single brotherhood, the Umma.'[8] After he died, it was the *ummah*, the community of believers, who had responsibility for proclaiming the message of Islam throughout the world.

In *Islam and Christianity*, Badru Kataregga (a Muslim) and David Shenk (a Christian) present the beliefs of the two faiths and respond to each other. Here are two extracts (the first by Kataregga, the second by Shenk) from their chapter on the *ummah*:

> As Islam spread, the Umma, which was essentially based on Islamic law, was quickly transformed from an Arab Umma into a universal Muslim Umma. It is not surprising that the Umma extended very quickly, after the prophet's death, far beyond the confines of the Arabian Peninsula. In the process, it brought together peoples of different cultures, races, and nations to form one great Umma. Today the Umma is still spreading. The universal message of reform (Islam) is now embraced by hundreds of millions of peoples from countries and cultures around the world.[9]

> Christians are impressed with the completeness of the Muslim concept of Umma, which includes a total programme for social, economic, cultural, political and religious organisations. All aspects of life are brought under the rule of the Shari'a within the Umma. This is an impressive achievement.[10]

At the same time it has to be said that the *ummah* is an ideal; it has never been fully realised.

4   Muhammad's Attitude to Christians

There is some evidence that, during the earlier part of his life and ministry, Muhammad met, discussed with, and learnt from Christians in Arabia. His wife Khadijah had a cousin, Waraqah ibn Naufal, who was a Christian, and there is a tradition that she encouraged Muhammad to consult him.

As Muhammad's own teaching became established, he hoped that others, including Christians, would embrace Islam. When they did not do so, he became more critical and hostile towards them. Nevertheless, from time to time, there were groups of Christians whom he and his followers tolerated.

There is more detailed discussion of this in Colin Champan's *You Go and Do the Same*.[11]

Activity
This may be the opportunity for you to discuss Muhammad's relationship to Christians with your Muslim friends. This will be helpful preparation for Chapter 11 where Christian-Muslim relationships are traced through history.

5   Muhammad and Inspiration

Was Muhammad genuine in his claim to receive his message from God? If not, did he deliberately deceive, or was he himself mistaken? The way in which these questions are answered is linked to the discussion on whether the Qur'an is the word of God. It would be helpful to look back at this in Chapter 5, section 10 **The Crucial Question**.

Doubt has been cast on the validity of Muhammad's claim to be a prophet and a messenger of God from the time of the earliest days of his ministry. Thomas Carlyle was the first person to suggest that an impostor could not have founded one of the world's great religions. Others have pursued this line of thought. Some have suggested that Muhammad suffered from some mental abnormality, such as epilepsy or hysteria.[12]

For the Muslim, there is not the slightest doubt that the messages which Muhammad received were inspired and that the source of that inspiration (*wahy*) was God himself. Muhammad is honoured and respected as the 'Seal of the Prophets' (33:44). His name is not spoken or written without the words 'peace be upon him' being added. We shall see in Chapter 13, section 4 **The Veneration of Muhammad and the Saints in Islam** how, after his death, many miraculous signs and events were attributed to

Muhammad, and the cult of his veneration developed.

Kenneth Cragg, in his book *Muhammad and the Christian*, sets out to clarify whether Christians are right in refusing to give Muhammad the same respect as they do Jesus. On the question of qur'anic *wahy*, he looks at *surah* 96: 'Recite ... Recite: And thy Lord is the Most Generous... ' (96:2), and writes: '*Wahy* here is a commanding awareness of the reality of God, made vocal in language of which God himself is the source — language to be spoken, commandingly, to the world. Nothing is here for private congratulation. All is for urgent public witness. The words are not for perusal but for utterance.'[13]

The content and argument of Cragg's book is complex and detailed. We cannot attempt to summarise it here. It is included in the book list at the end of this chapter.

In the concluding chapter Cragg writes:

> Hopefully we are now ready for the question, after careful review of all aspects of Muhammad's Islamic actuality in Qur'anic *wahy*, in *Hijra* and Statehood, in Tradition and devotion, in ethical and spiritual definition of Muslim society and culture. Christian response to the main theme of his prophethood has surely to be a positive acknowledgement of its significance.... But that lively sense of its relevance is left taking strenuous issue with the guiding principles of action by which the message was reinforced.[14]

Bell tries 'to get behind the usual mechanical interpretation' of the receiving of the Qur'an and pictures Muhammad in the throes of composition. He writes:

> In some way, then, Muhammad's claim to inspiration might be understood. It has analogies to the experience which poets refer to as the coming of the muse, or more closely to what religious people describe as the coming of guidance after meditation and waiting upon God. 'Guidance' is in fact one of the Qur'an's favourite words for the message.[15]

Dr. Nazir-Ali asks the question, 'What *were* the origins of Muhammad's religious consciousness?' In answer he suggests: his early meditations in a cave in Mount Hira, probably in imitation of Christian hermits, and his disgust with the idolatry of popular religion. He writes: 'He turned, therefore, in meditation to Allah, the supreme but ignored deity of the Arabs. Eventually he became aware of a "presence" and experienced a "revelation".'[16]

Activity

In Chapter 3/4, section 5:4, *The Prophets of God* we read: 'Muslims believe in Jesus as a bringer of Islam like Muhammad. This is why Muslims often, with sadness, ask Christians, "We believe in Jesus, why do you not believe in Muhammad?"'

If your Muslim friends should ask you this question, how are you going to reply?

We cannot reproduce a model answer to this question. How you answer will depend on how your own thinking has developed as you have studied Part 2 (Chapters 3/4, 5, 6 and 7). This activity is designed to help you not only grasp hold of its central theme, but also as a reviewing exercise. It will be worthwhile glancing back through these chapters before attempting your answer.

Recommended Reading

CHAPMAN, Colin. *You Go and Do the Same*, CMS/BMMF Int/IFES, London, 1983. Chapter 5 is especially relevant to this chapter, but the whole book is recommended for study, in conjunction with the appropriate chapters.

Additional Reading

ARBERRY, Arthur J. *The Koran Interpreted*, OUP, 1983.
CRAGG, Kenneth. *Muhammad and the Christian,* Darton, Longman and Todd, London, 1984.
LINGS, Martin. *Muhammad,* Islamic Texts Society and George Allen & Unwin, London 1983.
MAWDUDI, Abul A'la. *Towards Understanding Islam*, Islamic Foundation, Leicester, 1981. Recommended book for Chapter 3/4.

Notes

1 MAWDUDI, Abul A'la. *Towards Understanding Islam*, Islamic Foundation, Leicester, 1981, p46.
2 Ibid, p54.

3 TAMES, Richard. *Approaches to Islam*, John Murray, London, 1982, p24.
4 CHAPMAN, Colin. *You Go and Do the Same*, CMS/BMMF Int/IFES, London, 1983, pp22–23.
5 Ibid, p23.
6 BELL, Richard and WATT, W Montgomery. *Introduction to the Qur'an*, Edinburgh University Press, Edinburgh, 1970, p25.
7 GUILLAUME, Alfred. *The Traditions of Islam*, Khayats, Beirut, 1966, p13.
8 KATEREGGA, Badru and SHENK, David. *Islam and Christianity: A Dialogue*, Eerdmans, Grand Rapids, Michigan, 1980, p75.
9 Ibid, p52.
10 Ibid, p53.
11 CHAPMAN, Colin. *You Go and Do the Same*, CMS/BMMF Int/IFES, London, 1983, pp29–30.
12 BELL, Richard and WATT, W Montgomery. *Introduction to the Qur'an*, Edinburgh University Press, Edinburgh, 1970, p17.
13 CRAGG. Bishop Kenneth. *Muhammad and the Christian*, Darton, Longman & Todd, London, 1984, p89.
14 Ibid, pp140–141.
15 BELL, Richard and WATT, W Montgomery. *Introduction to the Qur'an*, Edinburgh University Press, Edinburgh, 1970, pp22–23.
16 NAZIR-ALI, Michael. *Islam: A Christian Perspective*, Paternoster Press, Exeter, 1983, p28.

Chapter 8

HISTORY AND POLITICAL DEVELOPMENT OF ISLAM

1 Study Guide

In this chapter we move from the life and times of Muhammad to consideration of the social and political development of Islam. To do this you are encouraged to spend time reading and studying in and around the subject, rather than simply assimilating the facts. Islam is much more than a religion in the narrow sense of the word and Christians have not always acknowledged or appreciated this. Some books are specifically suggested for study, but a browse in your local library, or a visit to a specialised library such as the FFM Library at All Nations Christian College, will certainly help you understand the heritage of Islam. Look out for those books which are either written by Muslims, or present Islam in a positive way. The questions in the text for you to consider are quite difficult. They will require not only thinking through, but, if you want to find adequate answers, some background reading. By now we hope that you will either have found others with whom you are discussing the course as you study, or an experienced person with whom you can think through the issues. Ron George has written this chapter, as well as Chapters 9 and 10.

Learning objectives
When you have completed this chapter you should:

1 Have assimilated an overview of the way Islam has developed historically and politically.
2 Have begun to explore some of the creative and artistic dimensions of Islam.

FAMILY TREE OF MUHAMMAD

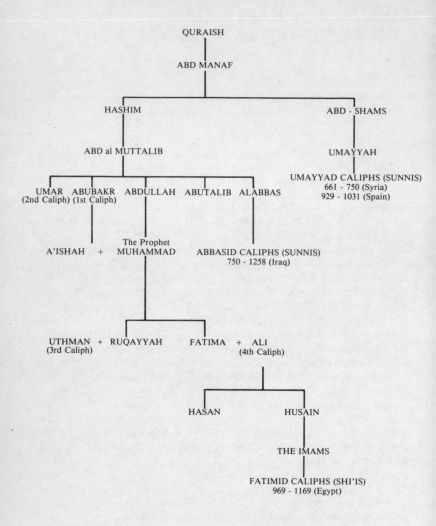

Used by permission of the Fellowship of Faith for the Muslims, from Canon R W F Wootton, *Understanding Muslim Sects*, p45.

2 Introduction

Islam today, driven by the challenges posed by western, twentieth century materialism, is seeking for a fresh appraisal of its content and call. The current resurgence of Islam is in the process of change; it is beginning to evidence strong religious fundamentalism. There is a potent nationalistic search within Islam, and Muslims are experiencing an upsurge of pride in their own culture as they discover that western materialism does not meet their needs. Allied to this, they watch the decadent West crumble in upon itself. Part of the resurgence of Islam is due to the fact that, rightly or wrongly, Muslims have felt themselves to be oppressed by the West.

Two major trends can be identified in the Islamic world today, which point the way towards reform of Islam (*islah*). First of all, there is the modernist, rationalist school which arises as a result of observing the West. It recognises a need for change, responding by modernising or updating Islamic thought and reinterpreting the sources of authority, such as the Qur'an and the traditions (*hadith*). The second movement has been to return to fundamental, traditional views in a reactionary way. The first school is exemplified by Salafiyyah, and was to have much influence in the creation of a modern Turkey, the establishment of the Shah's regime in Iran, and the building of modern Egypt. The fundamentalists look to ibn Hanbal, their example *par excellence*. He was a staunch defender of Islamic traditions when the government of his day (he died in 855) was trying to impose new Islamic thoughts upon the community. The Hanbaliyya believe in a literal reading of the sources, a strict puritanism, and a hatred for all things foreign. These have influenced Libya, the Muslim brotherhood, and present-day Saudi Arabia. (These trends are expanded in Chapter 12, sections 3 and 4 **Three Main Trends** and **Liberalism**).

We now turn to look more closely at the historical development of Islam in order to improve our understanding of the main influences at work in modern Islam.

By now, you will have met and discussed religious issues with Muslim friends. Which of the two major trends in the Islamic world today do you think they follow? What are the reasons which make you think that? (It may be that they follow neither trend, but are more interested in Sufism, that is the mystical expression of Islam. We shall be studying this in the next chapter.)

87

3 The History of Islam — After the Death of Muhammad

3:1 *First crisis*

Muhammad's sudden death in 632 AD presented the Muslim community with a major crisis. Who would replace Muhammad and rule the new community, which transcended tribal loyalty? Secondly, would the community stand the test of a transfer of power, since most of the tribes gave their loyalty to Muhammad and not to one another? In the event, the Arab leaders fell back upon the tried and trusted traditional Arab method of electing the most honourable and aged one amongst them. They chose Abu Bakr, the uncle of Muhammad. Not all Muslims agreed that Muhammad would have wanted Abu Bakr to be the first Caliph. (Caliph means successor.) Some claimed he had said that Ali, his son-in-law, husband of Fatima, his daughter, should take over from him. However, the Arabs did not respect Ali as being a wise and mature person.

Before he died, Abu Bakr, having consulted the senior companions, selected Umar to be his successor. Umar was known as Al-Faruq, which means one who distinguishes between right and wrong. He was a gifted orator and was concerned for the welfare of his people. During the ten years of his leadership Egypt and large areas of the Roman and Persian Empires were conquered. He was assassinated by a disgruntled non-Muslim, having previously appointed a committee to choose his successor.

The committee chose Uthman as third Caliph. He was a kind and generous man from a rich family. He was also pious and god-fearing. He was not, however, a strong ruler, so that discipline in his adminstration was lax.

He ruled from 644–656 AD. He was assassinated and many suspected the disgruntled Ali, or at least his followers were responsible. Uthman's cousin demanded that justice be done and the murderer be brought to court. This cousin, Muawiya, was governor of Damascus at the time. He laid no claim to rule Islam but used this quarrel in an effort to overthrow Ali. The two sides were drawn up in battle, but both parties agreed to submit the question to a panel of mature leaders who would arbitrate in the matter in order to save Muslim blood from being shed. At this, many of Ali's followers left him, since they claimed that only God had the authority to arbitrate between the two parties, that

God would be on the side of whoever was right and that the battle should have taken place. Ali, in his determination to bring them back into the fold, ended up slaughtering most of them, but that was only to lead to his own assassination by the hand of a survivor. Today Muslims look back with nostalgia upon the period of the first four Caliphs, considering that they were the rightly guided ones and a model for present-day Islam.

During this period, the Persian and Byzantine armies had become exhausted by continual warfare. The people of the Fertile Crescent, whom they had conquered, were oppressed by the high taxes they had to pay and were discontented. The invading Muslim Arab armies were seen as liberators and reformers, thus facilitating their conquest of the area.

Activity
What do you think might have been the particular problems which the early Caliphs faced?

The selection of the early Caliphs proved difficult. The unity of believers which had been such a feature of Islam during the life of Muhammad began to crumble. Glubb lists a number of reasons for this. He writes:

> In 652, twenty years after the death of the Apostle of God, the Arabs still exhibited in war the same reckless courage and patient endurance as before. But with the reduction in active operations many thousands of them now passed idle lives in their cantonments. Several factors appeared which tended to introduce internal schisms, as the white-hot religious enthusiasm generated by the Prophet began to cool.[1]

Other factors mentioned by Glubb are:

> Arab allegiance had always before been to their tribe, and intra-tribal conflicts began to surface again.
> The Caliph Umar had encouraged soldiers to bring complaints about their commanders to him, which had sown the seeds of insubordination.
> The Quraysh, Muhammad's own tribe, had become the most influential tribe, because of the prestige they gained from him. This led to conflict with the other tribes. Added to this the Quraysh themselves were

disunited, being split into two parties, one supporting the candidature of Ali for Caliph, the other that of Uthman.

3:2 *The First Muslim Kingdom*
With Ali's death in 661 the way was open for Muawiya to take control of the new Muslim community.

He set up his capital in Damascus and modelled his rule upon the Greek-Roman-Byzantine Empire that had been overthrown by the young and vigorous Muslim armies when they had broken out of Arabia. Thus begins the first Islamic kingdom named after his family, the Umayyads, which was to last from 661 to 750 AD. In turn they were overthrown by a reactionary movement from the East and replaced by a new empire called the Abbasids.

3:3 *The Golden Age of Islam*
In 750 AD the fourteenth Umayyad Caliph was overthrown by a new dynasty, which was to be know as the Abbasid dynasty. Professor Lewis observes that 'it was a revolution in the history of Islam, as important a turning point as the French and Russian Revolutions in the history of the West.'[2] It came at the end of a long period of dissatisfaction by elements of the population who felt that they were being treated as second-class citizens.

The new dynasty was descended from Muhammad's uncle al Abbas, and they were eventually to shift the capital from Damascus to a purpose-built city called Baghdad, which was an old centre of Judaism. The result of the geographical shift was to move the attention away from expansion in the West, particuarly in Spain and Europe, to a new expansion to the East.

3:4 *Persian models of government*
The old Persian Empire was to play an important part in providing a model for government, court etiquette, and the arts. Arab influences further declined and Persian culture took over.

> Under Harun al-Rashid (786–809), legendary caliph of the *Thousand and One Nights*, Baghdad flourished as an unrivalled centre of commerce and learning. His successor, al-Mamun (818–833), established in the capital a 'House of Wisdom', a combination of library, academy, translation bureau, and observatory. A few examples may indicate the achievements of Muslim scholars at a time when Europe was still half-barbarised. al-Khwarizmi (d. circa 850) made major advances in astronomy, wrote a pioneering treatise

on algebra, and popularised the use of 'Arabic' (derived from Indian) numerals. In medicine al-Razi (895–925) was the first to make a clinical distinction between measles and smallpox, while in philosophy al-Ashare (874–935) wrestled with the problem of reconciling predestination with free will.[3]

3:5 *The Empire disintegrates*
By the tenth century the political unity of the Islamic empire had begun to fragment. It was under increasing pressure from ambitious provincial governors and, in Baghdad, rival warlords were usurping authority.

These problems were further aggravated by Islamic ambivalence during this period. In Spain an autonomous caliphate was established by descendants of the Umayyad line (925). In North Africa yet another caliphate was set up by the Shiite Fatimids (909), who claimed descent from the prophet's daughter Fatima, and founded a new capital for themselves at Cairo. The Shiites are discussed in more detail in Chapter 9, section 4 **Theological Divisions**.

3:6 *Further expansion*
The tide of conquest rolled forward again in the eleventh and twelfth centuries with armed incursions into western Africa and northern India. At the same time the Abbasid Caliphate effectively fell under the control of Turkish invaders, the Seljuks, who briefly reinvigorated it — and, in effect, provoked the Crusades. Seen against this general background, the Crusades assume the perspective of local and temporary reverses in a general trend of expansion. The chivalrous and statesmanlike Salah-al-Din (Saladin), 1169, recaptured Jerusalem from the Christians, and succeeded in briefly reuniting Egypt and Syria under firm rule. Chapter 11 discusses the Crusades in some detail. It shows that this period of history has had a profound effect on Christian-Muslim relations, even up to the present day.

Activities
1 What do you think were the main reasons for the fragmentation of the Abbasids in the tenth century?

This quote from Glubb's *A Short History of the Arab Peoples* will help answer this question:

The Abbasids had obtained power by what today we should call subversive propaganda. Under the rule of the Prophet's own family, it had been claimed, the iniquities of the wicked Umaiyids would cease and the reign of peace, mercy, justice and happiness would spread over all the earth. These dreams had been quickly dispelled ... If the Abbasids were no worse than the Umaiyids, they were certainly no better.[4]

2 Islamic achievements in the arts and the sciences should be appreciated if we are to understand and to relate to Muslims. It is important to visit the Islamic sections of museums such as the British Museum, or the Victoria and Albert Museum. Try to visit the oriental department of your local museum as well.

4:1 The Mongols and After — New Influences in Islam

In 1258 the Mongol hordes of Hulagu, grandson of Ghengis Khan, struck deep into the heart of India. The last Abbasid Caliph was done to death and the glittering imperial capital of Baghdad was virtually wiped off the face of the earth. The psychological shock was tremendous, but short-lived. In 1260 the Mongols were checked in Palestine by an army of Mamluks, slave soldiers who had established praetorian rule in Egypt.

As Lewis has observed, '... Most scholars would now agree that the harmful effects of the Mongol conquests were not as great, as lasting or even as extensive as was once thought'.[5] Iraq and Northern Persia were badly affected, but most other areas were either never troubled or were subject only to the most distant suzerainty. And the Mongols, once converted to Islam, became great patrons of culture.

4:2 *New leadership*

It can be seen with historical perspective that the Seljuks, Mamluks, Mongols, and Ottomans gave Islam much-needed infusions of invigorating new leadership. The historian ibn Khaldun acknowledged their importance and later historians have seen them as the reason for the military resurgence of the sixteenth century. They brought with them not only traditions of courage and military skill but also techniques of statecraft and patterns of institutionalisation adapted from both Chinese and Byzantine methods. Cairo henceforth supplanted Baghdad as the hub of the Islamic world and its University of al-Azhar became the foremost seat of Muslim learning.

4:3 *The role of Islamic institutions*
If by the fourteenth century the Islamic Empire was no more than

a political fiction, the Muslim world did continue to retain the substance of cultural unity.

> Bonds of trade and law, language and learning were kept alive by thousands of travelling scholars, judges, merchants, and pilgrims. A civilisation consists of shared experiences and shared meanings, and for the Muslim world these were supplied by Islam — by five daily *prayers*, the fast of *Ramadan*, the rites of the *hajj*, the charitable hospices for merchants and travelling scholars, and the Arabic language of the *Qur'an*. This is amply illustrated by the story of the young ibn Battuta, who in 1325 left his home in Tangiers to undertake a pilgrimage to Mecca. He did not return until 29 years later in 1354, having visited every country under Muslim rule, from Spain to the Niger, from the Crimea to Mombasa, from Delhi to Sumatra. Wherever he went he was able to earn an honourable living as a judge administering the *shariah*, the sacred law of the faith.[6]

4:4 *New empires arise*

In the wake of the Mongol storm three great empires arose — the Ottoman of Turkey, the Safavid of Persia, and the Mughal of India. Each centred on a court of surpassing grandeur, dazzling to the eye of European visitors. Each bestowed lavish patronage upon the arts and, in architecture and miniature painting especially, gave birth to works of art of enduring significance. Each passed through a century or two of self-confidence and military ascendancy to enter upon a longer period of stagnation which would finally be terminated by more or less violent dismemberment at western hands during the colonial period.

> Of these three, the Ottoman Empire emerged the earliest and survived the longest. It expanded from an obscure thirteenth century kingdom in north-west Anatolia, until, by 1500, it had embraced the heartland and capital city of the former Byzantine Empire. The height of its glory was attained under Selim I, 'the Grim' (1512–1520) and Suleyman II, 'the Magnificent' (1520–1566) who conquered Egypt, Syria, Iraq, the coastlands of North Africa and the Red Sea, the island of Rhodes, and the Balkans as far as the Hungarian plain. Nearly a century later an English traveller was still moved to declare, 'He who would behold

these times in their greatest glory could not find a better scene than in Turkey' (H. Blount, 1634).[7]

4:5 *Europe and Islam*

Proximity to Europe made the Ottoman Empire an integral part of European diplomacy. Religious loyalties usually appear to have been overriden by pragmatic considerations of power and profit. In December 1525, for instance, Francis I, of France, appealed to Suleyman to attack Charles V. The Sultan obliged in 1526, overrunning Hungary in the process. This not only eased the military pressure on the French, it also distracted the Hapsburgs from persecuting the Lutherans and thus exercised a decisive influence on the development of Protestantism in its crucial early stages. The Ottomans twice laid siege to Vienna (1529 and 1683), but were unable to operate effectively so far from their Anatolian base. Nieuwenhuijze notes, '... Henceforth, Islam can spread only as a creed not as a realm; a most un-Islamic state of affairs since creed and realm are in principle indistinguishable.' The Treaty of Karlowitz (1699) under which, for the first time, the empire ceded conquered territory, marked a major turning-point in the fortunes of the Ottomans. By the eighteenth century prolonged inflation, military conservatism and political corruption had forced the Ottoman Empire onto the defensive. Despite sporadic but largely successful attempts at reform which were made throughout the nineteenth century, the fate of the empire was sealed by defeat in the First World War.[7]

4:6 *The Safavids*
In Persia the Safavid Empire lasted from 1503 until 1722. Militarily it was based on an elite of Turkish tribesmen, but administrative power was effectively in the hands of Persian judges and bureaucrats. The regime reached its zenith under Shah Abbas (1587–1629), who not only put down internal feuds and instituted much-needed reforms in the political structure of the state, but also embellished the city of Isfahan with unrivalled splendour. At its heart he laid out a vast park and polo field surrounded by arcades and palaces. But its greatest glory lay in the magnificent tile-decorated mosques which are among modern Iran's most prized national treasures.

4:7 *The Mughals*

In 1526 Suleyman the Magnificent laid the foundations of Ottoman power in the Balkans by annihilating a Hungarian force at the Battle of Mohacs. In the same year, but at the other end of the Muslim world, Babur, of Mongol descent, was the first to establish decisively a local supremacy with a victory at Panipat outside Delhi. His grandson, Akbar, doubled the area of his inheritance to take in all but the extreme south of the subcontinent. Whereas the Safavids and Ottomans owed their decline to mutually destructive border wars and Russian pressure, the Mughal power was gradually eroded by internal disintegration. The French and then the British intervened to fill the vaccum thus created, though the fiction of Mughal suzerainty was maintained until 1857.[8]

4:8 *Islah — reform of Islam*

Within the framework of these empires, significant internal changes took place. Historically, reform movements of a 'puritanical' variety have played an important part in the development of Islam. Not least among them is the Wahabi which arose in Arabia in the eighteenth century and currently dominates the religious practices of the Arabian peninsula. These movements invariably call for a return to the original principles and practices of Islam and protest forcibly against what they regard as idolatrous and superstitious accretions (e.g. veneration of saints, tombs, palm reading, etc.). They are invariably associated with political changes, providing as they do an ideological catalyst for discontent which rises up to challenge and overwhelm the existing authorities.

Not only were the reform movements which were puritanical in their outlook developing, but also some more liberal Muslim thinkers were expressing the view that Islam and modernisation were not incompatible, but rather should go hand in hand towards the goal of an Islamic society equipped for the modern age. These differing trends will be discussed in more detail in Chapter 12.

We look briefly now at two of the Muslim leaders of the beginning of this century and compare their differing approaches.

1 Kemal Ataturk

After the fall of the Ottoman Empire at the end of the First World War, Ataturk was Turkey's leader. He was a well-read, well-travelled man and was the culmination of a long line of reformers within Turkey. He had visited foreign countries when in the Ottoman army and was anxious that his people should have the benefit of modern education as other, particularly western, countries did.

2 *Muhammad Reza Khan*

As a result of a rebellion in the army, Reza Khan came to power in Persia. He did not come from an educated background; in fact, he was illiterate. He had had no contact with the western industrial countries and had little understanding of ruling a country or of introducing reforms. He seems to have tried to copy Ataturk.

Further developments in both Turkey and Persia (Iran) are mentioned in Chapter 12, when we look at Islam today.

Recommended Reading

GLUBB, John Bagot. *A Short History of the Arab Peoples*, Quartet Books, London, 1978.

Additional Reading

BROCKELMANN, Carl. *History of the Islamic People*, Routledge & Kegan Paul, London, 1982.
LEWIS, Bernard. *The Arabs in History*, Hutchinson, London, 1970.
SHABAN, M A. *The Abbasid Revolution*, CUP, 1970.

Notes

1 GLUBB, John Bagot. *A Short History of the Arab Peoples*, Quartet Books, London, 1978, p65.
2 LEWIS, Bernard. *The Arabs in History*, Hutchinson, London, 1970, p80.
3 SCHOOL OF ORIENTAL AND AFRICAN STUDIES. *The World of Islam: A Teacher's Handbook*, 1977, p61.
4 GLUBB, John Bagot. *A Short History of the Arab Peoples*, Quartet Books, London, 1978, p95.
5 Quoted in TAMES, Richard. *Approaches to Islam*, John Murray, London, 1982, p64.
6 SCHOOL OF ORIENTAL AND AFRICAN STUDIES. *The World of Islam: A Teacher's Handbook*, 1977, p62.
7 Ibid, p63.
8 Ibid, p64.

Chapter 9

HISTORY AND SIGNIFICANCE OF SECTS WITHIN ISLAM

1 Study Guide

This chapter goes through the development, particular characteristics, and influence of the different sects of Islam and should give you a good overall view. Little is said by Muslims about divisions in Islam, which is only natural and you may find your Muslim friends reluctant to talk about them. You should, however, be able to find out whether they are Sunnis, Shi'as, or adhere to one of the smaller groups. It ought to be possible for you to get a good basis for answering the discussion questions at the end of the chapter by studying the chapter itself, doing some further reading (as suggested in the additional reading list), and by chatting to Muslim friends. You may find the study of the sects somewhat complicated and should keep an eye on the genealogical tree as you read. The booklet *Understanding Muslim Sects* by Canon R W F Wootton gives a helpful summary. It is the recommended book for this chapter.

Learning objectives
When you have completed this chapter you should:

1 Be able to distinguish between the different sects and divisions of Islam.
2 Have assessed the relative political and social importance of the different sects in today's world.
3 Understand something of why and how the sects developed as they did.
4 Be in a position to consider how they may influence the future of the Muslim world.

HISTORICAL DEVELOPMENT
OF THE SECTS OF ISLAM

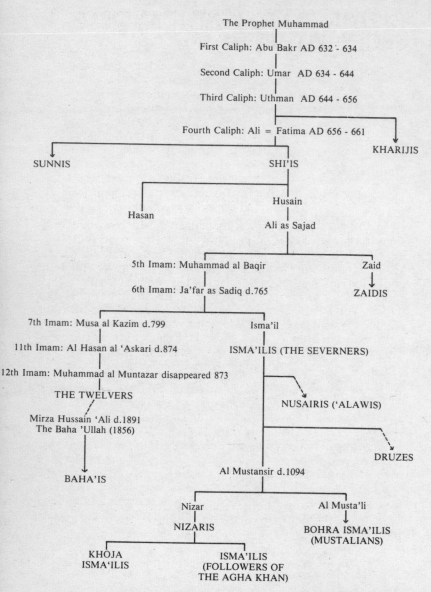

The Prophet Muhammad

First Caliph: Abu Bakr AD 632 - 634

Second Caliph: Umar AD 634 - 644

Third Caliph: Uthman AD 644 - 656

Fourth Caliph: Ali = Fatima AD 656 - 661

KHARIJIS

SUNNIS
SHI'IS

Husain

Hasan

Ali as Sajad

5th Imam: Muhammad al Baqir
Zaid

6th Imam: Ja'far as Sadiq d.765
ZAIDIS

7th Imam: Musa al Kazim d.799
Isma'il

11th Imam: Al Hasan al 'Askari d.874
ISMA'ILIS (THE SEVERNERS)

12th Imam: Muhammad al Muntazar disappeared 873
THE TWELVERS
NUSAIRIS ('ALAWIS)

Mirza Hussain 'Ali d.1891
The Baha 'Ullah (1856)

DRUZES

BAHA'IS
Al Mustansir d.1094

Nizar
Al Musta'li

NIZARIS
BOHRA ISMA'ILIS
(MUSTALIANS)

KHOJA
ISMA'ILIS
ISMA'ILIS
(FOLLOWERS OF
THE AGHA KHAN)

Used by permission of the Fellowship of Faith for the Muslims,
from Canon R W F Wootton, *Understanding Muslim Sects*, p46.

2 Sects and Divisions Within Islam

In *Islam in the World* Malise Ruthven compares Muslim sects and Christian denominations. This may be helpful in discussing the matter with Muslims. He writes:

> The divisions of Islam, in contrast to those of Christianity, have their origins in politics rather than dogma. This is not to say that dogmatic and theological questions do not form part of these divisions. However, the questions over which they first crystallised were political to the extent that they were primarily concerned with leadership of the community. Having a religious ideology built on the social foundations of tribalism, the Muslims expressed their aspirations first in terms of group loyalty, and only afterwards in terms of the doctrinal and theological accretions surrounding these loyalties.[1]

When we use the word 'sects' in connection with Islam, we are not referring primarily to a non-Islamic group which sprang out of the movement, but of sub-divisions which, although varying in many degrees from each other and what is accepted as orthodoxy, would still be regarded by the majority and by themselves (which is most important), as being Muslim.

There is a tradition which occurs in various forms which recognises that there are sects within Islam. Muhammad is alleged to have said, 'Did not the people of the book divide into 72 sects (*milla*) and in truth this community will one day divide into 73 sects, of which 72 will go to hell and only one to paradise.' Another form of this tradition speaks of the Jews having 71 sects, the Christians 72 and the Muslims 73.

There are different ways of classifying the very many groups within Islam. We can assume that Sunni Islam is the standard, because it has the most adherents. Other groups can then be evaluated on the basis of how far they digress from this standard. We can, alternatively, classify the sects according to their geographical origins, or by the names of their founders. In this section we look at some of the causes of division which have led to the development of sects.

3 The Role of Mecca

While examining the emergence of various sects in Islam, attention should be paid to the importance of Mecca in the spread of sectarian views. Whenever Muslims have gone on a pilgrimage to Mecca they come into contact with new ideas. Some returned to their own country influenced by the new ideas, and ready to propagate them amongst their own people. This has been true in the case of the Sufi brotherhoods as well as the more extreme of the fundamentalist groups.

4 Theological Divisions

4:1 *The status of the Qur'an*
The divisions which arose within Islam were often the result of either political conflict or theological disagreement. It is assumed by most Muslims that scholars of the first and second Islamic centuries held the doctrine of the uncreated Qur'an (that is that the Qur'an is eternal). Very few believed the Qur'an was actually a book that could be dated. It was only towards the end of the second Muslim century that the question was explicitly raised whether the Qur'an was created or uncreated, which led to the *mihna* (inquisition).

This resulted in conflict between the Islamic clergy and the caliph of the time. The assumption was that the Qur'an was the eternal book of God (an idea that developed after contact with early Christians who held that Jesus was the eternal Word of God). This was supported by the idea that the *hadith*, or traditions about Muhammad, had been handed on with complete verbal accuracy from the Companions to later generations of Muslims. There is, and always has been, an immense confidence in Islam that the Qur'an and traditions are true, and that what disagrees with them is false.

The question as to whether the Qur'an was created or was the eternal word of God, posed several problems. First and foremost, is the fact that if the Qur'an was the eternal Word of God, it would seem to imply that there are two eternities in heaven: God is eternal, and by associating the Word of God with God, some Muslims have argued that the sin of *shirk* is committed (that is, the sin of associating any thing or person with God).

4:2 *The question of guilt or innocence*
Another question which caused division within the early Muslim community was the question of guilt or innocence. In certain cases, men should not judge a question of guilt or innocence, but should leave the decision to God. This led to disputes over such matters as:

1   The choice of Uthman as leader and the demoting of Ali to fourth place in order of merit after Muhammad.
2   Not merely postponing the judgement of the grave sinner and treating him as a believer, but positively asserting that he is a believer, but has erred. It was understood that all Muslims would eventually go to Paradise provided that they do not fall into the sin of *shirk* or idolatry.

The Mutazila introduced dogmatic theology into Islam. They stressed man's responsibility for his deeds, because he has been given free will. They were concerned with the question of the grave sinner, and asserted that he was neither a believer nor an unbeliever, but was in an intermediate position.

The Kharidjites wanted to establish a pure theocracy. They questioned the need for the Caliphate, believing in the rule of Allah alone. They were far more aggressive, and positively held that a grave sinner was an unbeliever. They seemed to have placed a great majority of Muslims in this last group, since most claimed to believe that even a bad sinner could still be a Muslim.

4:3 *The doctrine of Qadr*
Another Islamic point of contention was the doctrine of *qadr*, the teaching that God alone has the power to create and produce things, which exists in contention with the concept of man's free will. The early controversies that divided the Muslim community into various sects in the Umayyad days were the outcome of differences concerning the true nature of faith. Was it, as the Murdjites maintained, simply 'knowledge and confession of God, together with knowledge and confession of his apostle and what he brought from God,' or was it, as the Kharidjites believed, a duty imposed by God upon his creatures so that every great sin is unbelief or polytheism?

The predestination-free will problem was first raised by Islam as recorded debates between Muslims and Christians in Umayyad times. It was summed up in the question, 'Can God be the cause of evil?' Christians and Muslims alike answered, 'No, the evil is from our negligence and the devil's cunning.' Further to this came the question of 'are you then a free agent?' Most of the Kharidjites and Shiites believed in the power of God and that God fore-ordained everything that happened, both good and evil. The Umayyads claimed that their right to rule was based upon the fact that they were already ruling. If it had been God's will that they should not rule they would never have been in a position of power. Thus, theological arguments were mobilized to undergird and legitimise a 'corrupt' Umayyad dynasty.

5   Political Division

5:1 *Sunnism*

Sunnism gradually became the orthodox, most widely accepted position held by some 90 per cent of Islam and all other groups came to be considered as sectarian. As various leaders and teachers arose within these groups, they set up their own schools of thought and teaching and became sub-sects. This was particularly evident with the argument concerning who should lead the community after Muhammad died. Some claimed that it should be left to a democratic process amongst the elders of Islam; others claimed that it was an inheritance left to Ali. The followers of Ali (the party of Ali, Shiat Ali) eventually became known as the Shiites.

5:2 *The emergence of the Shi'a sect*

The Shi'a sect emerged from the argument as to whether Ali should have been the first Caliph or not. They also developed a different view of government. The Sunni Muslims held that the *sunnah*, or practice of the prophet, was an authoritative source of law-making. On the other hand, the Shi'as held that an *imam*, or leader, went into hiding in the ninth century and is still alive today, and so is the only legitimate ruler of the Muslim world. However, as long as he remains in hiding the government falls on the shoulders of his representatives, the Islamic clergy. The Iranian revolution is a return to Shi'a fundamentalism. Shi'as differ in some respects from the majority of the Muslims. The traditional creed is expanded to include the term 'and Ali is the friend of God.' They reject the idea of the Muslim being able to have a concubine; but alternatively they introduced the idea of *muta* marriage which is legal, temporary marriage whilst a man is on pilgrimage or on a business trip.

As we have seen, the Shi'as claim Ali was the rightful successor to Muhammad. When he was killed he left a line of descendants. There have been two great schisms concerning the succession of leaders (*imams*). The first was after the death of Ali Zainu Abidin, when part of the sect adhered to his son, Zaid, the founder of the Zaidiyyah sect. The second was on the death of As Sadiq, when his father nominated his second son, Musa Alkazim, as his successor, instead of allowing the caliphate to go to Ismail's family. This was because of Ismail's alleged alcoholism. Those who follow Ismail are called the Ismailiyyah; today they are led by the Aga Khan. The greatest number of the Shi'as acknowledge Musa Alkazim (the second son of As Sadiq) and his descendants as the true line. They are thus called the Ithna Ashariyyah or *the Twelvers*. A dispute over the political leadership of the Shi'a sect resulted in a theological difference as well. A small minority regarded Ismail's drunkenness as evidence that he accepted the hidden meaning of Islam but not the legal precepts. Of the proverbial 73 sects of Islam no fewer than 32 are assigned to the Shi'as and possibly as many as 70. Many of the Shi'as have carried their dedication to Ali as far as to raise him to the position of a divine person (most of the sects make their *imams* partakers of the divine nature).

The Ismaili or *the Sevener* line of *imams* provided the Fatimid Caliphs of North Africa and Egypt (909–1171). One of the Fatimid Caliphs was al-Hakim (996–1021) who claimed to be God incarnate. He was actually quite mad and eventually had to flee the throne and found refuge in the Lebanese mountains. His followers are the present-day Druze.

5:3 *The Druze*

The Druze are a community living mainly in the Lebanon, Israel, and around Damascus. The name is derived from Beth Darazi. It is probable that the people of this area were already racially distinct before the founding of their religion and that they were never truly converted to Islam. They have sometimes been regarded as the descendents of Persian colonists. In the seventeenth century they were thought to be survivors of the Latin Christians who escaped the massacre of Acre in 1291, but this has been disproved. The Druze claimed that they were descended from Godfrey Bouillon, one of the Crusader knights. The Druze religion is a system of doctrine which only the *Uqqal* (learned) know. Those who do not know this system are called the *juhhal* (the ignorant). The religion was founded in the time of the Fatimid Caliph Hakim (996–1021) as a splinter group from the Shiite Ismailis. They held the view that God became incarnate in man. The Caliph Hakim represented God in his unity and is worshipped and called 'Our Lord.' His eccentricity and cruelties are explained symbolically. He was the last incarnation of God and did not die but is still living, hidden in a secret place.

6:1 Sufi Orders

Between one-third and one-half of the Muslim world is involved in some kind of Sufi brotherhood. The Sufis represent a more mystical, poetical dimension of Islam, and are found in most of the schools, or sects, of Islam. It was al-Ghazali who began to combine classical learning with mystical Islam around 1111 AD.

The word '*suf*' usually is interpreted as meaning 'wool' and represents the woollen garments that the early Sufi mystic used to wear. This was a carry-over from the monkish habit of the Christian ascetics of the sixth and seventh centuries: for Islam, however, Muhammad himself is seen to be the prime example of a mystic, because of the mystical nature of the revelations and visions that came to him.

In the developing centuries of Islam, the study and practice of the law was seen to be far more respectable than the gyrations of babbling, wild-eyed, ascetic mystics. It was not until al-Ghazali became disenchanted with his academic, legalistic studies and took up the practice of meditation and the Sufi internalisation of the law that Sufism became respectable. Traditional Islamic law is an external imposition of rules and regulations. The Sufi sees beyond the external and seeks to internalise an experience with the help of either his particular teacher, or with Muhammad, who will then be able to lead the initiate into communion with God. Muhammad is seen to be the pole round which the universe is ordered because he pleased God. Disciples strive towards this 'pole' or 'axis' of pleasing God.

The Sufis are divided into numerous religious orders of *dervishes* or *faqirs*. Although they differ in name and in some of their customs, such as dress, meditations, and recitations, they are all agreed in their principal tenets; particularly those which inculcate the necessity of absolute submission to a *murshid* or 'inspired guide.' It is generally admitted that, irrespective of minor sects, the Sufis are divided into those who claim to be only the *ilhamiyya* or 'inspired of God' and those who assert that they are *ittihadiyyah* or 'in union with God'.

6:2 *Early Sufis*

One of the first known teachers of Sufi ideas was al-Sufi, who was a Shi'a chemist in Kufa. Hasan al-Basri, who died in 728, was a teacher of mysticism and is famous for the statement, '*Ana al haqq*', which means 'I am the truth.' Many people took him to mean by this statement that he was God; he was saying, however, that he had come to such a height of spiritual experience that he had found complete union with God. The Sufis have a genealogy of spiritual teachers, which gives a considerable hierarchy of believing souls reaching back to Muhammad (and God).

During this period 900 to 975, four poets from Basrah were responsible for the collection of what is called the *rasa'il* or 'letters', numbering 51 or 52. Incorporated into this is a collection of Hindu folk laws, amongst which are stories and fables of a ringed dove (taken as the symbol of fellowship). Their followers came to be known as the Brethren of Purity (*Ikhwan al Safa*). The collection was divided into four parts:

1 Mathematical sciences, arithmetic, geometry, astronomy, music.
2 Physical sciences, medicine, logic, chemistry, biology.
3 Intellectual/moral sciences, soul, intellect, resurrection.
4 Metaphysical, jurisprudence, rational perception of certain subjects, astrology, magic under a religious title.

The whole of life was reduced to a single creative impulse having as its objective the release of the soul and union with the universal. (Here we can see the influence of neo-Platonic Greek thought as well as Zoroastrianism and Hinduism upon Islam.)

6:3 *Sources of revelation*

The Sufis claim that divine reality is perceived by three organs of human perception. First, *qalb*, or 'the heart', which is the seat of the emotions; secondly, *ruh*, or 'spirit', through which knowledge is perceived; and thirdly, *sira*, or 'secret', which would be a secret developed or revealed by a teacher, who passes it on to his disciples when he feels they are ready to receive it.

The Sufi disciples are gathered together in orders known as *tarikas*. Each *tarika* develops its own ritual and style. Common to many of them is the *dhikr*, which is the constant repetition of the name or names of God. This constant repetition induces a trance-like state and is accompanied by drum beating, the playing of various musical instruments, and the rhythmic movement of the body. In contrast, another technique is meditation where silence provides an atmosphere within which the disciple thinks about the names of God. Finally, there is the use of dreams to reveal inner truths.

One way in which Islam spread, particularly into black Africa, Central Asia, and India, was through travelling holy men or *awliya*, known as *pirs* in the Indian sub-continent. They were popular with the local people, since they brought with them special powers of healing and miracle working and were not strict in their position on Islamic law. They were the possessors of a certain type of charisma know as *baraka*. (In fact, when these men died, tombs were erected over their graves and they became places of pilgrimage. Just to touch the tomb was believed to transfer the *baraka* or blessing of the dead to the one coming to receive a blessing.)

The miracle worker, *karama*, was also a popular figure. He would write verses of the Qur'an on pieces of paper and then dip them in water; people would be healed by drinking the water. The miracle worker might also be someone to go to for advice concerning a marriage, planting of crops, or to seek the inducing of conception.

The organisation of Sufi orders into *tarikas* brought a standardisation within the order and the possibility of promoting its goals amongst the general population. In Turkey the Bektashiya and the Meveleviyya are probably the most well-known. In 1240 a widespread revolt against Islamic authority in Turkey prepared the way for the arrival of *Hajji* Bektash and his message of popular Islam. From this came the Bektashiya movement to which *Hajji* Bektash lends his name. Among them are the whirling *dervishes* who spend their time meditating on the names of God spinning on their feet, another technique of inducing a trance. The Bektashiya is a Turkish movement which has strong links with Central Asia. During the 1480s to 1520s the Bektashiya became a source of recruitment for the *janissaries*, who were the guards of the Ottoman Empire.

6:4 *The Sufis in India and Africa*
Islam arrived in India around the 750s and as the Muslim armies conquered the main cities and set up their garrisons, wandering holy men would travel from garrison to garrison teaching and preaching an ascetic form of Islam. One movement that developed in India was the Chistiyya, and again there was an incorporation of pre-Islamic ideas from India. Three others were the Deobandi, Suhrawardiyya and Naqshbandiya. In West Africa, probably the most widely known order is the Tijaniyya. The Tijaniyya was founded by Ahmad al Tijani who died in 1815. He claimed to be the Qutb al Aqtab, i.e., 'the pole of poles', and the Khatm Awliya, 'the seal of the saints'. He claimed that his followers were superior to all other orders, a claim which proved to be very popular in West Africa.

7   Modern Movements

With the coming of European domination in Egypt, Iran and India in the eighteenth and nineteenth centuries, Islam reacted either by absorbing and adapting to western ideas, or by rejecting them and adopting a conservative form of Islam. This conservatism is exemplified by the Wahabis of Saudi Arabia, who are a fundamentalist group within the Muslim world.

Probably the most well-known and aggressive Muslim movement today has come out of British India and is known as the Ahmadiyya.

The Ahmadiyya sect was founded by Mirza Ghulam Ahmad, a chief of the village of Qadian in the Punjab. Religious syncretism seems to have run in Ahmad's family, and the Ahmadiyya movement has become very adept at this process. Whilst remaining a Muslim he posed as a guru (teacher), professing to have come into the spirit and power of Jesus Christ, and to be the promised Messiah. He also claimed to be in the spirit and power of Muhammad and to be the promised Ahmad ('Praised One'), as well as the spirit and power of Krishna and the promised, future incarnation expected by all Hindus. His attempt to unite the main religions of India, (Islam, Hinduism, and Christianity) could be seen as a pacifist attempt to combat the rule of the British in India and to re-establish Indian glory. To have embarked upon a bloody, holy war against the ruling British would have been suicidal for him: and thus, one of the central claims of the Ahmadiyya movement has been non-violence.

In order to clear the way for his own messianic claims, he held that Jesus Christ did not die on the cross, but actually went to India to preach to the descendants of the ten lost tribes in Afghanistan and Kashmir. Jesus is said to have died a natural death in Kashmir, where his tomb exists today.

Ahmad claimed that Jesus was on the cross only a few hours and that his legs were not broken. He only became unconscious through the loss of blood and finally was revived in the darkness and coolness of the tomb and left the area to go to India. This is a revival of the nineteenth century 'swoon' theory. Ahmad interpreted Jesus' claim to be the 'sign of Jonah' as confirmation that Jesus never died. Jesus said, 'For as Jonah was three days and three nights in the belly of a large fish, so the Son of Man will be three days and three nights in the heart of the earth' (Matthew 12:40). But, says Ahmad, Jonah entered the belly of the fish alive and remained there alive and came out alive; so must Jesus have entered the tomb alive, remained there alive, and come out alive in order to make the analogy complete. This has been discussed in Chapter 6.

Finally, he points to the spiritual death of Christianity since the fruits of Christianity in the West are obviously corrupt. The Ahmadiyya were the first Islamic group to establish a mosque in Britain (Woking, Surrey), and have embarked upon an aggressive 'evangelistic' campaign to convert Europeans to the Muslim cause.

In September 1974, following the recommendations of an

International Muslim Conference held in Saudi Arabia in February of that year, the Ahmadiyyas were declared a non-Muslim sect by the government of Pakistan. The reason for this is that Ahmad claimed that he, not Muhammad, was the final prophet. The Ahmadiyya have been severely persecuted since then in Pakistan, and many have lost their lives.

Activities
1   Describe and explain the historical origins of the Shi'a sect. You will find a brief summary in Chapter 8, section 4:1, **The Mongols and After — New Influence in Islam**. Basically the schism arose over a disagreement about the caliphate succession. There is, of course, much more to it than this. Your further reading will help you to understand more of the background loyalties and the characters of Ali and the contending caliphs.

2   Describe any one of the sects of Islam in existence today. Look out for any mention of it in the news. Use the knowledge gained in this chapter to explain the background of the news item to a friend.
It will be helpful to choose one sect and to do some further reading on it. If you can also find a Muslim who is an adherent, this will be better still.

3   From your reading and from the newspapers, do you think that the link between politics and religion is as strong as this chapter suggests?

Recommended Reading

WOOTTON, R W F. *Understanding Muslim Sects,* FFM, 1983.

Additional Reading

GIBB, H A R, and KRAMERS J H. *The Shorter Encyclopedia of Islam*, E J Brill, Leiden, 1974. See articles under the titles 'Mutazila', 'Kharidjites', 'Ismailiya', 'Murdjia', 'Shia', and 'Ahmadiyya'.
HUGHES, T P. *The Dictionary of Islam*, Premier Book House, Lahore, 1964. See articles under 'Sects of Islam', pages 567–569, and 'Sufi', pages 608–617.
RUTHVEN, Malise. *Islam in the World*, Pelican, Penguin

Books, Harmondsworth, Middlesex, 1984.

Note

1 RUTHVEN, Malise. *Islam in the World*, Pelican, Penguin Books, Harmondsworth, Middlesex, p181.

Chapter 10

ISLAMIC LAW

1 Study Guide

Without going into too much detail, this chapter gives a sound basis which will help you understand something of how Islamic law is structured and applied. Although this material may not seem essential in learning how to relate to Muslims, it does in fact explain some of the problems Muslims have in living in non-Islamic countries. It also helps us to understand the changes some Islamic countries are introducing in order to become more Islamic. We asked Ron George to write this chapter.

The chapter divides the subject into three parts:
1. The introduction: Pre-classical Islam.
2. The Classical period: Tenth century to 1800.
3. The Modern period: 1800–1980.

Learning Objectives
When you have completed this chapter you should:

1. Understand the framework of Islamic law.
2. Be able to explain the sources of the law and its development from these sources.
3. Know something of the application of Islamic law and the difficulties encountered in this.
4. See how relevant Islamic law is to the Muslim world today.

2 Introduction

Islamic law is of central importance to Islam, and the heart of

Islamic law is family law. No study of Islam is complete without an attempt to understand this legal system which has developed over 1300 years, from the time of Muhammad. Muslims will often claim that Islam is a complete system and in a way that is quite true. Within Christianity the church and state have different responsibilities, even where there is a state church. In Islam legal matters are considered to be a revelation from God. The holy law of Islam, the *shariah*, is regarded as the revelation of God to man, to order his affairs, guide his life and give him an answer for every question of right and wrong.

3   Schools of Law

Islamic law is known as the *shariah*, a word which describes 'the path the camel takes to the water hole'. It is a path to follow which should ultimately end in refreshing the follower. The *shariah* has both legal and religious content. It includes, for example, subjects such as marriage, how and what to eat, how and when to pray.

It is not a unified single system of law. Within Islamic law there are different schools or *madhabs*. Within the Sunni, or orthodox sect, there are four schools, the largest of which is the Hanafi which exists primarily in India, Pakistan, Turkey, Syria, Jordan, Iraq, Lebanon and Afghanistan. The second largest school is the Maliki which exists in North Africa, Morocco, Algeria, Tunisia, Egypt, West Africa, and Kuwait. The Shafi School is the third most numerous and is scattered within the Middle East, Lower Egypt, East Africa, Malaysia and Indonesia, since it was a legal system carried by traders. Finally, the Hanbali School exists predominantly in Saudi Arabia and Qatar. Most of our comments concerning Islamic law will be concerned with the Hanafi School. The differences between the various schools are small.

4   The History of Islamic Law in the Pre-classical Period

This covers the period from Muhammad up to the tenth century. It was only after the Arab conquest of Syria that a distinct Muslim code of law began to emerge. The simple tenets of belief that 'God is one', that 'the Qur'an is the word of God', and that 'Muhammad is the last and ultimate messenger of God' were unable to provide solutions to the problems of governing an empire. By 900 AD, at least four sources of authority that were to be important in the development of Islamic law, had gradually emerged. These were mentioned in chapter 3/4, part 1, section 3, **What is the Meaning of Islam?** Can you remember what they were?

5 The Sources of Authority for Islamic Law

5:1 *The Qur'an*

The Qur'an is not a book of law; of the 6,219 verses only 600 deal with law. These are in the later Medinan *surahs*. It contains only six offences punishable by law. These punishable offences are called '*hadd*' crimes (4:3,4). They are: illegal sexual intercourse, a false accusation of lack of chastity, theft, drinking of wine, highway robbery, and apostasy.

The Qur'an does not deal with the problems of the law in detail. There are few definitions of terms or of penalties for breaking the law; for example, usury (*riba*) is prohibited in *surah* 2:275, but there is no definition of what *riba* is or of the consequences of practising it. There is further discussion of *riba* in Chapter 12, section 3:2, *The implications of a return to the shariah*. The qur'anic revelation is not a comprehensive legal code and a number of the pronouncements relate to Muhammad personally. For example, the effect of *qadhf* or slander, *surah* 24:4, is concerned with the defamation of women. This law was the result of an incident involving Muhammad's wife, Aisha, who had lost her shells and was found wandering around the camp. A soldier took her to Medina, and she was accused of unchastity. Aisha's innocence was revealed in *surah* 24:1. It was in judging this incident that the necessity of having four witnesses to the act, and the punishment of 80 lashes for the offender, were established. In the case of Muhammad wanting to marry his adopted son's wife Zainab, as we saw in Chapter 5, section 5:3, *The Medinan period*, *surah* 33:38 proclaimed that God had allowed this. Following this incident adoption was prohibited in Islam.

5:2 *Hadith*

As was seen in chapter 7, section 3:2, *Main events in the life of Muhammad*, the sayings and practices of Muhammad and his early followers and companions were later recorded in the *hadith*. There are six main collections. Muhammad al Bukhari (died 870 AD), was the first and best-known main collector. There were literally hundreds of thousands of sayings which were said to have been handed down. Bukhari and the other collectors sifted these through with the utmost care, rejecting many, as these could not be authenticated to their satisfaction.

Each *hadith* consisted of two parts: the *isnad*, which was the chain of people who were supposed to have passed the tradition down from the time of Muhammad to when it was actually written down; and the text itself, the *matn*. The collectors investigated the *isnad* of each tradition, those found satisfactory were included in the *hadith*. Bukhari arranged some 7,300 of these traditions in 97 'books'. They were arranged according to their subjects.

The *hadith* covers both religious practices and details of everyday life. Here are just two subjects, chosen because they are issues in present day society:

Jihad, which is described by Maulana Muhammad Ali in *A Manual of Hadith*, as follows:

> *Jihad* means *the exerting of one's power in repelling the enemy* or *in contending with an object of disapprobation*. It carries a twofold significance in Islam, being applied to both the purely missionary activities of a Muslim and his defence of the Faith, when necessary, in a physical sense.[1]

Here is one of the traditions which Maulana Muhammad Ali quotes:

> A man came to the Messenger of Allah, and said, 'Guide me to a deed which is equal to jihad.' He said, 'I do not find it.' [Then] he said: 'Is it in thy power that when the one engaged in jihad goes forth, thou shouldst enter thy mosque and stand in prayer and have no rest, and that thou shouldst fast and break it not?' He said, 'Who can do it?' (Bukhari 56:1)[2]

A second example concerns the *role and status of women*. Guillaume quotes 'The World, all of its property (could mean enjoyable or valuable) and the best property in the World is a virtuous women.' (reported by Abd Allah b. Umar)[3] and: 'A woman may be married for four things: her money, her birth, her beauty, and her religion. Get thou a religious woman (otherwise) may thy hands be rubbed in dirt!' (reported by Abu Huraira)[3]

C E Bosworth writes in the preface to *A Manual of Hadith*:

> ... For the Muslim believer, *hadith* is of supreme importance in this faith, because it gives first-hand guidance, once the chain of transmitters and guarantors of the tradition in question is accepted as authen-

tic, on how the Prophet and the early Muslims acted and felt in the contexts of a multiplicity of situations in everyday life.[4]

5:3 *Ijma*

There is a *hadith* which says that Muhammad claimed that his people would never agree upon error. On the basis of this *hadith*, the ideas of *ijma* was developed (see Chapter 3/4, section 3, **What is the Meaning of Islam?**). *Ijma* means consensus of opinion and, therefore, means that if the followers of Muhammad agree upon something they themselves become a source of lawmaking. Originally it was the companions of Muhammad who agreed. Now it is the Islamic teachers, not just any group of Muslims. This is true for the Sunnis. The Shi'as have a similar system, in the office of the *imam*. Consequently, by agreeing upon a principle or rule they became law-makers themselves.

5:4 *Qias*

Finally, analogical deduction was used (*qias*) (see Chapter 3/4, part 1, section 4). If an analogy or parallel could be drawn from a verse in the Qur'an or *hadith*, then this was a valid way of applying those traditions to many a situation. These sources of law are in order of authority. *Ijma* must be on the basis of the Qur'an and *hadith*, *qias* on the basis of the Qur'an, *hadith* and *ijma*.

Activities
1 Consider whether the following were all purposes for which Islamic law was promulgated:
Reform of bad practices.
Protection of society.
Standardisation within an empire.
Communication of the will of God to the world.
Check your answers when you have completed the chapter.
2 Find out what your Muslim friends consider. Read what is said in newspapers about the introduction of Muslim law into countries such as Pakistan and Sudan. This will be good preparation for further consideration of the implications of a return to the *shariah* in Chapter 12.

6 Historical Development

6:1 *Practical application*
One example of the application of Islamic law did effect some improvement in the status of women compared with the pre-

Islamic Arab customs that were prevalent. Women were allowed to inherit possessions from their deceased husbands, the harshness of divorce was tempered, and polygamy was limited to four wives only. A woman was also to receive her dowry directly instead of it going to her father (see Chapter 2, section 6:4 *Women in Islam*.

The institution of *idda* was developed. The divorced wife must observe three menstrual cycles after divorce before remarrying. During this time the husband could revoke his divorce, but different schools varied in what must happen to the wife during this *idda* period. The Hanafis say that she must be maintained by the husband. The Shafi School says that she does not have to be maintained.

In the pre-Islamic system the nearest male in the male line took everything after death. The Qur'an reformed this (2:177), making bequests in favour of kinsfolk obligatory. In *surah* 4:7–12 a second step is taken where each relative is given a specific share of the deceased's estate. A husband takes half of his wife's; a wife takes one-quarter of her husband's.

The Qur'an is not a legal code or legislation. Muhammad was not concerned with establishing a new legal order but only introducing some essential reforms of tribal society. As a result, the major formulative period of Islamic law is from the tenth century onwards.

6:2 *The classical period*

As the Arabs broke out of the Arabian peninsula in the seventh century, instruction had to be given as to the treatment of the conquered peoples and their lands and possessions. Umar (634–644) began to adopt certain aspects of Byzantine and Persian law in the form of adminstrative directives for this purpose. For example, he made use of the *diwan* system from Persia — a register of soldiers and their families which recorded their pensions. Umar expelled all non-Muslims from the Arabian peninsula and commanded that no Muslim could own land outside Arabia. Arabs could own land in Arabia if a tithe and the *zakat* tax were paid. Land was to be left in the hands of the existing population if they accepted Islam. We see that as a result of the new conquests, land law begins to develop during this period.

7:1 The Developing Law

As the law began to develop it was divided into five categories:
    1   *Wajib:*   compulsory and binding on all Muslims.

2	*Mandub:*	recommended and meritable.
3	*Mubah:*	indifferent and open to choice by the individual.
4	*Makruh:*	disapproved of, hateful, but still permitted.
5	*Haram:*	forbidden acts.

The tendency was to define actions according to these categories rather than to develop general legal principles by which a judge could officiate. For example, in marriage a body of law developed which made distinctions as to whether the marriage was *sahih* (full and valid) or *batil* (meaning void and not legal) and thirdly, *fassid*, (a marriage that was irregular, but still legally valid).

7:2 *Qadis*

After the first century of Islam, *qadis* or judges were appointed by governors of the Abbasid central government. They took over appointments and acted on the advice of the chief *qadi*. These *qadis* had to fulfil a number of criteria.

1 Have a good character (*adl*).
2 Be a member of the *ulema*, learned in the sacred law of Islam.
3 Be of full sight and facilities, not blind in one eye.
4 Not be a *dhimmi*, that is, a person of another religion, eg Jewish or Christian.
5 Not be a woman.
6 Hold his court in the mosque.

When judging a case, valid witnesses to any transaction in Islamic law had to be present, and written evidence was not acceptable. Two eyewitnesses had to be available for any transaction. But a woman's testimony was only worth half that of a man. (See Chapter 2, section 6:4, *Women in Islam*).

Procedure and evidence

To initiate a case before a *qadi* the claimant had to go to the *qadi* and take the offender with him. Later on, summons were introduced. The burden of proof lay with the plaintiff and witnesses were required by the claimant. One *hadith* states that the plaintiff proves his case by two witnesses, but the defendant clears himself by an oath. Witnesses were not cross-examined. Only their character could be brought into question.

7:3 *Conflicts of law*

In cases of succession one must apply the school of law to which the deceased belonged, and in litigation the law of the defendant must be applied. This is particularly difficult in a country where more than one school exists.

When there was a conflict between a Muslim and non-Muslim, any litigation had to go to the *qadi* and Islamic law was applied. If a Muslim had committed a tort, or civil wrong, against a non-Muslim he only had to pay half the blood money. If the conflicts were betwen protected peoples (such as Christians and Jews) of the same community then the dispute had to go to an ecclesiastical court. Alternatively they could ask to go before a *qadi* who would then apply Jewish or Christian law as long as there was no conflict with Islamic policy. If people from different communities had a conflict, then the issue had to come to a *qadi* who applied Islamic law.

In particular, conflicts arose when conversion was involved. If a Jewish husband had a wife who converted to Islam it caused considerable problems, because it is illegal for a Muslim woman to be married to a non-Muslim man. The husband was given three months to convert or else the marriage would be dissolved. In India many Hindu wives used this technique to escape from marriages.

As the Jews found, it was possible to keep the letter of the law whilst breaking the spirit of it. Within Islam a system of *hiyal* was developed. These were legal ways of doing something that was illegal. For example, interest or usury is forbidden in Islam. Therefore, double sales were developed to avoid this. For example A buys X from B for P pounds. B buys back from A for (P + T) pounds sometime in the future. T is the 'interest' involved.

No interest is actually charged, but the process of buying is perfectly legal. The Hanafis always accepted such devices, whereas the Shafis originally rejected them, but later saw that they were useful and therefore accepted them. The Maliki School rejected *hiyal* since they were interested in the internal intention of the law, and the Hanbalis violently rejected it.

Another example is, in certain cases, the law of pre-emption. This means that a neighbour has first right to buy a piece of land from a seller. However, if a third party offers a higher price for the land a *hiyal* can be used to go through with the transaction. A minute strip of land is gifted to the new potential purchaser who then becomes the new neighbour. Then the seller can go ahead and sell the rest of the land to this new neighbour.

Law officers
Along with this legal system there were men who were trained in varius aspects of the law and who could administrate it. The

office of the *qadi* was linked with the *shariah* law only, but the government under the caliph was to carry out the execution of that law. The *shurta* acted as police and the *muftis* as legal consultants. In the courts there was the *khatib* or the court clerk and *udul* were the notaries.

8 Modern Period

Beginning in the eighteenth century, European countries began to take over Islamic lands. The result of this expansion was that either Islamic law was influenced by European law, or it was set aside in preference of European law. For example, in India, British courts were established primarily as company courts under the East India Company. Indians frequently submitted themselves to company courts rather than the caste court. In 1718 an act established the East India Company as the appeal court and in 1772 its jurisdiction was extended throughout India. This was essentially a British system which led to misunderstanding and misinterpretation of Islamic law. As a result, much of the Muslim law was changed out of all recognition. Gradually over the period of British rule in India, Anglo-Muhammadan law developed. It is this law that Pakistan is attempting to purge in order to re-establish a purer form of Islamic law.

In other countries, for example Tunisia and Egypt, new ideas and concepts were introduced to the country and Muslim jurists attempted to assimilate them into Islamic law by looking again at the Qur'an and *hadith* and re-interpreting the law. For example, the Qur'an allows up to four wives for a man, but only if he treats all four equally. Tunisia claimed that it was impossible to treat four women equally and said that therefore Muhammad was actually teaching monogamy. In Ottoman Turkey there was a long period of change as a result of contact with the West. This began in 1839 with the Imperial Edict of the Rose Chamber and introduced the Tanzimat — a period of reform. By 1850 there was a new commercial code. In 1858 a criminal code and in 1879 a code of criminal procedure was introduced. As a result of this gradual process, by 1955 the Islamic *shariah* courts had been abolished in favour of secular courts.

Muslim countries continue to amend their legal systems either by re-interpreting the existing Islamic law in the light of new influences, or by returning to a purer form of the Islamic legal system.

The *shariah* has never been fully applied either in the past or the present. Certain attempts have been made but they have usually failed. The most notable examples of this are the purist reactions of the Almoravid movement in eleventh century Spain, and in the nineteenth century the attempts of the Fulani sultans in Nigeria. Even the Wahabis in present-day Saudi Arabia find it impossible to practise all the law all of the time.

Present-day reform in Islam is discussed in more detail in Chapter 12.

Activity

Do you think the carrying out of Islamic law is practical in the world today? Chapter 12 will, hopefully, throw more light on this, too.

Don't forget to check your answers from activity 1, at the end of section 5, **The Sources of Authority for Islamic Law**.

Recommended Reading

There is no book in this category for Chapter 10.

Additional Reading

COULSON, N J. *A History of Islamic Law*, Edinburgh University Press, 1964.

DOI, Abdul Rahman. *Shari'ah: The Islamic Law*, Ta Ha Publishers, London, 1984.

GUILLAUME, Alfred. *The Traditions of Islam*, Khayats, Beirut, 1966.

MUHAMMAD ALI, Maulana. *A Manual of Hadith*, Curzon Press, 1944, 3rd edition 1978.

PEARL, David. *A Textbook of Muslim Law*, Croom Helm, London, 1979. See chapters 2 and 11.

Notes

1 MUHAMMAD ALI, Maulana. *A Manual of Hadith*, Curzon Press, 1944, 3rd ed. 1978, p252.
2 Ibid, pp253–254.
3 GUILLAUME, Alfred. *The Traditions of Islam*, Khayata, Beirut, 1966, p124.
4 MUHAMMAD ALI, Maulana. *A Manual of Hadith*, Curzon Press, 1944, 3rd ed. 1978, preface, p5.

Chapter 11

CHRISTIAN-MUSLIM RELATIONSHIPS

1 Study Guide

In this chapter we have asked Ronald Waine to examine Muslim-Christian relations through a brief outline of their history and by considering the lives and witness of some leading missionaries of the past. It is important to have a clear understanding of what has happened in the past in order to understand the present situation. You will find it helpful to do some background reading and there is a book list at the end of the chapter from which you might like to select one or two titles.

Learning objectives

After completing this chapter you should:
1   Be able to sketch an outline of the history of Muslim-Christian relationships since the death of Muhammad in 632 AD.
2   Have seen how attitudes have varied over the years.
3   Have noted some key 'turning points', such as the Crusades.
4   Have looked at the lives of some who have contributed to the debate, or whose lives and witness have set an example to the Church.

2 The Development of Christian-Muslim Relations

2:1 *In the time of Muhammad*
Islam, the faith proclaimed by Muhammad, grew and expanded

rapidly in the fertile soil of a disunited and, as some would assert, a decadent Church. By 600 AD two factors characterised the eastern wing of the Church.

1 It had allied itself to the power of the State.
2 It was occupied more with doctrinal disputes and heresy hunts than with the declaration of the Gospel.

The early relationship between Islam and Christianity might perhaps have been different if:

1 Muhammad's knowledge of Christianity had been more accurate. He seems to have gained his knowledge from his acquaintance and association with a decadent form of Christianity.
2 The Church had been stronger and nearer in doctrine to the apostolic teaching.
3 Muhammad had been able to consult the Bible in his own language. There was no translation of the Bible available in Arabic before 737 AD, more than 100 years after his death.

As has been discussed in Chapter 7, section 4, **Muhammad's Attitude to Christians**, at first it seems that Muhammad was hoping for some sort of alliance with the Jews and Christians of the Arabian peninsula. This soon proved to be an impossible dream and as his teaching developed, his attitudes changed from one of friendly association to open disagreement. However, he did recommend to his followers that they should not dispute with the 'people of the Book': 'Dispute not with the People of the Book save in the fairer manner, except for those of them that do wrong; and say, "We believe in what has been sent down to you; our God and your God is One, and to Him we have surrendered"' (29:45).

Some Christians welcomed the Muslims as 'liberators', and the Muslim armies spread the new faith through the lands surrounding Arabia. The two faiths, either in friendship or on sufferance, managed to live side by side.

2:2 *During the spread of Islam*

As early as 633 AD, one year after the death of Muhammad, army detachments had penetrated Syria to the North and Persia to the East (see Chapter 8, section 3:1, *First crisis*). An astonishing number of towns, regions, and states were conquered in an incredibly short time. A list of the dates the towns fell helps us appreciate the speed of the advance.

Damascus	635
Jerusalem	640
Alexandria	642

Isfaham	643
Tripoli	647
Cyprus	649

Tunisia, Algeria, and Morocco were occupied and toward the end of the seventh century the Atlantic coast was reached.

One writer of these times expressed it thus:

> When at last there appeared, coming out of the desert, the news of a new revelation, this decadent and divided Christianity wavering in its fundamental dogmas and dismayed with uncertainties could no longer resist the temptations of a new faith which swept away at one stroke all doubts and along with a simple clear creed, 'There is no God but Allah and Muhammad is his prophet,' offered undisputed material benefits as well. [1]

Non-Muslim citizens in Islamic domains were to some extent disadvantaged. They had, for example, to pay special taxes, which took the place of the Islamic *zakat* (Chapter 3/4, part 2, section 7:3, *Welfare contributions*).

The Arab conquest swept aside old frontiers. From the seventh century onwards the Coptic and Syrian Churches do not seem to have played a decisive role in the history of their own territories. Theirs was a culture in isolation and decline and the interest of their story lies in the consequences of the reception given to the Muslim armies by the church leaders: thereafter it is a tale of the dour struggle for survival. In spite of the fact that millions of Christians were to live in close contact with Muslims, no organised chuches composed of Muslim converts to the Christian faith emerged.

At first the Muslims did not seek to propagate their faith amongst their subjects except those of the Arab race. During the first 70 years of Muslim expansion the subject people were left very much to their own devices. But, by 705 AD the church of St John at Damascus, which till then had been shared for Muslim and Christian worship, was completely taken over by the Muslims. From then on Arabic began to replace Greek as the language of administration.

With the fall of the Umayyad Caliphate in 750 AD, the Abbasids (see Chapter 8, section 3:3, *The golden age of Islam*) intensified the hostility against Christians.

History records the forcible conversion of the 'last Christian tribe in Syria', the Banu Tanukh. They had been resisting Islam for many years and had appealed to, and received help from, the

Byzantine Emperor, but on the order of the Caliph al-Mahdi (775–785 AD) they were compelled to become Muslims.

There was always the danger that some fanatic might invoke the *shariah* (Islamic law) as an excuse for destroying Christian churches. By 807 AD the Caliph Harun-al Rashid had ordered Christians and Jews to wear distinctive dress and his grandson, al-Mutawakkil, revived these orders and added further decrees designed to humiliate Christians.

Meanwhile the Muslim armies had crossed the straits from Tangier and captured Spain and were only halted between Tours and Poiters (a mere 100 miles from Paris) in one of history's decisive battles in 732 AD. Spain was to remain Muslim for a further 700 years and for much of that time the land enjoyed peace and prosperity. It was only after the dreaded Inquisition that Muslims were finally expelled from Spain in 1492.

2:3 *The first translation of the Bible into Arabic*

Up to the middle of the eighth century, as we have seen, relations between Muslims and Christians were varied.

The appearance of the first translation of the Bible into Arabic seems to have stirred some Christian writers into action. Perhaps the best known was John of Damascus whose work, *Sources of Knowledge*, includes an important section on Islam which he calls the 'deceptive error of the Ishmaelites'. The title derives from Ishmael who was born to Abraham by Hagar. At this time Muslims were often called Hagarenes (after Hagar). John of Damascus notes that they call themselves 'Saracens' which he seemed to think was derived from the Greek referring to their being 'sent away empty by Sarah'. More extensive is John's work, *Dialogue Between a Christian and Saracen*. (Translations of extracts of these works in English are to be found in issues of the *Moslem World* 1934 and 1935 which may be consulted in the Fellowship of Faith for Muslims Library.)

For the next century or so Muslims and Christians remained in close contact. In some places, like Spain, the contact and relationships proved, on the whole, peaceful and beneficial. In others they were marked by enmity and hostility, while elsewhere the two faiths existed side by side almost indifferent to each other.

An important piece of apologetic writing came from the pen of a Nestorian Christian serving in the court of the Caliph of Baghdad at about this time. Known as *The Apology of Al Kindy*, this was translated by Sir William Muir. Up till the tenth century this style of polemic writing continued. It seemed to be a kind of a game. But it was a 'pretty barren substitute for evangelism.'[2]

Activity

Some important reasons for the enmity between Christians and Muslims have been mentioned. What are they? Through your reading about the early history of Christian-Muslim contact, can you add to and enlarge on these?

3 The Crusades

Until now the Muslims had been the dominant, and except in Europe, the most successful disputers in the dialogue. But now follow 200 years of conflict between the powers of Islam and the armies of the Christian powers of western Europe. These armies aimed to conquer the lands held by Muslims and to wipe out Islam by force. Not for the first or the last time were atrocities committed in the name of religion.

It has to be admitted that the first intention in the minds of the Crusaders was to win, for Christ, a kingdom by the sword. There was no desire to make converts; Islam was the enemy. Laurence Browne, former Principal of the Henry Martyn School of Islamics, says in his book *Eclipse of Christianity in Asia*: 'One cannot help regarding the Crusades as the greatest tragedy in the history of Christianity, and the greatest set-back to the progress of Christ's kingdom on earth.'[3]

The eastern and western armies of the Church had enjoyed a period of comparative equilibrium and most Christians had been granted permission to rebuild all destroyed churches. At the same time, through long contact with groups of Muslim tribesmen, some Christians had abandoned their links with Nestorian Christianity and become zealous, if unconventional, followers of Islam. Then gradually the Muslim rulers of Southern Syria and Palestine began to surrender to the Turks, who by 1070 had captured Jerusalem.

This was the situation which led the Byzantine Emperor and the Pope to call Christians to action to save the Empire and rescue the holy places from the Turks.

By 1217 a truce was declared and in 1229 access to Jerusalem and the Christian holy places was granted. But by 1244 the Muslims were again in control and Jerusalem was to remain in Muslim hands until 1918.

Activity

This turbulent period in the history of Christian-Muslim relationships has, understandably, been interpreted differently by Christians and Muslims. You may have opportunity to discuss the Crusades with your Muslim friends. How far do you think these events in history influence present-day relationships?

4 Christian Missionary Activity Begins

With the founding of the Franciscan and Dominican Orders in the thirteenth century a new chapter in the history of Muslim-Christian relations was opened. For the first time since the Nestorians (who under the Abbasid Caliphate had exercised some Christian witness particularly in the court of Baghad) we can record a deliberate attempt to abandon forceful means to re-establish Christ's kingdom, and to organise missions to win converts by peaceful means.

Francis of Assisi seems to have taken the initiative or set an example by actually visiting the Sultan of Egypt while the Fifth Crusade was still going on. His visits proved fruitless but at least he had started something. Later the same year, some of his newly formed order went to Morocco. At least five were martyred. A similar mission to Tunis proved impossible because of the opposition of the Christian merchants in the city who thought the preaching of the Gospel might interfere with business.

In 1225 groups of Franciscans and Dominicans entered Morocco but worked mainly amongst Christian slaves. There is no record of any missionary success as a result of this witness. Yet some attempts were made to understand the Muslim faith and the Qur'an was translated into Latin at about this time by Peter the Venerable, the Abbot of Cluny.

5 Ramon Lull: A Case Study

Ramon Lull is still one name which stands out in the history of Christian approaches to Islam. He has been recognised by both Roman and Protestant Churches as the man who, more than any other, demonstrated by his own writings and example a new way of reaching Muslims for Christ. As a scholar and philosopher he was typical of his time. But as a missionary enthusiast, whose main aim was to win Muslims for Christ, he was far ahead of his time. As a teacher and thinker he was successful and as a missionary zealot he almost always encountered misunderstanding and failure.

Born around the year 1232 of wealthy parents in Palma, Majorca. Ramon Lull became companion and tutor to the sons of King James of Aragon. When one of the sons, James, became King of Majorca, Ramon became an adviser at court. Around this time he married, and apparently lived completely unconcerned about the things of God. It was not until he was 31, while busy one day composing a 'love song' to his latest mistress, that he seems to have experienced a moving vision of Christ on the cross. After a long and agonising struggle he finally yielded to Christ. With the failure of the Crusades Ramon Lull came forward to proclaim the power of loving persuasion as the only means worthy of Christ. Within weeks of his conversion a plan was taking shape in his mind. This involved three separate but related objectives:

1   To write books of apologetics that would win by 'irrefutable logic' the minds and hearts of unbelievers and infidels.
2   To work towards the founding of schools for the training of missionaries.
3   To give his life, to martyrdom if necessary, in the service of Christ as a witness to Muslims.

He was soon hard at work on the first of his works. The *Book of Contemplation*, a huge volume of nearly one million words, covered the whole range of theology and the devotional life. At several points he restates his conviction that to win Muslims is of prime importance and he calls on the Pope to send missionaries to Islam. A college was founded during this time at Miramar in Majorca, but after only 25 years the college was closed and there is no evidence that any of its students became missionaries. Towards the end of the century the University of Montpellier was founded (1290). Although this was not a missionary college, there were faculties of both Arabic and theology and it was here that Ramon Lull continued his work as student and teacher for many years.

When he was 60 he seems to have discovered new reserves of will-power and sailed for Tunis where for a time he was able to confront groups of learned Muslims with the arguments he had been developing over the years. His approach seems to have aroused a certain amount of antagonism as a consequence of which the local ruler and his council condemned Lull to death. The decree was changed to banishment and reluctantly he returned to Naples. In 1301 he set out to visit the Holy Land but got no further than Cyprus where he stayed a few months, returning via Armenia to Majorca.

Six years later in 1307, after a period of lecturing and writing in Montpellier and Paris, once again he set sail for North Africa, landing at Bugia (now Bejaia) about 100 miles east of Algiers.

This was just at a time when a Muslim reformer had succeeded in arousing the conservative elements of the area to a degree of fanaticism that had been aggravated by recent warfare between Bugia and Tunis. Lull preached openly in the market place and attempted to expose the falsity of the Muslim creed. This so aroused the anger of the crowd that only the intervention of the *qadi* saved him from death.

After a period in prison, during which he continued to dispute with some of the learned Muslims who visited him, he was deported and, having survived a shipwreck off the Italian coast, landed at Pisa. He set about completing a work he had begun in prison in Bugia. As a result of these trials, Ramon Lull appears to have been deeply troubled by doubts concerning the methods he had been advocating, and instead of the 'persuasion by argument and love' called for a new crusade to assail the Muslim Kingdom of Granada (Spain), the Barbary Coast (North Africa), and the Holy Land.

Lull now moved his sphere of activity to Paris and there for two years set out to disprove the teaching of ibn Rushid (known better by his Latin name of Averroës). He continued to pester the Pope with the request that missionary colleges be established. His requests were accepted by the Council of Vienne, but there is some doubt as to whether the decision was ever implemented.

In 1314, at the age of 82, he sailed once again for North Africa. He seems on this occasion to have exercised a little more discretion and, after presenting letters of commendation from King James of Aragon to the Ruler of Tunis, was permitted to engage in preaching tours and even to enter into debate with some of the leaders of Islam.

At some time during the end of 1315 and the spring of 1316 he seems to have been seized by his desire for martyrdom and, leaving Tunis for Bugia, there, in the open market place, defiantly proclaimed his message. He was stoned by an angry mob and probably died on board the ship that had attempted to rescue him.

Ramon Lull was something of a paradox, part scholar, part mystic, and eventually martyr; it is not easy to evaluate his contribution to Muslim-Christian relations. Certainly his was a new approach; equally certain was his lack of success. Yet to stand on the beach at Bejaia is to feel even today, over 650 years later, the challenge of this amazing man.

Activity
Are there things we can learn from Ramon Lull's life and work which might help us in our ministry to Muslims today? As you

look over this short account of his life, we suggest you list any points which might be helpful.

6 Muslim Ascendancy in the Middle and Near East

In spite of many reverses and changes of fortune with which the history of Mongol, Turkish, Egyptian, and the western powers are interwoven, the Muslim armies gradually achieved the ascendancy once more and by the middle of the fourteenth century, Christian dominance had been virtually eclipsed in the lands of the Middle and Near East.

The Mediterranean had virtually become a Muslim sea and Europe, cut off from its eastern markets, turned westward toward the Atlantic Ocean.

The Ottoman Empire continued to expand and reached its zenith in the middle of the sixteenth century. By this time theological interest in Europe was no longer focused on Islam but on the new doctrines being expounded by Luther (1483-1546). Zwingli (1484–1531), and Calvin (1509–1564) in Europe, and in England by Thomas Cranmer (1489–1556) and William Tyndale (d.1536).

For nearly two centuries there was little missionary vocation in the churches of the Reformation. The foremost leaders, named above, displayed neither missionary vision nor missionary spirit. For Luther, the real Antichrist was not Muhammad but the Pope. The Turks were simply vicious enemies and he protested at turning the war against them into a religious crusade.

7 The Moravians

Until the end of the eighteenth century the only Protestants, except for a relatively obscure band of German Pietists, to show any zeal for evangelism among the Muslims were the Moravians. Dr Hocker, a Moravian doctor, worked in Cairo. On the other hand, the Society of Jesus (founded by Ignatius Loyola) had entered India. From a base in Goa, a small Portuguese outpost, they sent a small band of missionaries to the court of Akbar the Emperor with the aim of winning the people of India for Christianity. The results of this mission were meagre and reports of converts from Islam were so rare that in two decades the genuine converts from Islam could probably be counted in dozens.

8 European Colonialism

The colonial era which stretched from the end of the fifteenth to the mid-twentieth centuries probably made a much greater impact on Muslim-Christian relations than even the Crusades had done. Except for Turkey, Iran and Afghanistan, nearly all Muslim countries became colonies or protectorates of European 'Christian' powers. When the Mughal Empire declined, the British, at first through the East India Company, then through the crown and the state, ruled the vast country of India. The Dutch colonised Indonesia, and the Muslim countries of North and West Africa and the near East were divided between France, Britain and Italy.

Islam had spread and conquered along trade routes and had held power not only through conquest but also through control of trade. In the eighteenth and nineteenth centuries, European powers spread their influence though their developing maritime power. This enabled them to set up trading posts and to appropriate riches from an increasing number of areas of the world, among which were countries formerly under Muslim rule. During and after the Industrial Revolution, the needs of capitalist countries for increasing resources, both to feed their work-forces and to be used in their industries, necessitated further acquisition of territory and obtaining economic and political control.

The effects of colonialism were profound. The whole manner of life of those colonised was changed. Colonies were split into two classes, the colonisers and the natives, so that the natives themselves came to believe that they were inferior. Work patterns were changed, with labour demands causing people to leave subsistence farming to work in mines and on plantations set up by the colonial power. The extremes of exploitation were sadly not abolished with slavery, but lived on in other types of forced labour and land dispossession.

In some ways this was an era of great missionary opportunity. The 'Christian' colonial powers not only exploited, but felt a genuine responsibility to share their civilisation and their material progress with the people of the colonies they had acquired. The heritage they believed they should pass on was a Christian one, so missionaries were, for the most part, encouraged and respected. They were even able to influence the colonial administrators from time to time, and to pass on insights they had gained through their pioneer work and their closeness to the indigenous people.

In spite of their diminishing power in the world, most Muslims remained firm in their Islamic faith. Christians found them resistant to the Gospel and, in the main, the only real contact between the two religions was polemical, in the setting up of public debates between Christian and Muslim scholars.

9   Missionaries to the Muslim World

As we have seen, from the time of Ramon Lull to that of Henry Martyn at the beginning of the nineteenth century, the only serious attempts to reach Muslims are those of the Moravians in Egypt and the Jesuits in India.

In 1734 a translation of the Qur'an appeared in English. This work, by Dr. Sale, revived an interest in the Muslim world. In 1786 William Carey addressed a conference of Baptist ministers on the subject of mission: 'the Commandment given to the Apostles to teach all nations in all the world must be recognised as binding on us also, since the great promise still follows it.'

Thus begins a new era in missions. This, coupled with a renewed awareness of the Muslim world, resulted in a new missionary approach to Muslims.

9:1 *Henry Martyn*
In 1781, Henry Martyn was born. He was one of the first Protestant workers to direct his energies almost entirely towards Muslims. Arriving at Calcutta in 1806 he wrote, in his diary, 'now let me burn out for God'. He did just that. Educated at Truro Grammar School and St John's College, Cambridge, he was a brilliant student who intended to read Law but, after the death of his father, and his conversion to Christ, felt that God was calling him to the ministry of the Church. Following a curacy served under Charles Simeon in Cambridge, he turned his back on the prospect of marriage to his beloved Lydia, and upon appointment as Chaplain of the East India Company he set sail for India in July 1805.

He was a keen linguist and even before he had set sail he had a desire to translate the scriptures into the languages of India. In June 1807 he wrote of being 'constantly engaged in works of translation and languages' and by the spring of 1808 was well into his greatest achievement — the translation of the New Testament into Urdu. Subsequent translations into Persian and Arabic owe much to his scholarship. He did not live to see any of his translations in print, for he died at Tokat in Turkey in 1812.

Vivienne Stacey states in a short biography of Henry Martyn that he 'still challenges Christian students and young people of each generation with their reponsibility of sharing the good news about Jesus Christ.'[4] His life and work made a major contribution to the task of presenting the Gospel to Muslim peoples by making it possible for many to read the New Testament in their own tongue.

During the last decades of the nineteenth century and those of the early twentieth century there are two men who stand out as having made a particularly valuable contribution to the history of Muslim-Christian relations: Samuel Zwemer (1867–1952) and Temple Gairdner (1873–1928).

9:2 *Samuel Zwemer*

Zwemer, who has been variously called the 'Flaming Prophet' and the 'Apostle to Islam', was born in the USA of Dutch-Huguenot parents. During his senior year in college he became linked with the Student Volunteer Movement that was exercising such a big influence on college campuses both in the USA and the UK. Zwemer was fired by the challenge of the movement's watchword, 'The evangelisation of the world in this generation', and as his part in this task, he formed the Mission to Arabia. He spent 23 years of sacrificial service in the Arabian peninsula. He founded and edited the magazine *Moslem World* (now the *Muslim World*), and for many years devoted all his energies to promoting the work of evangelising the Muslim world. First and foremost he was always a personal evangelist. 'Books were a passion with him. But people, especially Muslims, were his first love.'[5] It was said of him that 'it will be primarily for his loving that they (his friends) will recall him, a loving heart which was the reflection of God's love in Christ.'

9:3 *Temple Gairdner*

If Henry Martyn's life work concentrated on the need for the Muslim people to have the Word of God in their own language, and Samuel Zwemer's emphasised that the Muslim needs to see a practical demonstration of the life and love of Christ, Temple Gairdner, the third of our nineteenth-twentieth century heroes, used his life to approach the educated Muslim through the church in a fresh and positive manner. Born in Scotland, where he spent his early years, he went up to Trinity College Oxford in 1892, becoming president of the Oxford Inter Collegiate Christian Union in 1895. He gave his whole life to the service of Christ amongst the Muslims of Egypt, attempting to use contemporary Arabic musical, poetic, and dramatic forms in reaching them. During his early days in Cairo he wrote, 'It takes faith, believing in Christ and his church and ministry in this Muslim city, but oh my word, it takes more faith to believe in these when one thinks of the Chruch itself as it exists here — sect upon sect, each more intolerant than its neighbour ... and that in the face of an Islam which loathes all alike.'

The unity of the Church of Christ was one of the major passions of his life, and in this he challenges us today. Yet he had no use for any synthesis reached by ignoring the facts; he saw the intense importance of our denominational distinctions even while working for unity 'because they enshrine fragments of truth that are necessary to the perfect whole.' It was said of him that his greatest contribution to the quest for Christian unity, and to the challenge of the Muslim world, was that he refused to stop thinking and he refused to stop hoping. May these two attributes of this godly man, who died in his fifty-fifth year, guide and challenge us as we contemplate the opportunities before us in the world of Islam.

9:4 *Abdul Masih*

Having come this far in our study we see that relations between Islam and Christianity have fluctuated through the centuries. Apart from a movement of Muslims towards the Church of Spain in the thirteenth century, and the recent large-scale conversions in Indonesia, there has been no significant turning from Islam to Christ.

This makes the story of *Abdul Masih*, the only known Muslim convert from the ministry of Henry Martyn, all the more remarkable. We are indebted to Vivienne Stacey for the following summary of his life.

Abdul Masih was the only known Muslim who came to Christ through the ministry of Henry Martyn. He was one of those listening from afar to Martyn's outdoor preaching to beggars on Thursdays. He was a man of importance in the court of the King of Oudh. His original name was Sheikh Salih. He was converted after Martyn left India. The main influences in his conversion appear to have been Martyn's life and the reading of the New Testament when he was entrusted with its binding by Martyn. He was baptised at Calcutta by the Rev D Brown on Whit Sunday 1811. He was the first agent of the Church Missionary Society, being engaged as Catechist in 1812. The Rev Daniel Corrie located him to Agra in 1813 and worked with him there for two years. In 1820 he received Lutheran orders. The ordination helped his standing among former Muslim friends. They said, 'The English do indeed regard him a brother.' In 1825 he received Anglican orders being made Deacon by Heber, Bishop of Calcutta. He was the first Muslim convert to be ordained in India. He died at Lucknow in 1827.

Abdul Masih became an outstanding evangelist in his own right. On the river boat from Calcutta to Agra he held services and preached to the boatmen, Christian children and servants. He refused to visit the tomb of a Muslim saint, explaining that he had been a Muslim and had now come to visit the living. He gave them the Gospel of Matthew as a valuable present. He did not eat with his brother and nephew until they understood the reasons for his conversion. Abdul Masih's brother believed but delayed baptism so that he could explain his faith to his friends first. Through Abdul Masih's preaching and teaching over 40 Muslims joined the congregation at Agra. He composed hymns and set them to indigenous tunes, and also put Christ's conversation with Nicodemus into verse for use in evangelism. His general evangelistic method was to explain the Books of Moses and the Gospels. Whenever Muslim customs seemed to be from the Bible he indicated this. He never discussed their prophets but asked if they could show anyone to compare with Jesus. He usually expounded a chapter rather than a verse. The converts were set to spinning, weaving and ploughing in order to maintain themselves but further development plans were interrupted by the illness of the Rev D Corrie who left Agra after working for two years with Abdul Masih. Abdul Masih effectively continued the work. He ran a small school and also dispensed medicines. Abdul Masih suffered from poor health and in July 1825 was forced to leave Agra for this reason. Subsequently he was able to return to Agra under the care of Dr Luxmore who took him into his own house. He was to die shortly afterwards.

The Chaplain at Agra, the Rev John Irving, wrote to the Archdeacon of Calcutta about Abdul Masih: 'The more I see of him, the more I have reason to respect him — so unassuming, and yet so steady. I confess I do sometimes lose my patience when I am asked by Englishmen if I think him a sincere convert; for there are few of us who might not, in some point or other, take pattern from him.'

Activity

An extensive reading list is provided with this chapter. We are sure you will find some of the books, particularly the biographies, both interesting and helpful. You could list relevant points in the lives and teaching of Henry Martyn, Samuel Zwemer, Temple Gairdner, and Abdul Masih as you did when you read the life of Ramon Lull, section 5.

Christian attitudes towards Islam today vary enormously. Some would advocate a working arrangement between the two faiths in the interest of harmony and expediency. Others would insist that Islam is still, in this generation, the major challenge to the Christian Church and would advocate a fresh approach making full use of current anthropological and sociological thought.

This subject is taken up in Chapters 14 and 15. A useful book on current evangelical thought is *New Paths in Muslim Evangelism* by Phil Parshall, the recommended book for Chapter 15.

Recommended Reading

There is no specific book for this chapter. We hope you will be able to find time to read some of the books listed below.

Additional Reading

We do encourge you to read at least some of these books, or extracts from them.

On the historical developments of Islam:

> BOER, Harry. *A Brief History of Islam*, Daystar Press, Ibadan, 1963. Available in FFM Library.

> VERHOEVEN, F R J. *Islam, Its Origin and Spread in Words, Maps and Pictures*, Routledge and Kegan Paul, London, 1962.

On the Crusades:

> *History of Christianity*, Lion Publishing, Tring, Hertfordshire, 1977. See pp269–274.

> BOER, Harry. *A Brief History of Islam*, Daystar Press, Ibadan, 1968. Available in FFM Library.

Early Approaches:

> ADDISON, J T. *The Christian Approach to the Moslem*, Columbia University Press (OUP in UK), 1942. See part 1 in particular. Available in FFM Library.

> NEILL, Stephen. *History of Christian Mission*, Pelican, Penguin Books, Harmondsworth, Middlesex, 1964. History of Church, v.6. See chapters 3 and 4, p61–139, and chapter 10, p359–369.

Approach to Muslims since 1500 AD:

> VAN DER WERFF, Lyle L. *Christian Mission to Muslims: The Record*. William Carey Library, South Pasadena, California, 1977.

Biographies:

BENTLEY-TAYLOR, David. *My Love Must Wait*, IVP Leicester, 1975. Biography of Henry Martyn.

PADWICK, Constance. *Temple Gairdner of Cairo*, SPCK, London, 1929. Out of print, but available from FFM Library.

PEERS, E Allison. *Fool of Love*, SCM, London, 1946. Biography of Ramon Lull. Available in FFM Library.

STACEY, Vivienne. *Henry Martyn*, Henry Martyn Institute of Islamic Studies, Hyderabad, India, 1980.

WILSON, Christy. *Apostle to Islam*, Baker Book House, Grand Rapids, Michigan, 1952. Biography of Samuel Zwemer. Available in FFM Library.

For More Advanced Reading and Further Study

ARBERRY, Arthur J. *Religion in the Middle East*, CUP, 1969. Volume 2.

BROWNE, L E. *Eclipse of Christianity in Asia*, CUP, 1933.

EVERY, G. *Understanding Eastern Christianity*, SCM, London, 1980.

KATEREGGA, Badru and SHENK, David. *Islam and Christianity: A Dialogue*, Eerdmans, Grand Rapids, Michigan. 1980.

KHAIR-ULLAH, Frank. 'Evangelism among Muslims', p823–824, in *Let the Earth Hear His Voice*, J D Douglas, ed., World Wide Publications, Minneapolis, Minnesota, 1975.

RUNCIMAN, S. *History of the Crusades*, Penguin Books, Harmondsworth, Middlesex, 1971. 3 volumes.

SAUNDERS, J J. *History of Medieval Islam*, Routledge and Kegan Paul, London, 1965.

Notes

1 Attributed to CAETANI. quoted in ADDISON, J T. *The Christian Approach to the Moslem*, Columbia University Press, New York, 1942.
2 Ibid, p29.
3 BROWNE, Laurence. *Eclipse of Christianity in Asia*, CUP, 1933, p144.
4 STACEY, Vivienne. *Henry Martyn*, Henry Martyn Institute of Islamic Studies, Hyderabad, India, 1980, p75.
5 VAN DER WERFF, Lyle L. *Christian Mission to Muslims: The Record*, William Carey Library, South Pasadena, California, 1977, p227.

Chapter 12

ISLAM TODAY

1 **Study Guide**

This is the second bridging chapter mentioned in the study guide to Chapter 7. It links Part 3 (Chapters 8, 9, 10 and 11), which deals with the historical and political aspects of Islam, with Part 4 (Chapters 13, 14 and 15), which looks at social and cultural matters. It does this by focusing on present-day trends in the religious, political, social, and economic spheres. Rather than attempting to present a detailed analysis, it covers a wide spectrum of ideas and considers a number of the countries of the Muslim world, albeit briefly. Anne Cooper has put this chapter together. Much of it is based on *Islam: A Christian Perspective* by Dr Michael Nazir-Ali, the recommended book for the chapter.

Learning Objectives
When you have completed this chapter you should:

1   Have begun to understand the different emphases in present-day development and interpretation of Islam.
2   Begin to understand economic and political factors which influence the expression of Islam today.
3   Have been introduced to the Christian Church in Muslim areas.

(MAP OF MUSLIM WORLD)

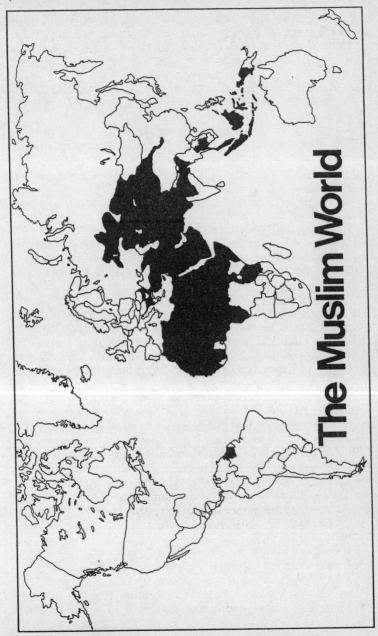

The Muslim World

Bishop Stephen Neill, in his last book, *Crises of Belief*, published just before he died in the summer of 1984, discerns three distinct tendencies in present-day Islam of which we should be aware as we approach our Muslim friends. We have added the fourth tendency, in the light of recent developments.

1 *A 'Back to the Qur'an' tendency*. The fully orthodox believe that the answer to all problems would be solved if the Muslim world were to return to the teaching of the Qur'an.

2 *A tendency to maintain traditions without being tied to them.* This means adaptation to modern scientific, technological, and economic developments. This has been summed up by A A Fyzee, formerly Indian ambassador in Egypt and vice-chancellor of the University of Kashmir:

> 'I believe that the Koran is a message from God. It is the voice of God heard by Mohammed ... I believe that in every age these words must be interpreted afresh and understood anew. I believe it is the duty of every Muslim to understand this message for himself.'[1]

3 *A mystical tendency*. Many who maintain a perfectly orthodox appearance may well have this inner hope of 'union' with God, as a personal mystical experience. Should this tendency become dominant, Islam would undergo a re-creation comparable in impact to that experienced by Christianity in the Reformation.

4 *A tendency to emphasise Meccan surahs*. Recently there has been an attempt to centre on the Meccan *surahs* as inspired and not to give such prominence to the Medinan ones. In this way the *ulema* are emphasising Islamic teaching as a spiritual movement and releasing it from the political and legal bonds that are rooted in seventh century life.

We must always recognise as we reach out to our Muslim friends, that one or other of these trends may be predominant. We shall be wise to adapt our approach accordingly.

Activities

1 This may be a good point to find out from your Muslim friends which trend they follow. If you have already done this (Chapter 8), you could discuss some current events together.

2 You might also find it helpful to consider whether the same trends are recognisable among Christians. Do you have one

of these tendencies yourself?

3 Three Main Trends

We take the first three trends now, as a framework in which to consider the development of Islam in today's world.

3:1 *Fundamentalism*
Under the heading 'Islamic Revival', Richard Tames, in *Approaches to Islam*, asks the question, 'What is to be revived?', and answers:

> For a thousand years after the Prophet's death Islam's history was a history of temporal success. A man from Mars arriving in the seventeenth century might well have thought that the world was on the eve of complete Islamisation. Then the political tide turned against Islam. History started to go wrong. Over the course of subsequent centuries 'revivalists' did what they had often done in the previous thousand years — criticised the current state of society and preached a 'return' to pure Islam, thus offering both an explanation of present ills and a programme for their remedy.[2]

Three movements in modern times have exhorted Muslims to return to the simple, but essential, tenets of the faith, as taught by Muhammad and his companions. Rather than finding this impractical for the world today, they urge that this is the only way which leads to harmony and justice.

1 *The Wahabi Movement* originated in the eighteenth century. It is still the important religious influence in Saudi Arabia and some of the Gulf States today. The movement emphasiscs complete reliance on the teaching of the Qur'an, the extreme importance of the *shariah* (see Chapter 10, section 2, **Introduction**) and the suppression of saint worship and mystical practices (see Chapter 8, section 4:8. *Islah — reform of Islam*.)

2 *The Muslim Brotherhood (Ikhwan al Muslimun)* was founded in 1827. It is still particularly active in Egypt, Syria, and other middle eastern countries. Concerning the aims and teaching of the Brotherhood, Michael Nazir-Ali writes:

> The basic aims of the society were to restore *shariah*

as the instrument of government, to remove superstition, to do away with the cult of saints, to counteract the popularity of Sufism (see Chapter 9, section 6:1 **Sufi Orders**) and to create a society which reflected the ideals of primitive Islam.[3]

The Muslim Brotherhood tends to be fanatical in outlook and to advocate the persecution of religious minorities. They have been responsible for a number of terrorist acts, perhaps among them the assassination of President Sadat of Egypt.

3 *The Jamaat-i-Islam* was founded by none other than Mawlana A A Mawdudi, the author of *Towards Understanding Islam*, the recommended book for Chapter 3/4, from which we have quoted extensively. The *Jamaat-i*-Islam is active in Pakistan and is also involved in social work among Pakistanis living in Britain.

Mawdudi advocated the setting up of a theocracy to govern the Muslim *Ummat*. In such a theocracy the *shariah* would be supreme and no law could be promulgated which was repugnant to the *shariah*. There could, however, be legislation on matters not covered by the *shariah*. The Qur'an itself does not provide a complete code of conduct whereby the whole social, political and religious life of the *Ummat* may be ordered. Along with the Qur'an, God also sent his Prophet, and his Sunnah complements the Qur'an and shows us how the divine commands are to be implemented.[4]

Fundamentalism in Saudi Arabia is a powerful influence both internally and among foreign Muslim visitors. Owing to the large oil revenue many expatriate Muslims go there to work and many others visit during the Pilgrimage. They are impressed by the Islamic order and the sense of unity and worship and may have been influenced by Islamic fundamental teaching when they return home.

The revolution in Iran
A type of religious fundamentalism has been in operation in Iran since the revolution which overthrew the Shah in 1979. The present rulers, the *ayatallahs*, are Shiite doctors of religious law. They have reintroduced *shariah* in Iran and are ruling the country in a way very different from the more liberal westernised rule of the late Shah.

Some reports from Iran seem to indicate that some thinking Muslims are disappointed if not disillusioned. V S Naipaul in *Among the Believers: An Islamic Journey* records:

> They had believed that the restoration of the Islamic faith in its purity would solve all problems, would bring about the jama tauhid, the society of true believers. The revolution had come, Islam was again triumphant — and yet the problems had not been solved.[5]

3:2 *The implications of a return to the shariah*

The public has been well-informed about the reintroduction of flogging and amputation of the hand for certain types of theft. There is no doubt that in countries where *shariah* has become legal public flogging does take place regularly and amputation occasionally. There have also been cases of the death penalty being enforced for adultery. There have also been what may seem to Christians retrograde steps in the restrictions imposed on women. You might turn back to Chapter 2, section 6:4 *Women in Islam* to remind yourself of some of the issues discussed there. In Saudi Arabia, for example, women are not allowed by law to drive cars!

In this section two other major issues which relate to the introduction of Islamic law are taken up.

1 *Apostasy* Verses in the Qur'an suggest that punishment and withdrawal of God's guidance will be the result if a Muslim should change his religion.

> Whoso desires another religion than Islam, it shall
> not be accepted of him; in the next world he shall
> be among the losers.
> How shall God guide a people who have disbelieved
> after they believed, and bore witness that the Messenger
> is true and the clear signs came to them?
> God guides not the people of the evildoers.
> Those — their recompense is that there shall rest
> on them the curse of God and of the angels and
> of men, altogether, therein dwelling forever;
> the chastisement shall not be lightened
> for them; no respite shall be given them.
> But those who repent thereafter, and make amends —
> God is All-forgiving, All-compassionate.
> Surely those who disbelieve after they have believed
> and then increase in unbelief — their repentance

shall not be accepted; those are the ones who stray.
Surely those who disbelieve and die disbelieving,
there shall not be accepted from any one of them
the whole earth full of gold, if he would ransom himself thereby;
for them awaits a painful chastisement, and
they shall have no helpers (3:79–85).

Whoso disbelieves in God, after he has believed —
excepting him who has been compelled, and his heart
is still at rest in his belief — but whosoever's breast is
expanded in unbelief, upon them shall rest anger
from God, and there awaits them a mighty chastisement; ... (16:107–108).

Whether the punishment refers to this life, or to the after-life,
is questionable; but as Michael Nazir-Ali says: 'All jurists
agree that an adult male apostate is to be put to death if he is
in possession of his faculties and has not acted under compul-
sion.'[5]

In practice, the lives of many converts from Islam are
endangered and countries such as Egypt, Indonesia, and
Pakistan have tried to restrict the conversion of Muslims to
other religions, by restricting what is termed proselytising. As
yet, no Muslim country has a law either forbidding conversion, or applying the death penalty for apostasy, although
there has been such a bill before the Egyptian parliament.

2 *Islamic banking* The Qur'an forbids the practice of usury
(*riba*) and this is taken to mean the exacting of interest in
money-lending exchanges.

Those who devour usury shall not rise again except as
he rises, whom Satan of the touch prostrates ... God
blots out usury, but freewill offerings He augments
with interest. God loves not any guilty ingrate
(2:276).

O believers, devour not usury, doubled and redou-
bled, and fear you God; haply so you will prosper
(3:125).

In reintroducing *shariah*, the receiving of interest on money is
discontinued. Instead of this a concept of partnership between the bank and the investor is put into operation. A person or private company wishing to invest in a business enter-

prise, or other project, enters into a partnership with a financing agency on a profit and loss-sharing basis. If the project succeeds, the bank receives a share of the profits; if it fails, the bank is entitled to take over some of the assets, on a previously agreed basis. Because of the qur'anic restriction on *riba*, many Muslims will not receive interest on personal banking accounts. Mortgages are handled through partnership schemes similar to those operated by banks. Islamic banking has been in operation inside Saudi Arabia for some time. It is being introduced in Pakistan.

Income tax has been declared non-Islamic. The Islamic *zakat* (Chapter 3/4, part 2, section 7:3, *Welfare contributions*) is being reintroduced. This is a religious tax collected by the government. It consists of taxing land and goods which can be assessed; also personal effects such as jewellery, in which case it is left to the conscience of the individual to make appropriate payments.

It can be readily appreciated that there are enormous difficulties in avoiding *riba* in today's world.

> The paradox is that interest in Islamic countries is becoming taboo at the very time that oil-rich countries are investing their new-found wealth in interest-paying western banks and other financial institutions. At the other end of the scale, poor countries like Pakistan plan to phase out interest within the country but arc paying enormous sums, as interest on loans borrowed from foreign countries and banks.[7]

4:1 *Liberalism*

Both liberalism and fundamentalism have arisen from the same driving force, a desire to purify and strengthen Islam.

> The difference, in the main, between the conservatives and the liberals is that the former think that all problems can be solved simply by returning to the Qur'an and primitive tradition, whereas liberals realise that the purification of the House of Islam must go hand in hand with modernisation.[8]

The introduction of liberalism was first expressed through individual thinkers and writers, some of whom were also politicians. Perhaps the best known example of such a person is Muhammad Iqbal. Iqbal was the first to present the idea of a homeland for Muslims, an idea which was fulfilled, at least in theory, when Pakistan was established. He 'was in favour of a social democracy which embodied the egalitarian ideals of Islam.'[9]

Turkey was the first Muslim country where modern liberalism was put into practice. The Ottoman Empire ended by defeat in the First World War. Kemal Ataturk then became leader of the Turkish Republic and set about introducing a programme of modernisation and development along western cultural lines. In his view, this was incompatible with much of the old Islamic structure. His programme of reform included the abolishing of the caliphate (1924), disestablishing Islam as the state religion (1928), replacing the *shariah* with a new legal code (1926), and having a new secular constitution (1937). During the period 1946–1950 there was a reaction to the secularisation programme; Islamic practices, such as taking part in the Pilgrimage and the Call to Prayer, were re-established. Politically, a multi-party system was in operation and Ataturk was defeated at the polls in 1950. Since that time, Islam has had to compete with nationalism, a powerful force in the country. There is no doubt, however, that Islam holds the hearts and minds of many of the ordinary people and the tendency is towards a return to a more Islamic way of life.

Activity
At the end of Chapter 8, Kemal Ataturk is compared with Muhammad Reza Khan. We saw that their characters and their approach to leadership were very different. How far do you think this accounts for the way in which their reform movements subsequently developed and were ended?

4:2 *Islamic socialism*
The Arabic word for socialism, *ishtirakiyya*, was first used by Jamaluddin Afghani. 'By *ishtirakiyya* he meant a right sharing of wealth as practised by the Prophet and the first four Caliphs.'[10] Others, including Iqbal, believed that Marxist teaching could be adapted to Islam. This would mean that, 'The theism of Islam could convert the lamentable amorality of communism, thus ensuring that social justice was achieved on the basis of a code of morality.'[11]

For a short period, under Zulfikar Ali Bhutto's People's Party, Islamic socialism was experimented with in Pakistan. The Pakistan People's Party did not, however, survive in power, due partially to pressure from the religious leaders, but also because of the traumatic break with East Pakistan, now Bangladesh. Bhutto was executed for conspiracy to murder and his party slogan, 'Islam is our faith, democracy our polity and socialism our economy', proved to be an empty one. Pakistan has now, under

President Zia ul Haqq, veered towards a strongly fundamentalist policy, modelled on that of Saudi Arabia.

A number of Muslim countries do have left-wing governments at the present time. These include Afghanistan, Algeria, Egypt, Iraq, Libya, Syria, and the Republic of South Yemen. For some, such as Afghanistan, Marxist government has led to much unrest; it is strongly opposed by more orthodox Muslim elements within the country.

5 Mysticism

This subject is dealt with more fully in Chapter 9, section 6:1, section 6:1, **Sufi Orders**, where Sufism is discussed and in Chapter 13, **Folk Islam.**

It is, however, important to understand at this point that, although the political leadership in a country may be either right-wing orthodox, or left-wing liberal or Marxist, for the majority of ordinary citizens, the 'popular' religion of folk Islam has an enormous influence. This influence appears to be increasing; it certainly affects the everyday lives of large numbers of Muslim people.

6 The Changing Face of the Muslim World

Activity
Stephen Neill, in his book, *Crises of Belief*, entitles his chapter on Islam, 'Islam in Crisis'. From your study of the course so far, can you suggest any reasons why Islam should be in crisis? Please pause to consider this before going on to the next section.

One reason which Bishop Stephen Neill points out is that Islam is a much more success-oriented religion than Christianity. Whereas the Christian longs for the time when 'at the name of Jesus every knee should bow ... and every tongue confess that Jesus Christ is Lord ...' (Philippians 2:10–11), this is for the future; the present is slow and painful progress, with many disappointments. For the Muslim, however, as Bishop Neill says, '... for a century at least, history seems to have gone wrong.'[11] He continues, 'To put the contrast in straightforward human terms, Jesus was a failure and Mohammed was a success.'[11]

We look now at some of the other reasons why Islam can be said to be in crisis.

6:1 Colonialism and Independence

Again quoting from *Crises of Belief*:

> In two generations the situation of the Islamic world has entirely changed. In 1918 it was at its lowest point of humiliation — poor, exhausted, and at almost every point subject to Christian domination. In 1978 it stood before the world free, aggressive, and with a new self-confidence.[12]

Most of the major Muslim countries became independent from foreign powers in the period after the Second World War: Indonesia from the Dutch; Libya from the Italians; Algeria, Morocco, and Tunisia from the French; also Syria and Lebanon in the Middle East, Pakistan, what is now Bangladesh, Egypt, and Sudan from the British. This has meant each has had to go through a period of finding a national identity, at the same time as learning how to govern a country, relate internationally, and set up judicial and political systems. This has been a mammoth task and has not been accomplished without heartache and even bloodshed.

6:2 *The Discovery of Oil*

Nearly half the known oil resources of the world are in the Muslim countries of North Africa and the Middle East. The ownership of this 'black gold' has catapulted these formerly backward and deprived areas into the secular, materialistic world of modern economics and commerce. Personal riches have far outstripped educational opportunities. As to the future, these are not bottomless wells; the supply will dry up one day, in 15 years, in 20 years? What then?

The people of Islam have been aware of these forces around them. The mainly Muslim OPEC countries have striven to keep control of the production of oil, but with diminishing success. There have been a number of Islamic summit meetings where 35–40 Muslim nations have looked for the unity and the brotherhood of the early days of Islam. This has not been forthcoming; Egypt and Libya at loggerheads, Pakistan being torn apart, Egypt forming an alliance with the middle eastern Muslim countries' arch-enemy Israel, perhaps most damaging of all the Iran-Iraq war dragging on, both sides claiming to be involved in *jihad* (holy war) and the rift between Sunnis and Shiites growing larger all the time.

No wonder, as Stephen Neill writes: 'So the Islamic world has entered on a new phase of prosperity. And yet, for all its power, that world seems to be pervaded by a sense of anxiety'.[13]

6:3 *Migration*

Another factor which has encouraged a sense of unease in the Muslim world is the considerable amount of migration which has recently taken place. As has been mentioned, the richness of the economies of the oil-producing countries has attracted migrant workers from other, mainly Muslim areas. These include other Arabic-speaking people, but also workers from countries such as India and Pakistan.

At the same time, quite large numbers have gone from countries with less well-developed economies to work in industralised areas. Some have gone temporarily to find work, others to settle permanently. Turks have gone to mainland Europe, Pakistanis and Bangladeshis, with their Commonwealth links, to Britain. Even conservative estimates agree that there are now more than a million Muslims living in Britain.

Some Muslims are displaced persons, like the Palestinians who had to leave their country when Israel was formed, or those who have taken refuge in the Lebanon and now find themselves homeless and rootless once again.

Note One way to keep up to date with what is going on in the Muslim world is to obtain a Muslim current affairs magazine. Such a publication also gives helpful insights into the Muslim way of thinking. One such magazine is *Impact International*, 33 Stroud Green Road, London N4 3EF. This magazine is published twice a month. In the December 28th–January 10th, 1985 edition there were main articles on Muslim workers in Europe, Christmas in Britain, the political situation in Bangladesh, the military government in Nigeria, the Sikhs demand for Khalistan, the Indian election, and China's aid programme. There were a number of shorter articles and news items as well!

7 The Church Today in Muslim Societies

It has often been pointed out that a very small proportion of missionary resources is available for the greatest challenge missionaries have, namely Muslim areas of the world. Certainly there are restrictions and missionaries are not welcomed in many Muslim countries, but that is not true of all. Chapter 15 describes some areas where there are great opportunities and encouragements.

We end this chapter by looking at three other possibilities for nurturing the growth of Christian-Muslim relationships in today's world.

7:1 *The Ancient 'orthodox' churches*

Martin Goldsmith writes in *Islam and Christian Witness*: 'Perhaps the greatest grounds for optimism lie in the old traditional churches which have survived through centuries of Muslim pressure in Egypt, Lebanon, Jordan, Israel and other countries.'[14]

These churches have survived much persecution over the centuries and, perhaps as a result of this, have become inward-looking and ritualistic in their worship. However, there are already some signs of a fresh spiritual awakening. The Coptic Church in Egypt and the Mar Thoma Church in South India are already involved in evangelistic outreach. There is much to be learnt from these churches. They need the support and prayers of other Christians.

7:2 *Churches of the modern missionary movement in Muslim lands*

In a number of Muslim countries, churches have been planted as a result of missionary activity over the last two centuries. These churches are now autonomous. It may be necessary to ask the question, 'Is there more Christians can do to help one another in Muslim areas?' In several of these countries there is still a missionary presence and perhaps we need to heed the words of Michael Nazir-Ali, now a bishop in the Church of Pakistan:

> An astonishing feature of Christian missions in the post-colonial age has been the reluctance of many western missionaries to take a back seat and to let nationals manage the affairs of the local church. In spite of much talk of partnership and of missionaries going to serve the national church, the mentality is still, in many cases, imperialistic.[15]

7:3 *Secular Christians working in Muslim areas*

Christians in secular employment, sometimes called 'tent-makers', referring to Paul in Acts 18:3, are going in increasing numbers to work in the oil-rich countries of North Africa, the Middle East and the Gulf States. They have opportunities denied to professional missionaries. By relating to Muslims as colleagues, working alongside them, they may witness and share in a non-confrontational way. Many of these Christians come, not from the western world, but are themselves migrant workers, often from another Muslim country.

148

Activity

Please think through what you have read in Chapter 11 about past missionary activity among Muslims, comparing it with the last section of this chapter, section 7, **The Church Today in Muslim Societies**. How do you think Christian evangelistic outreach can best be accomplished in Muslim areas? Again, there is no model answer to this question. It is designed to help you prepare for your study of the next part, particularly Chapter 15.

Recommended Reading

NAZIR-ALI, Michael. *Islam: A Christian Perspective*, Paternoster Press, Exeter, 1983.

Additional Reading

GOLDSMITH, Martin. *Islam and Christian Witness*, Hodder & Stoughton/STL Books, London/Bromley, 1982.
NAIPAUL, V S. *Among the Believers: An Islamic Journey*, Andre Deutsch, London, 1981.
NEILL, Stephen. *Crises of Belief*, Hodder & Stoughton, London, 1984.
RUTHVEN, Malise. *Islam in the World*, Pelican, Penguin Books, Harmondsworth, Middlesex, 1984.

Notes

1 FYZEE, A A. *A Modern Approach to Islam*, OUP, Delhi, 1981, p110.
2 TAMES, Richard. *Approaches to Islam*, John Murray, London, 1982, p93.
3 NAZIR-ALI, Michael. *Islam: A Christian Perspective*, Paternoster Press, Exeter, 1983, p97.
4 Ibid, p98.
5 NAIPAUL, V S. *Among the Believers: An Islamic Journey*, Andre Deutsch, London, 1981, pp197–198.
6 NAZIR-ALI, Michael. *Islam:A Christian Perspective*, Paternoster Press, Exeter, 1983, p128.
7 Ibid, p133.
8 Ibid, p102.

9 Ibid, p118.
10 Ibid, p117.
11 NEILL, Stephen. *Crises of Belief*, Hodder & Stoughton, London, 1984, p58.
12 Ibid, p61.
13 Ibid, p63.
14 GOLDSMITH, Martin. *Islam and Christian Witness*, Hodder & Stoughton, London, 1982, p155.
15 NAZIR-ALI, Michael. *Islam: A Christian Perspective*, Paternoster Press, Exeter, 1983, pp151–152.

Chapter 13

FOLK ISLAM

1 Study Guide

This chapter is, on the surface, a straightforward account. If you are able to tackle this whole area of the religious thought patterns of ordinary people, you will learn a great deal about how to communicate. This chapter naturally centres on Islam, but many of the ideas in it can be applied to other religions as well, even to our own! There is nothing very difficult or obscure, so enjoy your study and the background reading we hope you will be able to do. Ron George has written this chapter and has included extensive quotations from various other writers who have also lived and worked among Muslims.

Learning objectives
After completing this chapter you should:

1   Understand the difference between 'theological' and 'popular' Islam.
2   Have seen something of why 'popular' expressions of religious faith arise.
3   Begin to understand how in Islam religious faith and practices become adapted in popular belief.

2 Popular Islam

2:1 *Different expressions of Islam*
Bill Musk, in *Popular Islam: The Hungar of the Heart*, writes:

Islam looks the same the world over. The 'Five Pillars' are famous, and any missionary to Muslims can expound on the 'iman' and 'din' of Islamic religious life.

But, beneath the surface, throughout the Muslim world, there is at least one major divorce. In popular Islam, the *meanings* attached to the forms of religious expression are radically different from those understood by Bishop Cragg's muezzin (Cragg 1964) or Professor Anderson's students (Anderson 1970). It is a division between 'high' or 'ideal' Islam, and 'low' or 'popular' Islam.[1]

The realities of the ordinary Muslim's everyday life are rarely perceived by the unsuspecting western student of Islam:

> ... Popular Islam has added a whole life-way of animistic beliefs and practices. The use of the rosary for divining and healing, the use of amulets and talismans, the use of hair-cuttings and nail-trimmings, the belief and practice of saint-worship, the use of charms, knots, magic, sorcery, the exorcism of demons, the practice of tree and stone worship, cursing and blessing — these and many other animistic practices belie the gap between the theological religion and the actual religion.[2]

A member of the Indonesian Bible Institute (located in Batu, East Java) has asserted:

> Working for many years in a Muslim country, I have come to the conclusion that the power of Islam does not lie in its dogma and practices, nor in the antithesis of the Trinity, against the Lordship of Christ and his redeeming death, but in the occult practices of its leaders, thus holding sway over their people.[3]

2:2 *Form, function and meaning in 'theological' and 'popular' Islam*
Bill Musk describes the outworking of belief in practice in popular Islam as follows:

> A brief look at the foundational statements of faith and practice in Islam, as they are primarily understood by ordinary Muslims, will demonstrate the divorce before us.

Creed: The Muslim creed ('iman') includes a statement of belief in the only God, his angels, his books, his apostles, the Last Day (of judgement) and predestination. In popular Islam, the belief in the only God revolves largely around a magical use of the names of God.[4]

Phil Parshall expands this thought as follows:

There is great significance in the continual repetition of the word *Allah*. The tongue should linger at the palate of the mouth as A-lllll-aaaa-h is pronounced. During this time all extraneous thoughts are to be banished from the mind. However, it is permissible and even good to concentrate upon one's *pir* during *dhikr*. For variety, the pace can be quickened and the name *Allah* repeated in harmony with the heartbeat. This is a method of actually bringing Allah into one's being. It is easy to discern the mystical element in this performance. The repetition is to be continued until the mind is completely submerged within the divine radiance of almighty God.[5]

Musk continues:

Certain formulas compel God to do what is requested, and it is especially the use of the names of God that produce these results. There are many books on the magical use of the names of God, and the associated magic of numbers. The doctrine of *angels* includes, in popular Islam, demonology and *jinn*-worship. Involved in this doctrine is the concept of the familiar spirit, or Qarina — that is, the double of the individual, of opposite sex and progeny of Satan, born at the same time as the individual:

'The popular idea is that qurana come into the world from A'alam al Barzakhiya (Hades) at the time that a child is conceived. Therefore during the act of coition Muslims must pronounce the word *bismallah*. This will prevent the child from being overcome by its devil and turned into an infidel...' (Zwemer, 1939).[6]

The doctrine of *God's books* is turned into bibliomancy and bibliolatry in popular Islam. The Qur'an has the power of a fetish:

'Certain chapters are of special value against evil

spirits ... The cure for headache is said to be the 13th verse of the chapter called 'Al-Ana'am' or the Cattle, which reads: "His is whatever dwells in the night or in the day: He both hears and knows"...' (Zwemer, 1917).[7]

In popular Islam, the doctrine of *God's apostles* revolves largely around their dealings with the spirit-world. Both Solomon and Muhammad stand out in the popular mind because of their reputed intercourse with demons and *jinn*. Muhammad's hair has become famous as a fetish, and has power to heal.

The doctrine of the *last day* relates, in the popular mind, to death and spirit-life. There is a belief in some saints as mediators between God and the faithful — Fatima and Jesus especially hold this position. The spirits of mortals remain near their graves; hence the habit of visiting graveyards on Thursday nights, and leaving food on the graves.

The doctrine of *predestination* (*qadr*) has its effect on the popular mind also. The 15th Shaban (the eighth month of the Muslim calendar, also known as 'the Prophet's month') is a holy night in which God determines the fate of mortals during the coming year.[8]

Another aspect of popular Islam is described by Jones:

Many Muslims, when ill, follow a ritual that seems baseless to the scientific-minded westerner. A verse from the Qur'an will be written in ink or sandalwood paste on a plate or on the inside of a basin. The container will then be filled with water, which dissolves the writing. The water is poured into a glass and given to the patient to drink. Another method is to write the words of the Qur'an on a piece of paper and wash them off into a glass of water. Or, even more simply, an imam recites from the Qur'an and then breathes over a container of water. This then is given to the sick person to drink.[9]

A similar illustration comes from North Africa:

At the mosque in Mammam the boys learn the Qur'an from wooden slates which are coated with whiting or chalk. The chapter of the Qur'an which is to be

154

memorised is copied on to the slate with a pen made from a split reed. This is dipped in ink made from charred sheep's wool and gum. The water used to wash the slates clean is called the 'Holy Water' and is kept in a large earthen jar outside the mosque. It is reputed to be a certain remedy for many complaints. The patients drink it and this, of course, is equivalent to drinking the word of God.[10]

3   The Hunger of the Heart

In his paper with this title in *The Gospel and Islam*, Bill Musk writes:

> A Muslim in a village in northern Sudan receives a vision of Christ, and sets out to find a Christian to explain to him its meaning. An official in high Islamic circles in Egypt turns to Christ as his little child is miraculously healed. Or an Afghan student, lying sick in bed in America, recalls:
> 'I could not get out of my bed, or stand or walk. The Christian woman sat beside my bed and prayed for me constantly as she took care of me.... As the Christian lady prayed, I sensed something beyond her own sincerity and earnestness. I knew she believed in Jesus, but I also came to know something else that night. There was another power, another presence, another person who was alive and drawing near to me. The conviction was inescapable. Jesus heard and answered prayer....'[11]
> Our view of popular or 'low' Islam brings before our eyes, ordinary Muslims. Their beliefs and practices, and especially their relationship to Islamic religious authority, belie huge felt-needs. Popular Islam betrays a hunger of the heart.[12]

4   The Veneration of Muhammad and Saints in Islam

As in any other religious system that goes through a process of evolution, present-day Islam has emerged as a result of several factors. The development of Islam has been influenced not only by outwardly acceptable ideas, but also by ideas which existed in the society before the advent of Islam. These ideas were unacceptable and in oppostion to the new teaching, but they have been unconsciously transformed and assimilated.

The area in which the original doctrines of Islam have been most influenced is that of the veneration of Muhammad and the saints. Islam in its pure form teaches that there is an insurmountable barrier between weak and finite humanity and an unapproachable God. The natural human longing for union and communion with the Creator is therefore diverted to something more readily at hand. The qur'anic injuction to follow God and his apostle was transformed and came to mean that Muhammad was an intercessor, an intermediate between the common people and God. Muhammad's own view of himself was that God chose him to teach all mankind, but that he was as weak and mortal as other men.

The Qur'an seems to confirm this view. He is described as 'the first of them that surrender' (6:14). He has a definite role, which is descibed in *surah* 33:44: 'O Prophet, We have sent thee as a witness, and good tidings to bear and warning...'

There appears to have been some discussion concerning Muhammad's humanity which is clarified:

> Say: 'Glory be to my Lord! Am I aught but a mortal, a Messenger?' And naught prevented men from believing when the guidance came to them, but that they said, 'Has God sent forth a mortal as Messenger?'
> Say: 'Had there been in the earth angels walking at peace, we would have sent down upon them out of heaven an angel as Messenger.' Say: 'God suffices as a witness between me and you; surely He is aware of and sees His servants' (17:95–96).

Yet in the *shahada* the Muslim creed links the name of God inseparably with that of Muhammad: 'There is only one God and Muhammad is the Prophet of God.' Even this has been seen by some in Islam as committing the sin of *shirk* by associating something with God. The Qur'an speaks against the veneration of saints and that they only achieve blessedness through Allah's mercy. There is an enormous gap between this concept held by early Islam, and the place that the veneration of and appeal to saints occupies today. Perhaps it is the need to try to fill this gap that has led to veneration of Muhammad and of various saints in popular Islam.

During Muhammad's lifetime unbelievers, possibly even his friends, could not understand his very human behaviour.

> They also say, 'What ails this Messenger that he eats
> food, and goes in the markets? Why has an angel not
> been sent down to him, to be a warner to him? Or why
> is not a treasure thrown to him, or why has he not a
> garden to eat of?' The evildoers say, 'You are only
> following a man bewitched!' (25:8–9).

It was after Muhammad died that the way was open to ascribe to
him many types of miracles. As we have seen in Chapter 3/4, part
1, section 3, **What is the Meaning of Islam?** and in Chapter 10,
section 5:3, *ijma* (consensus of opinion) is one of the four ways in
which Islamic beliefs and laws develop. In this way, even
orthodox Muslims began to teach that Muhammad had been a
worker of miracles and that he had been given the key to all the
treasures of the earth. It was not long before a thousand miracles,
such as feeding, quenching thirst, and healing, were ascribed to
him.

Thus the gap between the divine and human was bridged.
There was another step in the process. The popular view of Islam
had to be validated by a scriptural base. This was found in the
qur'anic concept of the *wali* (plural *awliya*) (17:33, 27:53, etc.). In
religious language, this idea of nearness was extended also to the
relation of man with God. The pious holy men are said to be in
close relationship to God. The cult of saints grew up around
those who manifested visible signs of *wali*-ship. Muslims call any
person inspired by God, possessing ecstatic or spontaneous
illumination *majdhub*. This experience is a result of their closeness to God.

The developing order of *walis* did not wait for others to sing
their praises but began to teach how great they were themselves.
Tradition has it that the chief saint Arslan (died 700) was able to
produce a change in the four seasons within one hour. Others are
said to be able to be present at several places simultaneously and
change shapes at the same place; they changed gold to blood in
order to show vainglorious rulers what is the nature of this glitter.
Spatial distance disappears for the saints; animals and stones are
able to speak; they cure sickness, and their prayers are always
granted. Wild animals become tame at their bidding, they ride on
lions and can appear to be different personages to different
people at the same time. Sheik Abu Abd Allah Alqurashi had
one eye and was a leper. However, he was able to win the love of
a young girl by appearing to her as a beautiful youth whilst at the
same time he appeared to the rest of the world in the form of an
ugly cripple.

The further we move on in time the more marked became the reverence towards holy memorial places. This explains the 99 graves of prophets that were found in Mecca between the Black Stone and the Zamzam Well.

In Medina the sites of the houses of the first caliphs can be visited and the cistern of water which became sweet through the prophet's spit. Outside Medina there is a stone from which olive oil dripped at the prophet's order. Celebration of the more important historical moments are also an occasion to declare certain spots sacred. Once the process had begun, old pagan sanctuaries were gradually adopted and used as the graves of past Muslim saints. Gradually a cult of graves developed and they became places of local pilgrimage. To guard against shipwreck and other mishaps at sea, it was usual for a symbolical image of the prophet's shoe to be hung from the mast as a protection against the raging of the elements.

The primary function of the veneration of the saints in Islam is to satisfy the instinct to look for perfection within the human sphere, which is worthy of veneration and admiration.

The Caliph al Ma'mun wished to spare the ruins of Persepolis in southern Iran and therefore called it a place of prayer. Persian pre-Islamic festivies were incorporated into Islam such as the Nawruz or New Year. This is celebrated on 21st March every year. The justification for this is that Ali was supposedly appointed by the prophet as his successor, on this date, according to Shiite belief.

This is a Persian version of the tradition of *jamshid's* accession to the throne on Nawruz Day. Ali is said to abide in the clouds and causes thunder and lightening. Thus he is the god of thunder. In Persian mythology red evening skies are said to be the blood of the boar killed by Adonis or Aphrodite who was wounded by thorns. The Shiites claim that the red evening sky is the blood of the martyred Hussain. Islamic legend transferred the miracle of the arrest of the sun on Tibon to Muhammad. The late afternoon sun is said not to have set until the prophet captured a hostile town. (Muhammad is now claimed to be the *insan al kamil*, the most perfect man.)

Once the door has been opened to this process it is not difficult to move from the veneration of individuals to the veneration of trees, stones, streams, mountains, valleys and caves. Objects such as rings, beakers, cups, shoes, bits of bone, hair, clothing, and handwriting are all part and parcel of this awe and magical influence in popular Islam.

Activity

Please cover the right hand column of the diagram below, headed 'Christian Answer to Felt Needs.' Read the other columns, then write down your answers to the felt needs. Then compare your answers with those in the column.

FELT-NEEDS IN POPULAR ISLAM	ANIMISTIC ANSWERS TO FELT-NEEDS Not acceptable ... More Acceptable			CHRISTIAN ANSWER TO FELT-NEEDS
fear of the unknown	idolatry stone worship	fetishes talismans charms	superstition	security in Christ as Guide, Keeper
fear of evil	sorcery witchcraft	amulets knots	exorcism(?)	exorcism, protection in Christ
fear of the future	angel worship	divination spells(?)	fatalism fanaticism	trust in Christ as Lord of the future
shame of not being in the group	magic curse or bless	hair/nail trimmings		acceptance in fellowship of believers
powerless-ness of individual against evil	saint worship		baraka saint/angel petitioning	authority and power of the Holy Spirit
meaning-lessness of life		familiar spirit(?)		purpose in life as God's child
sickness	tree/saint worship	healing magic(?)		divine healing

Excerpted from 'The Gospel of Islam: a Compendium', Don McCurry editor. Published and used by permission only by MARC International, a division of World Vision.

5 Present-day Folk Islam

Folk Islam, like other forms of folk religion, is living and dynamic. This means that it undergoes gradual change. Samuel Zwemer, you may remember from Chapter 11, lived and worked at the beginning of this century. He made a study of popular Islam and many of the practices outlined in this chapter were described by him. Present-day folk Islam is not necessarily the same in detail. We shall also find considerable variations depending on the geographical area, as well as the cultural background, of the people concerned. Phil Parshall in his book *Bridges to Islam* writes mainly about South-East Asia:

> The folk Muslim is a practitioner. To him, nothing can be so barren as cognitive religion. Existence takes on meaning as it is experienced on the stage of life where the actors are permitted the freedom to improvise their contribution to the drama of humanness. Little does it matter if he is misunderstood or maligned. Actually he is convinced that it is the world — not himself — that is out of synchronisation with life.[13]

Here are some of the aspects of folk Islam which are listed:

5:1 *Animism*
Pointing out that animistic practices are usually left over from the time before conversion to Islam, Phil Parshall writes: 'More often than not, the initial Muslim missionaries were Sufis or at least mystically influenced. They were in favour of accommodation and compromise rather than strictly holding to the letter of Islamic law.'[14]

5:2 *Dhikr*
Dhikr is another practice of folk Muslims. It consists of the continual repetition of words such as 'Allah' with special intonation and concentration: the aim being to bring the performer closer to God. See Chapter 9, section 6:1, **Sufi Orders.**

5:3 *Mystical leadership*
We have already discussed this in relation to the rise of the *walis* after the death of Muhammad. Nowadays there are many *pirs* seeking to give charismatic leadership. These *pirs*, or Muslim

saints, usually exhibit some kind of magical powers. 'In my opinion, this ability to perform miracles and meet felt needs is the root of the charisma of most *pirs*'.[15]

Pirs teach through the telling of stories set in the culture and society of their listeners. Some have large followings and their needs, including financial, are cared for by their followers. Their teaching is syncretistic and they do not argue or debate. 'A good mystic would rejoice to hear of a friend who has found God — regardless of the path utilized in his pursuit.'[16]

Just as we saw in the last section, section 4, **The Veneration of Muhammad and Saints in Islam**, that the graves of Muslim saints are honoured and revered, so are the anniversaries of their deaths. Known as *urs*, they are times of great celebration and religious worship. See Chapter 9, section 6:1 **Sufi Orders**.

5:4 *Building bridges*
Folk Islam is the religion of the heart. As we learn and experience more, we can, perhaps, begin to build bridges.

> Bridges are a necessary part of life ... Bridges are also valuable in a religious sense. They can function as connectors between people of entirely diverse viewpoints and world views. Islam and Christianity can be likened to two continents opposite each other. Antagonism, suspicion, and even hatred swirl in the raging waters that separate the two. A few brave people have set out in small boats in an attempt to cross over to the bank with a message of peace, understanding and sensitivity. A few of these boats have crossed safely; others have been swept away in the tumultuous current.
>
> What is needed is a new structure to bridge the gap.[17]

Activity
It will be interesting to find out what view your Muslim friends hold about the matters presented in this chapter. You may have opportunity to discuss them together.
Note: More orthodox Muslims consider these practices un-Islamic and there are pressures to get rid of them. We need to be sensitive in discussing them.

Recommended Reading

PARSHALL, Phil. *Bridges to Islam*, Baker Book House, Grand Rapids, Michigan, 1983.

Additional Reading

JONES, Violet Rhoda, and JONES, L. Bevan *Women in Islam*, Lucknow Publishing House, India, 1941.
MARSH, Charles R. *Too Hard for God*. Echoes of Service, Bath, 1970. Republished by Scripture Union in 1980 under the title *The Challenge of Islam*.
MUSK, Bill A. 'Popular Islam: The Hunger of the Heart', pp208–221, in *The Gospel and Islam: A 1978 Compendium,* Don McCurry, ed, MARC, Monrovia, California, 1979.

Notes

1 MUSK, Bill A. 'Popular Islam: The Hunger of the Heart' pp208–221 in *The Gospel and Islam: A 1978 Compendium*, Don M McCurry, ed, MARC, Monrovia, California, 1979, p209.
2 Ibid, p211.
3 DOUGLAS, 1975, p385, quoted in MUSK pp209–210, as above.
4 MUSK, Bill A. 'Popular Islam: The Hunger of the Heart' pp208–221 in *The Gospel and Islam: A 1978 Compendium*, Don M McCurry, ed, MARC, Monrovia, California, 1979, p210.
5 PARSHALL, Phil. *Bridges to Islam*, Baker Book House, Grand Rapids, Michigan, 1983, p77.
6 ZWEMER, Samuel M. 1939, chapter 5.
7 ZWEMER, Samuel M. 1917, p2.
8 MUSK, Bill A. 'Popular Islam: The Hunger of the Heart' pp208–221 in *The Gospel and Islam: A 1978 Compendium*, Don M McCurry, ed, MARC, Monrovia, California, 1979, pp210–211.
9 JONES, Violet Rhoda and JONES, L Bevan. *Women in Islam*, Lucknow Publishing House, India, 1941, p365.
10 MARSH, Charles R. *Too Hard for God*, Echoes of Service, Bath, 1970. Republished by Scripture Union in 1980 under the title *The Challenge of Islam*. pp67–68.
11 HANNA, 1975, p63, quoted in Musk.
12 MUSK, Bill A. 'Popular Islam: The Hunger of the Heart' pp208–221 in *The Gospel and Islam: A 1978 Compendium*, Don M McCurry, ed, MARC, Monrovia, California, 1979, p212–213.

13 PARSHALL, Phil. *Bridges to Islam*, Baker Book House, Grand Rapids, Michigan, 1983, p71.
14 Ibid, p72.
15 Ibid, p84.
16 Ibid, p87.
17 Ibid, p113.

Chapter 14

THE GOSPEL AND CULTURE

1 Study Guide

This chapter gives a brief introduction to cultural anthropology as it relates to evangelism among Muslims. It looks in some detail at the cultural implications in meeting those from a differing cultural background. Dr Bill Musk has written the major portion of the chapter. There is also a contribution from Dr David Burnett. The unit is designed to give a theoretical framework into which Chapter 15 will fit. Some simple sociological concepts are explained, which we hope will be a basis for practical assignments and for further reading on this important subject.

Learning objectives
When you have completed this unit you should:

1 Understand more of the significance of culture in our own lives.
2 Be able to relate this to meeting and sharing with Muslims.

2 Introduction

The Lausanne Covenant recognises the need for Christians to be more culturally aware. Clause 10 reads:

2:1 *Evangelism and Culture*
The development of strategies for world evangelisation calls for imaginative pioneering methods. Under

God, the result will be the rise of churches deeply rooted in Christ and closely related to their culture. Culture must always be tested and judged by Scripture. Because man is God's creature, some of his culture is rich in beauty and goodness. Because he has fallen, all of it is tainted with sin and some of it is demonic. The Gospel does not presuppose the superiority of any culture to another, but evaluates all cultures according to its own criteria of truth and righteousness, and insists on moral absolutes in every culture. Missions have all too frequently exported with the Gospel an alien culture, and churches have sometimes been in bondage to culture rather than to the Scripture. Christ's evangelists must humbly seek to empty themselves of all but their personal authenticity in order to become the servants of others, and churches must seek to transform and enrich culture, all for the glory of God.[1]

2:2 *The Willowbank Report*

In January 1978 a conference was held on the subject of the Gospel and culture. It was convened by the Lausanne Committee's Theology and Education Group. Its report, Lausanne Occasional Paper no 2, is known as the Willowbank Report.

In defining culture, the report says, 'In the broadest sense, it means simply the patterned way in which people do things together.'[2] It also points out that the word is used to refer to units which are larger than the nuclear, or extended, family.

Other important facts about culture are defined in this section of the report. 'Culture implies a measure of homogeneity' and if the unit is large enough sub-cultures will be recognisable within it. 'Culture holds people together over a span of time.' Cultures are handed down from one generation to another, not by inheritance, but by subconscious learning and assimilating. During this process they undergo gradual change. Culture 'covers everything in human life' and indicates the *world view* of its members. We shall be looking at world views more closely later in the chapter. The phrase is defined as 'a general understanding of the nature of the universe and of one's place in it.'[2] A person's world view is of great importance as 'from this basic world-view flow both standards of judgement or values ... and standards of conduct.'[3] 'Culture is closely bound up with language, and is expressed in proverbs, myths, folk tales, and various art forms, which become part of the mental furniture of all members of the group.'[4]

We have seen in Chapter 13 something of how Islamic culture

has developed along these lines. This may be a good point in the course to stress the importance of learning the language of those with whom we wish to relate. This is a formidable task, but not an impossible one; there are now new and challenging methods of learning another language. Especially helpful, not least because it is so closely linked with the significance of culture, is the LAMP method developed by the Brewsters.[5]

To return to the Willowbank Report, it stresses the importance of a stable cultural background and the sense of loss and instability if, for any reason, a person is excluded from this. One reason for exclusion might be conversion; we consider the receiving and welcoming of Muslim converts into the church in Chapter 15. 'Men and women need a unified existence. Participation in a culture is one of the factors which provide them with a sense of belonging. It gives a sense of security, of identity, of dignity, of being part of a larger whole, and of sharing both in the life of past generations and in the expectancy of society for its own future.'[4]

2:3 *Christian Witness in the Islamic world*
This introductory section ends with another quote from the Willowbank Report, under the above heading:

> There is a need to recognise the distinctive features of Islam which provide a unique opportunity for Christian witness. Although there are in Islam elements which are incompatible with the Gospel, there are also elements with a degree of what has been called 'convertibility.' For instance, our Christian understanding of God, expressed in Luther's great cry related to justification, 'Let God be God,' might well serve as an inclusive definition of Islam. The Islamic faith in divine unity, the emphasis on man's obligation to render God a right worship, and the utter rejection of idolatry could also be regarded as being in line with God's purpose for human life as revealed in Jesus Christ. Contemporary Christian witnesses should learn humbly and expectantly to identify, appreciate and illuminate these and other values. They should also wrestle for the transformation — and, where possible, integration — of all that is relevant in Islamic worship, prayer, fasting, art, architecture, and calligraphy.

3 The Culture Factor

We look now at an article by Dr David Burnett which appeared in 1978 in *Third Way*. This gives general information about culture which will be helpful in learning to relate to Muslims.

3:1   The sun shone out of a deep blue tropical sky as I walked along one of the main streets of Madras with one of my students. He was an upright young man who had come to the Bible Institute to train for Christian work. For the few months that I had been in India I had tried to get alongside the young men at the college, but I was aware that there was a distance between us. As we walked down the street talking in a friendly way, he quietly took my hand.

What should I do? To me the act of two men holding hands held all the connotations of homosexuality. I knew that it was common practice for young men, who are friends, to hold hands in India, as it is in many areas of South East Asia. For him this act was in no way linked with homosexuality, only friendship, yet this knowledge did not help my embarrassment. If I drew my hand away he could interpret it to mean I did not want us to be friends. Once more I had come up against the culture factor.

During the last few years there has been a growing awareness of the importance of the culture factor amongst evangelicals ... what is 'culture' anyway? It is not a preference for Beethoven over the Beatles. It is not a matter of good table manners, nor a liking for opera. It is, by anthropological definition, an integrated system of learned behaviour patterns, ideas and products characteristic of a society.

3:2   *Culture is learnt*
Birds do not learn how to make nests typical of their species. They build nests in that way because it is part of their make-up. Dogs raised apart from other dogs with never 'meow' like a cat, nor hiss like a snake. They will whine, growl, yelp or bark in a manner characteristic of their breed.

With human beings the situation is more complex. A Chinese baby raised entirely in an English-speaking environment will grow up knowing only English, and not a word of Chinese. Language does not depend upon genetic structure, but it is learnt as are

167

many other factors of life. A child is born cultureless, but it soon begins to learn what are the acceptable ways of the society it has been born into. So before a child is old enough to evaluate, he is being conditioned to speak and act along certain patterns. Like little David whose mother scolds him: 'Don't eat your sausages with your fingers, use your fork.' Or little Rajan in South India who is told to leave his sandals at the door and not copy the bad manners of the foreign people who wear their shoes indoors.

This process of conditioning continues throughout our lives and gradually these patterns become a habit, as knowledge of the standard behaviour of our society becomes a part of our very selves. The result is that the people of a particular culture assume that their ways are best. Westerners are frequently surprised to discover that many people are proud of their own ways and do not accept the western way of life as obviously the best. In fact, when the early explorers contacted the Eskimos, the Eskimos thought that they had come to learn good manners from them!

The name the Hottentots use of themselves means 'men of men', implying that among the nations they are the 'real' people, and such feelings of racial superiority are common to most peoples. Some white Americans have been trying to prove that the IQ of a white American is intrinsically superior to that of one of his black countrymen. The Nazi dream was of a 'pure' Aryan race. It is this belief that one's own ways and people are best which, unexamined, leads to prejudice, and looks down on other peoples' language and customs, calling them primitive and heathen.

3:3 *Culture is ideas*

At the centre of any culture are basic presuppositions — ideas which are shared by all the society, shown in the way they organise their world, setting goals and judging actions. Frequently, a western teacher working in a tribal situation will get frustrated at how slow the children are at understanding. They are not, as he may feel, 'simple', but have different ways of arranging their thoughts.

Western man finds security in establishing orderly limits in the area both of ideas and of daily life. Clarity of thought is for him a sign of intelligence. These are products of a graeco-roman heritage, subsequently fortified by the influence of Descartes and Locke. Ideas must be precise. They must be scrutinised, analysed and classified; each idea must be separated from its neighbour by a fence so as to keep its true identity.

In contrast, the Baoule of the Ivory Coast thirst for unity. They desire cohesion, and abhor separating, clarifying and specifying. They need to feel surrounded and included; they like fluidity, mixture and mystery. They are grounded in the universe to the point of being barely distinguishable from it, whilst the white man stands at a distance and observes.

During a class on sex education, geared to illiterate Baoule, male and female physiology was explained and diagrams and pictures were used to show the development of the foetus. It was all very clear, perhaps too clear, for at the end of the session the people were saying, 'We saw a lot of things on that screen, but that is not the way one has children; there is something invisible behind all that, something one cannot see, the mystery of fertility and of life. And that is where truth is.' To them, what can be clearly seen is not life, nor is it truth.

3:4   *Culture is behaviour*

Ideas express themselves in the way people behave; how we dress, eat, sleep, bathe, conduct a meeting, work or get married are all a result of our culture. All these activities, and thousands of other ways of acting which seem so natural and right, are a result of our culture. How else can you eat, but with a knife and fork? Yet millions of peole in the world find the knife and fork as strange and awkward as we do chopsticks.

British exporters are at last becoming aware of these cultural factors in their overseas trade encounters. Getting 'straight down to business' may be well-received in the west, but other areas may find this crude and distasteful, preferring pleasant, friendly, casual conversation, which will finally lead on to the matter of business. Or take for example the distance that two business men stand apart to talk. The British stand at about arms' length, and are very careful not to touch each other. On the other hand, the Latin American likes to stand much closer, perhaps a little too close for our respectable British gentleman who unconsciously takes a step back, to an acceptable distance. This now leaves the Latin American feeling rather distant and unable to touch the person in the way he would naturally do with a business man from his own country. He therefore, unconsciously, takes a step towards the British man, who in turn takes a step back. And so the movement continues across the room! When the conversation is finished, the Latin American walks away with an unspoken feeling of how cold and aloof the British are. On the other hand, the British business man probably feels that Latin Americans are rather pushy and overwhelming. If cultural factors are ignored, it is too easy to criticise rather than to accept.

3:5   *Culture is products*

The making of material objects often stems from the attitudes and presuppositions of a culture, as well as from basic needs common to all cultures. It is necessary to realise that just because a society does not have such a complex technology as ours, it does not mean that that society is inferior to our own. A society will develop that aspect which it feels is most important; in the west, we have felt that technology is important and have concentrated on this aspect. Other societies may have developed along the line of artistic achievements, spiritual awareness, or close social relationships.

Take Malawi, for example, where the important social group is the clan, or 'extended family'. Everyone has a place and a position; everyone knows who he is in the family structure. Most Malawians live in rural areas and work on the land, either on their own smallholdings or big estates, and most are very poor by European standards. But the 'poor' villager lives in a stable society where both children and the old are well cared for. A 'latchkey' child, neglected by its parents, and a lonely old grandmother, living miles from her children, are unheard of and would shock a decent Malawian family.

3:6   *Culture is integrated*

Finally, it is necessary to stress that culture is integrated. A people do not just eat one way, dress in another way, work in another way or worship in another way without reference to the other activities. There is a 'oneness' about culture, which is very important to appreciate. It is therefore just not possible to 'pull out' the religion of a people, and 'plug in' Christianity without having an effect on the rest of the culture. We must acknowledge that anthropologists are correct when they say that missionaries have changed the cultures of people. The gospel will change cultures, acting like 'salt' (Matthew 5:13), purifying the culture of the people, and removing that which is tainted with sin. However, we must confess, as stated in the Lausanne Covenant: 'Missions have all too frequently exported with the gospel an alien culture, and churches have sometimes been in bondage to culture rather than the Scripture.'

The integrated nature of culture is clearly seen in the area of development and overseas aid. A home improvement programme was initiated in the high Andes of Ecuador. For reasons of hygiene, an attempt was made to get housewives to use a raised fireplace rather than a simple fire on the centre of the floor. However, all attempts to introduce this change have been largely unsuccessful, since the cultural factors were not explored thoroughly. The programme technicians viewed the fire as simply a cooking device, whereas it also served the equally important function of affording warmth to the household who slept around it at night. A raised hearth appreciably reduced the value of the fire for warmth.

In 1951 a yellow Cuban maize was introduced into the eastern lowlands of Bolivia. It had many apparant advantages. It grew well in the tropics, matured more rapidly, was less subject to insect attack, and produced a higher yield per unit of land. The new maize seemed to be an excellent means of improving the diet of the people, and it has indeed proved very popular — but not for the reasons anticipated. Its very hardness, desirable for the standpoint of storage, makes it difficult to grind, and people are unwilling to take the time and trouble to haul it to commercial mills in towns. But it makes an excellent commercial alcohol, and prices are high. Thus a seemingly desirable innovation has promoted alcohol instead of an improved diet.

Initially it was believed that the transmission of new technical skills to developing peoples was a simple matter of making available to them the scientific techniques that had worked well in industrialised countries. Now we have learned that the process is much more complex than we had thought, and the culture factor imposes other dimensions to technological innovation.

The term 'culture' is *a priori* concerned with people — people who have needs and seek to meet those needs in various ways. Every culture is an honest attempt to cope with these problems. Some might class them as being 'ridiculous', or even 'pagan', but they are a valid attempt by that society to do its best to answer the problems that it faces.

As an Old Testament example to us, Ezekiel had to 'sit where they sit' (Ezekiel 3:12–15). He had to appreciate the problems of the people amongst whom he was going to work and love them from that viewpoint. The Asian bus conductor may be different from the Anglo-Saxon housewife, yet both have needs which can only be met in a living relationship with their creator. We must be willing to cross the boundaries of culture, and overcome our natural prejudices in order to make Jesus Christ manifest to the peoples of the world, wherever they live.[6]

Activity
In talking with Muslim friends you will have noticed some of the cultural differences between you. Make a list of these. When you read the section marked *Comparative Study*, check your list with the comparison given in the text.

4:1 *Definition of culture*
When we speak about 'culture', we are dealing with something man-made. 'Culture' is the milieu in which we learn to relate to one another. Luzbetak has defined 'culture' as 'a *way of life*; culture is the *total* plan for living; it is functionally organised into a *system*; it is *acquired through* learning; it is the way of life of a *social group*, not of an individual as such.'[7] As one studies a specific culture, gradually one moves from a looking at the surface activities of the people of that culture, their customs, towards a deeper understanding of the motivations or assumptions underlying those customs, their world view. It is with this matter of world view that we are concerned in this section.

The 'world view' (German *Weltanschauung*) of a society is that inner, often inferred, corpus of attitudes which provides a society with its own unique genre. It is what makes an Arab Arab or an Englishman English. It is what makes a westerner an occidental or an easterner an oriental. The view of this writer is that there is no such thing as *the* 'Christian world view', since any world view is associated with a particular culture and cannot be either detached from a specific culture or universalised to apply to all cultures. The Gospel consists of God's supra-cultural message to people of every culture in the world. In the New Testament it would seem that the Jews, Jesus and Paul, go out of their way to try and accommodate to the world views of cultures other than their own in order to get across that divine message.

In Jesus' dealing with the Samaritans, for example, while he holds very strongly to the fact that 'salvation is from the Jews' (John 4:22), he concentrates on getting alongside Samaritans and on saying with his life that God is willing to meet the Samaritans within their own world view. In doing this he upsets his fellow-Jews so much that they even go so far as to accuse him of actually being a Samaritan (John 8:48). The great Jerusalem council of Acts 15 is precipitated by the conversions which took place in Antioch amongst the Gentiles. Paul and Barnabas come and represent to the council the view that Gentiles could become valid followers of Jesus Christ without first having to become Jews (Acts 15:1,2). The council upholds Paul and Barnabas' view as a whole but states some areas where they feel that the Gentile world view needs revision in order for it to be truly Christian (Acts 15:23–29). It would seem fair to conclude that every world view, as every culture, has some elements which come under the judgement of Christ, some which are perfectly acceptable in a Christian sense, and others which need transformation in order that that society becomes more truly Christian.

4:2 *Comparative study*

In order to illustrate the difference between cultures, let us take a contemporary look at what is loosely called 'western culture' and 'middle eastern culture'. At the risk of over-simplification, some broad generalisations may be made:

Western culture tends to be	*Middle eastern culture* tends to be
individualistic	family-centred
man-centred	God-centred
achievement-oriented	relationship-oriented
compartmentalised (sacred vs. secular)	integrated (sacred and secular)
materialistic	spiritual
enforced by guilt	enforced by shame

A helpful model here is that of three concentric circles representing, at the centre, the world view of a culture. Such a world view influences or gives shape to the philosophy of life or assumptions about life in terms of health, religion, politics, family, etc. Those assumptions in the different aspects of living give rise to the customs which are visible in people's words and acts. If this model is applied in some of its aspects to western and middle eastern culture, the following comparison can be made.

MODEL OF WORLD VIEW. AREAS OF LIFE. CUSTOMS.
(fig. 1)

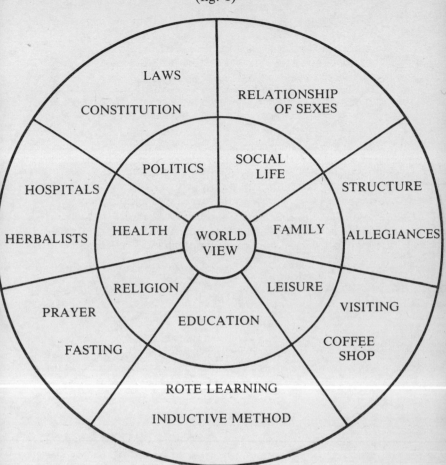

OUTERMOST CIRCLE - CUSTOMS
MIDDLE CIRCLE - AREAS OF LIFE
CENTRAL CIRCLE - WORLDVIEW

APPLICATION TO WESTERN CULTURE
(fig. 2)

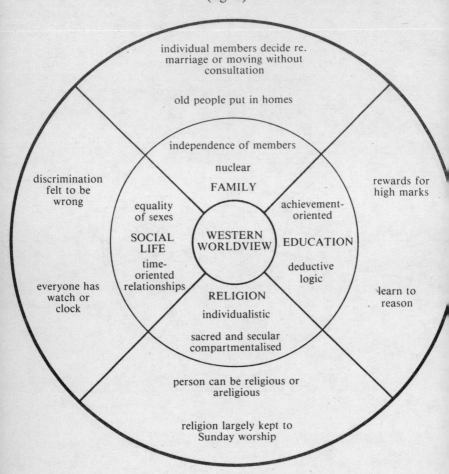

individual members decide re. marriage or moving without consultation

old people put in homes

independence of members

nuclear

FAMILY

discrimination felt to be wrong

rewards for high marks

equality of sexes

achievement-oriented

SOCIAL LIFE

WESTERN WORLDVIEW

EDUCATION

time-oriented relationships

deductive logic

everyone has watch or clock

learn to reason

RELIGION

individualistic

sacred and secular compartmentalised

person can be religious or areligious

religion largely kept to Sunday worship

APPLICATION TO MIDDLE EASTERN CULTURE
(fig. 3)

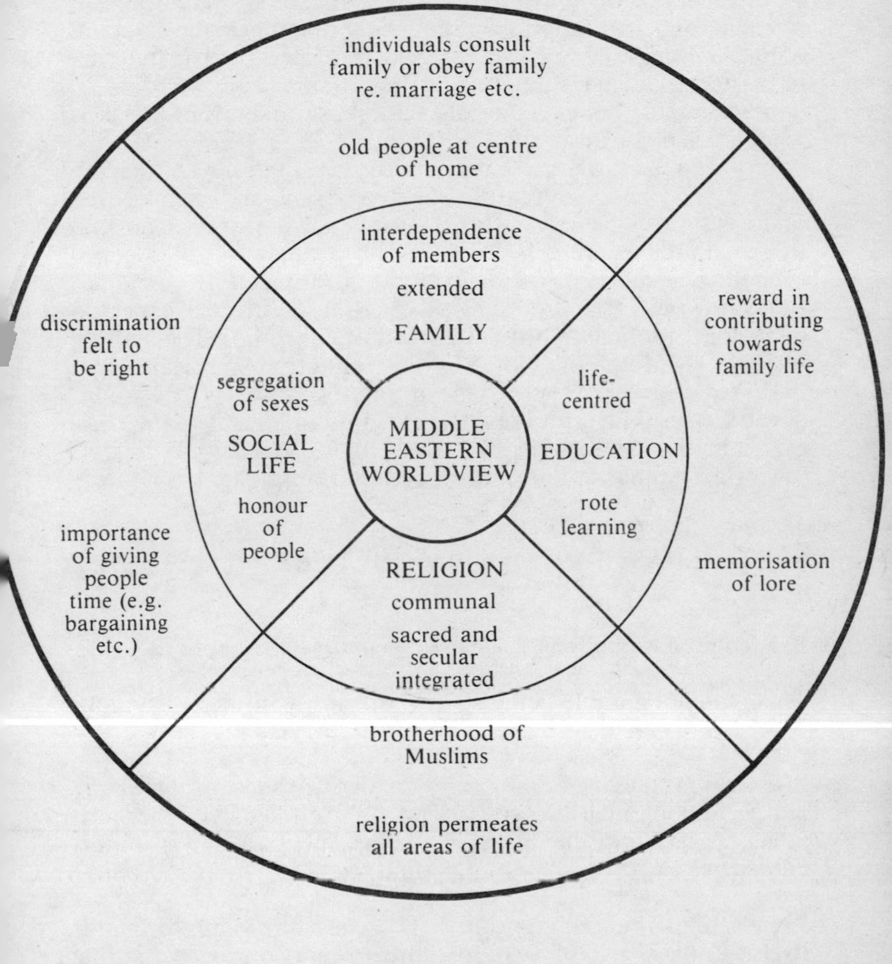
individuals consult family or obey family re. marriage etc.
old people at centre of home
interdependence of members
extended
FAMILY
discrimination felt to be right
segregation of sexes
SOCIAL LIFE
honour of people
importance of giving people time (e.g. bargaining etc.)
MIDDLE EASTERN WORLDVIEW
reward in contributing towards family life
life-centred
EDUCATION
rote learning
memorisation of lore
RELIGION
communal
sacred and secular integrated
brotherhood of Muslims
religion permeates all areas of life

4:3 *Assumptions behind cultures*

Another way of looking at a culture from the inside out, as it were, is to examine the assumptions behind its actions and words. Deepest of all would occur the existential assumptions of a society, those assumptions telling how things are, the essential nature of things. For example, it may be an accepted 'fact of life' or existential assumption in one culture that an ability to deceive another human being is one of the highest qualities of life; it is what life is really all about.[8]

Closer to the surface would occur those assumptions which are normative. These assumptions say that in such-and-such an area of life certain behaviour patterns must be the norm. Such normative assumptions are reflective of, and justified by, the deeper existential assumptions. For example, in the culture just mentioned it would be accepted as 'right', as normative, as expected behaviour, for man to grow in the art of deception. The activity of Judas Iscariot in the Gospel story would thus be acclaimed as 'right' and 'good'. Beyond the normative assumptions would occur the resulting attitudes, the customs and deeds of the society. For example, within middle eastern, Muslim culture, the following existential and normative assumptions seem to operate.

MIDDLE EASTERN, MUSLIM CULTURE

Existential Assumptions	**Normative Assumptions**
Man is an honourable being.	To bring man into dishonour (or shame) is sin.
The *world* is a living organism and is full of invisible spirit beings as well as visible material beings.	To live in harmony with the world itself, and with the spirit beings inhabiting it is important.
Time is linear but not a god in itself.	To reflect the value of man is the primary purpose of time (eg people with greater status come 'late' to meetings).
Causality (eg in sickness) is often seen as spiritual as well as mechanical.	To discover the source of the cause (eg in sickness) is important; one must look in the spiritual as much as the natural world for this source.

| *God* is transcendent. | To be brothers together, submitted to God is the aim of living. Possibly also the tendency towards fatalism. |

In terms of a people's view of the universe, of people, of 'the other world', of time, of space, of roles, of belief systems, of causality and so on, the existential assumptions of a society give cohesion to the culture. They are the core of the world view of a people. They say 'what is', what reality consists of.

In the case of Islamic cultures, where the religious area of life is very closely integrated with the core of their world view, these existential assumptions take on a religious flavour. In consequence the normative assumptions tend to be religious in nature and the whole of society is permeated by religion. A short visit to any Muslim, middle eastern culture soon convinces the westerner that religious words and acts are used all the time and in every transaction of life. From the call to prayer to saying good-bye, from arranging appointments to bargaining for produce, God is invoked and religious terms are used. To be a normal person in an Islamic culture is to be a religious person.

The religious story of an Islamic society has a strong effect upon how people interrelate (quite apart from its theological truth or untruth). Its content is usually consistent with reality as the people understand it. It deals with universal themes such as creation, the flood, after-life, etc. It speaks of the origins of the universe and of man. It talks about relationships, for example between God and man, between good and evil, between disease and healing. So the Islamic religious story (whether the Qur'an itself, or whether oral myths about evil *jinn*) has many functions. It explains the way things are: why drought, why earthquakes, why rich and poor, etc. It integrates the world giving the location of man in the universe meaning and value.

In the Middle East one discovers that man is only one of many beings in the world: there are dead saints, *jinn*, angels, etc all of whom have to live together in the world as the Muslim perceives it. The religious story undergirds society, suggesting rules, appropriate actions, taboos, etc. When should a woman be stopped from attending worship in a mosque? What places should a sick child be taken to for healing? These kinds of questions are answered by the religious story of Muslim middle eastern culture. The story also sanctions behaviour, exerting social control.

It renews life by re-enacting important events of life. For example, the need for and time of male circumcision, of female veil-wearing, of celebrating the birthday of the prophet Muhammad, are all defined by Islamic religious story and are foundational factors in the way society operates on a daily or yearly basis.

4:4 *The function of religion*
It is clear then that in this study of the Gospel and culture we are not dealing with religion in terms of its meaning, its essential truth. We are not talking about theology. Rather, we are asking the question (here of Islam), how does religion function? How does religion relate to the deep assumptions, to the world view, to the social structure of Islamic cultures? Of course, there are no simple, universally-applicable answers to these questions. But the contribution of cultural anthropology to evangelism in the Muslim world lies in helping us to ask the right questions and then leaves us to do our homework in each given culture or sub-culture. The aim of the 'right questions' is to help us understand how religion is already functioning in these cultures or sub-cultures:

1   What are some of the customs of this people, say, with regard to education (or health, or leisure, or time, etc)?
2   What is the normal behaviour expected of people in acting out those customs? What is the expected behaviour of the people concerned?
3   Why is that the expected behaviour? Why is visible prayer, five times a day, so important? Why does society operate more on 'who you know' rather than on 'what you know'? Why is Arabic a language of exaggeration?
4   What is man? Who is he? What does the religious activity and the religious story of this culture tell me about who man is?

Activity
Write down some of the assumptions you have on which your own culture is based (eg Does it matter in your culture whether man is a believer in God or not? Is 'being on time' important, and if so, why?)

4:5 *Introducing the Christian Gospel to a culture*
In introducing the Christian Gospel to another culture we are, wittingly or unwittingly, agents of change. We impart customs, concepts, perhaps even those deeper normative or existential

assumptions which have a lasting effect upon hearers from that other culture. The Muslim whose life is touched with the Gospel is changed at the most fundamental area of his existence. God speaks to him (as to us!) as the Lord of heart or spirit. He is changed from inside out. The meaning of existence is transformed in an encounter with Jesus Christ. In that process, he is also touched by the culturally-loaded communication of the Gospel via the agents of evangelism. He hears other assumptions about life from us, other views of the world from those who carry the Gospel to him. The questions which have to be asked by ourselves as evangelists lie precisely here.

1   What are the non-negotiable elements of the Gospel which need to be got across to the hearer so that he may make a faith-response to Christ? Where, like Christ with the Samaritans, can there be no compromise of Truth?

2   What are the extra, culturally-coloured implications of our preaching of the Gospel which are negotiable and not necessarily relevant to the hearer? Can the Gospel only be shared in English? Does a convert have to learn western hymn tunes in order to make music to the Lord? Is conversion measured only in acknowledgement by the mind of certain historical or theological facts? Or can conversion be more experience-oriented?

3   In terms of change and conversion, what kind of changes should be planned, or what may happen in an unplanned way if no cross-cultural sensitivity is developed? What kind of converts are sought — converts to Christ, or converts to Christ-via-western-world-view, or converts to western culture per se?

4   In terms of communication, how well understood by the evangelist is the recipient culture? Are its myths (both the official and the popular religious stories) well-known? Can the missionary 'see' the world as the Muslim sees it? For example, suppose the Muslim is afraid of evil spirits in the night. Is that just laughed at or can the witness give a biblical response to this fear? Or suppose sickness is seen as a result of sorcery. Does the Christian just say, 'Oh no, sickness comes from microbes,' or does he have a response which meaningfully meets the problem of sorcery? What are the appropriate forms of communication which 'fit' a society,

along which the Gospel may be transmitted? For example, if Muslims place a lot of emphasis on dreams, can the Christian learn to talk about the dreams of the New Testament as a way to introduce the Gospel?

In terms of being an agent of culture change, has there been a coming to terms with his own ethnocentrism by the missionary? Smalley defines ethnocentrism as 'the term used by anthropologists to represent that point of view which we all have to varying degrees, that our own culture, our own way of doing things, is best.'[9] Can the evangelist learn to identify with the world view of a culture not his own, or at least empathise with it? What kind of status and role can he meaningfully take in the recipient culture which enhances, rather than alienates, his opportunity to share the Gospel?

Activity

Write a 100-word paragraph in simple English expressing what you feel to be the essential non-negotiable truth of the Gospel which needs to be shared with all human beings.

Recommended reading

There is no specific book for this chapter. We hope you will be able to find time to read some of the books listed below.

Additional Reading

BREWSTER, E Thomas, and BREWSTER, Elizabeth S. *Language Acquistion Made Practical*. Lingua House, Toronto, 1976.
FAKHOURI, Hani. *Kafr El Elow: An Egyptian Village in Transition*, Holt, Rinehart and Winston, New York, 1972.
GULICK, John. *The Middle East: An Anthropological Perspective*, Goodyear Publishers, Pacific Palisades, California, 1976.
HESSELGRAVE, David J. *Communicating Christ Cross-Culturally*, Zondervan Publishing House, Grand Rapids, Michigan, 1978.
JEFFERY, Patricia. *Frogs in a Well: Indian Women in Purdah*, Zed Press, London, 1979. A sociological study of *purdah*.
KRAFT, Charles H. *Christianity in Culture*, Orbis, Maryknoll,

New York, 1979.
LUZBETAK, Louis J. *The Church and Cultures*, Louis J Luzbetak, Divine Word Publications, Techny, Illinois, 1970.
NIDA, Eugene. *Customs and Cultures*, William Carey Library, South Pasadena, California, 2nd ed., 1975.
—. *Religion Across Cultures*, William Carey Library, South Pasadena, California, 1979.
RICHARDSON, Don. *Peace Child*, Regal Books, Ventura, California, 1974.
SMALLEY, William A, ed. *Readings in Missionary Anthropology*, William Carey Library, South Pasadena, California, 1974. Enlarged edition, 1970.
Willowbank Report, Scripture Union, London, 1978.

Notes

1. *Lausanne Covenant*, World Wide Publications, Minneapolis, Minnesota, 1975.
2. *Willowbank Report*, Scripture Union, London, 1978, p17.
3. Ibid, pp17–18.
4. Ibid, p18.
5. BREWSTER, E Thomas and BREWSTER, Elizabeth S. *Language Acquisition Made Practical*, Lingua House, Toronto, 1976.
6. BURNETT, David. 'The Culture Factor', Third Way, June 15th 1978.
7. LUZBETAK, Louis J. *The Church and Cultures*, Divine Word Publications, Techny, Illinois, 1970, p60.
8. See, for example, *Peace Child* by DON RICHARDSON, Regal Books, Ventura, California, 1974.
9. SMALLEY, William A, ed, *Readings in Missionary Anthropology*, William Carey Library, South Pasadena, California, 1974.

Chapter 15

CASE STUDIES OF CULTURAL SIGNIFICANCE

1 Study Guide

Having, in Chapter 14, been introduced to the theoretical aspect of cultural differences, changes and developments, this chapter begins to apply this to actual situations. Northern Nigeria is considered in an interview with Graham Weeks, an experienced missionary who worked in the area for many years. We asked Andrew Dymond, who worked in Iran, to comment on the interview and this is also included.

The second part of the chapter consists of comments by a colleague of Phil Parshall, the writer of the recommended book for this chapter, *New Paths in Muslim Evangelism*. Then we asked Gwendy Anderson, an experienced missionary who has worked in the Muslim world, to comment on the receiving of Muslim converts into the church. This important subject concludes the chapter.

Learning objectives
When you have completed this chapter you should:

1 See how the theories discussed in Chapter 14 are being put into practice.
2 Have some understanding of how a Muslim convert church might be formed.
3 Have learnt some lessons from the development of the Church in Nigeria.
4 See how the Muslim convert church in 'Bimbar' is being developed according to principles of contextualisation.

2 Introduction

Bill Musk provided us with the following comments:

> For tens of thousands of Indonesians in 1966 and
> 1967, the traditional doctrinal problems of Christian-
> ity (especially the Triune Godhead and the Son-ship
> of Christ) did not stop them from becoming Christ-
> ians: almost overnight the theological 'objections'
> vanished and large numbers of Muslims became
> Trinitarian Christians, worshippers of the Son. Why
> did this happen in Indonesia? Is it possible that the
> real obstacles to conversion for Muslims often have
> not been theological ones; that larger obstacles have
> been centred, not in the Gospel, but in the social bar-
> riers found in the heralds of that Gospel?

An important question is raised here. Are the barriers social
rather than theological? One thing is clear, that whereas growth
of the church in other Muslim areas has been through the conversion of ones and twos, this has not been the case in Indonesia. In
his book *Islam and Christian Witness* Martin Goldsmith, himself
formerly a missionary in Indonesia, writes: 'Indonesia shines as
the great exception in Muslim evangelism, for many thousands
become Christians every year and the church grows rapidly.'[1]

He also points out that it is particularly the migrant workers
going from the over-populated island of Java to the larger, less-
populated Sumatra and Celebes, who are most open and recep-
tive to the Gospel. The Christian church has a long history of missionary work in the area with steady and encouraging church
growth. By 1980 it was estimated that it numbered 25–30 million,
with an annual growth rate of seven per cent.[2]

In this chapter it is important to keep asking the question,
'Why do people become Christians?' One reason for the large
number of conversions in Indonesia may well be that Islam tends
to be less traditional and more 'popular' in the area than in the
middle eastern heartlands of the religion. This is one of the religious tensions mentioned in the section on 'The Comparative
Status of Christianity and Islam in Southeast Asia' in *The Gospel
and Islam*: 'First there was the tension, antagonism between the
hard-line traditionist Islam (strict in both faith and practice) and
the vigorous beliefs and practices, often labelled animistic.'[3]

Before going on to the next section, you might like to look

back at Chapter 13, particularly sections 3 and 5:4 **The Hunger of the Heart** and *Building Bridges*, where popular Islam is discussed.

3   Contextualisation

Before further study it is important to understand this term 'contextualisation'.

Phil Parshall writes at the beginning of *New Paths in Muslim Evangelism*:

> 'Contextualisation' is a word which has recently come in to popular usage among evangelicals. The word itself directs our attention to 'context'. This includes the total matrix of society which embraces the social patterns of a people, their economic policies, politics, and a host of other integrative areas.
>
> The gospel of Jesus Christ must be attractively presented into the context of any given group of people. This is a process which involves great sensitivity. [4]

We must also remember the need for a balanced presentation. Here's a quote from the writer of the second case study (see later section 6, **The Country of Bimbar**): 'Ultimately it is not going to be the method of contextualisation that is going to turn anyone to Christ, it is going to be the working of the Holy Spirit in the hearts of men.'

4   The Church in Northern Nigeria

Part of a conversation between Graham Weeks and Roger Malstead helps towards an understanding of its growth and development.

RM: Graham, could you give us a brief history of the Church in northern Nigeria from your experience?

GW: Northern Nigeria is a place for which we should really give thanks to God for the growth of the Church there in this century. Pre-1900, you could look at the whole area of northern Nigeria and say, 'No Christians; zero per cent Christians.' Today, according to surveys done, for example, by Rev Dr David Barrett (*The World Christian Encyclopedia*), there are places where the number of professing Christians would be as high as 69 per cent of the population. Yet, there are other areas where Barrett states that there are no Christians at all. Why the difference? Why is it that in one area, for example, on the Plateau, there are thousands of groups of worshipping Christians, whereas you can go to a village 50 miles north of that area where there isn't a single Christian? Why? Why is there growth in one area and not in another?

The answer is to be found in the origins of these people. Where there are great numbers of Christians, some are converts, others are second and third generation Christians, and they come from a background of African traditional religions. In areas where there are no Christians the people are, by and large, Muslim.

RM: So there hasn't been much growth at all amongst Muslim communities. Haven't there been some signs of change in that area?

GW: If we look at churches throughout the north of Nigeria, and there are several thousand, I can only think of one where I know for certain that it originated from the conversion of Muslim peoples. In other churches you may find a few people who were Muslim before they became Christians, but on the whole this is not the case. There is a great divide, just as in the past the great divide existed between the Muslim and those who were animists and followers of African traditional religions. Today this divide continues because the Muslims have remained unmoved by the Gospel, while the majority of other groups have become Christians.

RM: Why do you think there is this divide?

GW: Perhaps it is because when the African traditional religionist looked at the life of the Christian missionary he realised that the totality of his life had something to offer that was better than he already had. But when the Muslim looked at the Christian missionary he didn't see that the missionary had anything better to offer. Why should he listen to him?

RM: That's very interesting. It agrees with what Phil Parshall is saying when he compares the life of the Muslim *imam* with that of the Christian missionary. (See diagram at end of this section.) Where is the one church that you were referring to? Is that in the heart of northern Nigeria, and is it the result of some missionary activity?

187

GW: The church to which I am referring is the Anglican Church in Oosasa, just north of Zaria; that church came from the work of one of the very first missionaries to the north of Nigeria. As far as I know he is the only man who ever planted a church in northern Nigeria from Muslim converts; and he only ever did it once, although he spent the rest of his life in Nigeria. One has to ask the question ... WHY?

RM: Do you think that there were some factors in his life that led to Muslim friends coming to Christ in that area? Or was it some accident? Some 'act of God' as some would say?

GW: I think one can see some reasons from the life of this man. His name was Dr Walter R S Miller. In one of his biographical works, he recounts how the first Hausa *imam* from northern Nigeria that he met in North Africa in the 1890s had said, 'Ah, my land is far away, but it is a beautiful land.' Miller replied, 'Yes, it is a beautiful land, a beautiful people, a beautiful language.' He appreciated the people and their culture and loved them. This is what comes across from reading the life of Miller. He also says some very harsh things about Muslims, but overall, his appreciation for the land, culture, language, and people really comes across.

RM: If there are no other examples of missionary success, are there, in your opinion, some areas in which the churches in northern Nigeria could build bridges to Muslims? What are some of the things in their lives or witness that might help Muslims understand the Gospel better?

GW: First of all, we must honestly face up to the reasons for our failure. Why has the Church failed to grow among Muslim people? I have to ask whether the Church in northern Nigeria is really interested in converting Muslims. If winning them involves a change in lifestyle, in cultural practices, and even in church practices, is it prepared to examine and face up to some of the deep historical factors which separate the Church from Muslims? When a Muslim Nigerian thinks about a Christian, is he thinking about some white missionaries or is he thinking about the Nigerian Christian down the road? And what is the relationship between the Muslim and Christian peoples of Nigeria? You have to remember that Christians and Muslims are not just separated by religion.

RM: So it's important for workers going into other areas, whether in Africa, the Middle East, or Asia, to be good students of history.

GW: You must not miss understanding the history of the area to which you are going. Read everthing you can from every point of view. From Christian points of view, secular, Marxist, pro-colonialist, and anti-colonialist. Read it from all the different points of view and evaluate it in the light of the wisdom Christ has given you.

RM: Can you think of any mistakes that have been made in the past by missionaries or national Christians from which we can learn as we think about the future?

GW: One of the basic mistakes is to think that the Africans can necessarily best evangelise Africa or that a Muslim African would rather hear the Gospel from an African Christian than from a foreign Christian. I think there's evidence to show that *some of the mistakes that have been made have, ironically, been a product of a sincere and indigenous approach to the Church, but one which failed to see the diversity of the African cultures*. There's one missionary society in Nigeria which more or less has a rule that says that no foreign missionaries should preach in public in Muslim areas. But converts from Islam have stated that Muslims would rather listen to a white man, who is taking pains to speak their language well, than they would listen to a black man who speaks it fluently but carelessly.

RM: So many bridges have to be built if there's going to be a communication of the Gospel cross-culturally. You mentioned church practices. How do these link up with cultural things in the lives of Christians which, though quite natural and good to them, they should perhaps think of changing in order to reach out cross-culturally?

GW: There is the area of worship. Many Nigerian Christians enjoy worshipping God to the accompaniment of drumming and other forms of African music, movement of the body and swaying and hand-clapping. It would be, if we can use the term, a sort of charismatic, free, and enthusiastic way of worshipping God. The women like to dress up in one uniform together, and if it has a picture of Jesus on the cloth, that's great! They will march through the town wearing it, singing Gospel songs, then preach in the market place proclaiming Christ. But all those things which

189

they are doing, and the way they're singing and dressing are in fact turning Muslims off! They're not listening, because to them what the Christians are doing is unacceptable. The outward form is speaking so loudly that they can't hear the words.

RM: So you are saying that the style of worship in which Christians delight might be naturally off-putting to Muslim people?

GW: Absolutely. First of all, the Hausa Muslim will say there are things which distract a man from worshipping God. Those things are women, children, and money and they should not be to the fore when a man is worshipping God. So for a man to worship God the sexes must be segregated, women must be kept apart from men, and there must be no intermingling. A Hausa Christian has told me he's quite happy if women sit on one side of the assembly and men on the other. He doesn't insist on what the Jews insisted on, that the women be behind a screen at the back, though that too would be understandable from his cultural background. In his worship, he woud like to have some singing, but not accompanied by drums which don't fit into the Islamic concept of worship. In his worship he wants a form in which he can be impressed with the grandeur of God. It's like asking a strict Presbyterian to be happy in the Assemblies of God. Of course, it isn't easy to say that Nigerian Christians shouldn't worship with drums and hand-clapping and dancing if they want to. But this type of issue must be faced up to.

Activity
Think of our own ways of worship. Could these cause offence to Muslims? If so, what should we do about it?

Popular Perceptions
of Muslim Priests and Christian Missionaries

	MUSLIM PRIEST	CHRISTIAN MISSIONARY
IMAGE	Passive disposition	Energetic — a doer
	Subjective outlook	Objective orientation to life
	People-oriented	Task-oriented

	Financially poor (with the exception of certain *pirs*)	Regarded as wealthy — possesses a car, camera, tape recorder
	Does not attend theatre, watch television, or go to movies	Does all of these
	Does not eat in expensive restaurants	Eats in expensive restaurants (at least occasionally)
	Does not eat pork	Eats pork
	Clothing identifies him as a religious person	Clothing identifies him as a secular person
	Wears a beard	Infrequently has a beard
	Wife wears a veil or modest, culturally-approved clothing	Wife does not always dress in clothing that Muslims consider modest; thus missionary wives are identified with the 'sinful' actresses seen in Western movies and television series
MINISTRY	Mosque is focus of life	Goes to church a few hours per week
	Prays publicly five times a day	Rarely prays in public
	Fasts for one month during daylight hours	Seldom, if ever, fasts
	Constantly uses religious vocabulary	Rarely uses religious vocabulary

Does not distribute relief funds or financial aid; receives local money only	Dispenses funds from foreign sources — in the form of relief funds, jobs, training institutions, hospitals
Has no employees	Has employees and thus acquires status
Puts little value on non-Quranic education	Puts great value on formal, secular education and degrees
Memorizes vast parts of the Quran in Arabic	Memorizes very little of the Bible — in any language
Involves himself in a ministry of healing — pours consecrated water on a sick person, puts charms on the diseased, chants the Quran, says prayers	Emphasizes the scientific, not the spiritual — offers a mild prayer for the sick with little faith or conviction; people go to the missionary for medicine, not prayer

From: 'Bridges to Islam' by Phil Parshall, published by Baker Book House, Grand Rapids, Michigan. Used by permission.

5   Comments from Mr Andrew Dymond

The interview you have just read highlights many of the problems and issues found by Christians and missionaries seeking to bring Christ to Muslims anywhere in Africa, the Middle East, or Asia. There are at least four great barriers to cross in Muslim evangelism and the growth of the Church in Muslim areas. These are:

1   The initial cultural and historical separation between Muslim and Christian peoples; questions of enmity and a lack of real contact.
2   The apparent strengths of Islam; its social, political, and cultural defences; its pride in claiming to be a superior creed and successor to Christianity;

the great reverence attached to the Qur'an as 'God's Word'.

3   The isolation, persecution, and loneliness which new converts must often endure.

4   The impediments to acceptance of Muslim converts by the churches. These stem from fear of infiltration by insincere or false believers, lack of trust, cultural inflexibility, or sheer unbelief that God's Spirit can bring about the conversion of Muslims.

Because of the magnitude and complexity of these problems, the world of Islam remains one field of Christian endeavour where the westerner — whether a Christian worker, tent-making missionary or professional — still has a major contribution to make: in commending the Gospel to the Muslim heart and mind, and in bringing the indigenous local churches closer to a position of effectiveness.

Experience has shown, however, that to have a significant impact, the expatriate should be prepared to combine a broad and sensitive understanding of the host culture, with a clear and open testimony. Muslims are impressed with the lives of people who demonstrate dedication and conviction in their service to God. Followers of Christ should display integrity in all they do and, whenever possible, speak and use the Word of God naturally and forcefully in conversation. (A Muslim friend of mine in Iran impressed me with the frequency with which he used the phrase 'God says', when invoking the Qur'an to explain his beliefs and practices.)

Expatriate Christians who make friends of Muslim people will find no end to the opportunities which arise to engage them in serious discussion. They will test your knowledge of Scripture and of the basic foundations of the faith. They will also bring you into much soul-searching; they will test your love and your patience and enjoy debating with you.

God will give you these opportunities, and the Word of God, spoken 'in season', will root and grow up in the world of Islam. But Muslims first of all generally need to be convinced that you are a true follower of Jesus, and to hear that you have thought through the theological issues of the Christian faith and are yourself convinced of the absolute truth of the Gospel when tested against Muslim arguments.

6   The country of Bimbar

The second case study is of a country we will call 'Bimbar'. In

New Paths in Muslim Evangelism, Phil Parshall writes: 'Bimbar is a country that presents a special challenge to Christianity. The people of this land are almost solidly Muslim. The gospel of Christ has made little overt impact in this nation.'[5]

6:1 Our case study writer comments:

There are about 15 per cent Hindu and 85 per cent Muslim with very small percentages of Christians and animists. The Church is largely from low-caste or out-caste Hindu background. The average Muslim therefore equates becoming a Christian with becoming a Hindu and the background is of Muslim-Hindu hatred over the last thousand years. In some ways we are in a unique situation. There are Hindus and Muslims, with the Church coming from the Hindu community. You do get analogies fairly close to this in other parts of the world where Christians tend to be from a minority group, for instance the Armenians in Iran. As I sold books all over the country, people would read them and say, 'These books are just right for Hindus. Why don't you sell to them?' I couldn't understand that. We had designed these books for the Muslims, and we wanted them to *go* to the Muslims. Then very gradually we began to understand through various people, particularly one, who is a Muslim convert, that the language in which we were communicating was the Hindu dialect and it just didn't apply to the Muslims at all. There are only about 50 words which are different, but they made a startling difference.

We began to realise that people were stumbling over the stumbling block of language and culture and not the stumbling block of the cross. I do not mind people stumbling over the stumbling block of the cross, because that is something we cannot change.

Christianity is God reaching out to us rather than us reaching out to God. I feel that if there are cultural stumbling blocks in the way, however, they have got to be removed. I think this is what contextualisation means. We are not adapting the Gospel but we are changing the vehicle so that the Gospel comes through in a way that the Muslim can feel at home with it, and feel that it is 'good news' to him. We want to use forms that are, perhaps, more Muslim.

I do not believe that a person must change his culture to become a Christian unless there are things in it that are definitely anti-scriptural. Se we began, almost sub-consciously, trying to make our presentation more and more suitable to the Muslims.

The practice of contextualisation
We have had three objectives in planning our witness to Muslims:
1   Reducing offence.
2   Increasing our credibility.
3   Setting the message in context.

6:2 *Reducing offence*

We have had to find out what behaviour is offensive to the Muslim in the way we live and the way we go about doing things. We want to reduce offence by things like wearing appropriate dress, not eating pork, and making sure that we treat our scriptures with care and with honour. We have tried to avoid Hindu ways of going about things. We have not allowed pictures, for instance, on our literature; especially there are to be no pictures of Jesus, which Muslims believe to be committing idolatry. If the Bible is a holy book then we should treat it with care. We have started to use wooden stands for keeping the scriptures on in order to prevent ourselves from treating them in a casual way.

Another way we have tried to reduce offence is by our women staying at home. This has been very frustrating for some of them who want to get actively involved among Muslim women, but we have felt that it has been the right thing to do. They do not go around visiting, other than in the immediate neighbourhood.

6:3 *Increasing credibility*

One of the things we have felt has been quite important is that we should actually take a role within society, so that people have taken the role of religious teachers, a role which is understood within the society. They have worn the Muslim dress of a religious man, hired a little shop out in a village centre or market, then invited people along to these shops to talk and debate. A great part of this kind of outreach can be simple story-telling, or the telling of parables in expounding biblical themes.

Another role in society is that of a business man. Islam was spread a great deal by its business men. I think we must have some sort of role within society so that we are understood, so that we have some kind of credibility. It is possible, if someone were to join the work who had the necessary gifts, that he could have a *pir* role. That is, a Sufi style of religious master, someone who has access to God, who can lead people close to him and pray for people to be healed.

6:4 *Setting the message in context*

The third area in which we have been involved, in practice, is the setting of the message in a Muslim context. This word 'contextualise' really means just that — to set it in the way that it is understood: set it in the Muslim culture. We feel that we must, if at all possible, encourage believers within their own culture so that a self-dependent church will be able to expand through the society. A church which will be within society rather than being some outcast foreign phenomenon.

The general pattern as far as baptism is concerned is that we have tended to delay it until there is a large enough group for its members to be able to stand together. We have not felt it wise to encourage baptism at the very early stages, particularly as it is seen as being a denial of culture and of family loyalty.

Another thing we have made a strong principle is that we should not be involved financially in helping the converts in any way. The average Muslim believes that a person only becomes a Christian because he is bribed to do so. We believe that if they need a church building, then they should build it themselves. We want this newly born, or being-born church, to stand on its own feet right from the beginning; we want to be very careful that there is no financial input which influences motivation.

6:5   To summarise, here are some of the points Phil Parshall mentions in developing a new strategy for Bimbar:

> There must be a continued emphasis on the spiritual dynamic in this outreach.... New missionaries should be recruited and trained in the methodology of effective cross-cultural communication of the gospel.... Short-term or 'secular' missionaries should not be encouraged.... The house-church model should be accepted. Homes in Bimbar are centres of social activity and thus can be regularly adapted as a church. They provide privacy and require no additional financial expenditure.'[6]

Activity

Please list what you consider are the main theological and cultural barriers to Muslims becoming Christians. Before doing this look back over the course, noting Chapters 2 and 6 especially. It will also be helpful to think back over the conversations you have had with your Muslim friends.

7   In this final section the important area of how to welcome and receive Muslim converts into the church is considered.

In Lausanne Occasional Paper No 13, 'Christian Witness to Muslims', we read:

> Many Muslim converts experience the same difficulties which Saul experienced as a new convert among Christians in Damascus and Jerusalem....
>
> We therefore need to give special care and attention to discipleship training for new believers, since this can sometimes be more difficult than the initial teaching of the gospel which brought them to faith. As far as possible, this teaching should be done in the context of the family.[7]

7:1 Receiving Converts into the Church

Costly practical implications surround the matter of receiving converts into the church. Whether we are in the West or in an Islamic land, we face searching questions.

Firstly, what is our attitude to Islam as a religion? If we believe that Islam is totally demonic, and Allah an idol, we will not receive a convert's background, but try to remove him totally from it. If we believe Islam contains elements of truth and beauty, we will encourage him to retain the good elements from his religious and cultural background. We should note (in context) the Pakistani's comment that 'Protestants seem to come here because they hate Islam and Catholics because they love God.'[8]

Secondly, is the convert an illiterate farmer? Is he or she from a less educated urban society? Is he or she a highly intellectual man or woman? Our gifts and calling need to be matched, to be more appropriate. Dialogue is important, and awareness of each person's background. 'Sitting where they sit' means orientation to the way a Muslim thinks, and where possible to his poetry, his proverbs, and his sense of humour.

Thirdly, can we avoid polarisation regarding the form of church gathering into which a convert is to be welcomed? Missiologists have two different emphases, two scripturally-based approaches, which will go on being debated.

1 *Converts are brought into the fellowship of the local church*. Are we praying that the ancient Christian churches still found in Muslim lands may yet become the receivers of Muslim converts? Are we seeing the welcome of the local church less as the endeavour of one teacher with one seeker/convert, and more as the house group/open family/*team* relationship? Is not 'you' in the New Testament predominantly plural, not singular? Wherever possible in a local church, are we encouraging a long period of education towards becoming sensitive to Islamic culture and being positive about some of the ways in which Muslims live and worship? Are we aware of the convert's difficulty with non-Muslim elements? Why should a Bengali convert have to use the name Ishwar (Hindi word for God) instead of Allah? (Or khuda, Urdu word for God, for that matter.) We must listen to the testimony of convert peoples and individuals, that there is continuity between faith in Allah and faith in the God and Father of Jesus Christ.

2 *Converts are organised separately into a 'Muslim church'*, defined as a company of people committed to Jesus Christ and

the teaching of Scripture, yet remaining within the community of Islam, and retaining many of the cultural forms of Muslim society. Can we identify with a 'Muslim church' in areas where there is no local church, or where temporarily at least the local church still shows too much resistance to positive involvement? Our Bimbar case study, in this 'Muslim church' category, is part of the experimental outworking of the 'homogeneous unit' principle enunciated by Prof Donald McGavran and many others. A 'Muslim church' that lessens the cultural and social isolation of converts, may increasingly be God's pattern for the future.

7:2 Does receiving converts mean welcoming them? The task is hard because the walls of prejudice are so high. Can we come with humble recognition that Christians have dominated and fought, instead of showing the love which still covers a multitude of sins? Is there any other way than love's endeavour, love's expense? Some Muslims are willing to sacrifice far more than Christians are. Thomas à Kempis wrote, 'Jesus has many who love his kingdom in heaven, but few who bear his cross.' In the West we find it hard to have real Christian empathy with suffering people. Perhaps our greatest need is for the emptiness that can receive his love, and so receive his Muslim children.

7:3 Colin Chapman in *You Go and Do the Same*, writes:

> Do we realise the possible cost for any Muslim who wants to become a disciple of Jesus? Do we realise the possible cost for ourselves?
>
> It is a sad fact that in spite of its tolerant attitudes in many areas, Islam does not find it easy to accept the idea of a Muslim becoming a Christian. Conversion to Christianity (or to any other religion) is generally regarded as apostasy, as a betrayal of one's family and society.
>
> Muslims who express an interest in the Christian faith are often subject to strong pressures; and those who finally take the step of being baptised frequently experience opposition and hostility in the home, at work and in society. Many converts have had to leave their homes for safety, and some have been killed.[9]

The whole of this chapter, 'Muslims and Conversion,' is recommended for further consideration and study. It concludes:

198

If you know a Muslim well enough to ask him about the Muslim attitude to apostasy, he may well say that there is no such thing as a law concerning it, whether written or unwritten. This may reflect politeness on his part, or ignorance, or increasing tolerance on the part of educated Muslims. The real test, however, is what actually happens in any Muslim society when a Muslim confesses his allegiance to Jesus Christ.[10]

Recommended Reading

PARSHALL, Phil. *New Paths in Muslim Evangelism*, Baker Book House, Grand Rapids, Michigan, 1980.

Additional Reading

BENTLEY-TAYLOR, David. *Java Saga: Christian Progress in Muslim Java*, OMF Books, London, 1975. First published as *Weathercock's Reward*, 1967.

COOLEY, Frank L. 'Indonesia' section of 'The Comparative Status of Christianity and Islam in Southeast Asia', pp321–327, in *The Gospel and Islam: A 1978 Compendum*, Don M McCurry, ed, MARC, Monrovia, California, 1979.

GOLDSMITH, Martin. *Islam and Christian Witness*, Hodder and Stoughton/STL Books, London/Bromley, 1982. Recommended book for Chapter 2.

LAUSANNE OCCASIONAL PAPER NO 13. *Christian Witness to Muslims*, LCWE, Wheaton, Illinois, 1980.

SHEIKH, Bilquis. *I Dared to Call Him Father*, Kingsway Publications/STL Books, Eastbourne, Sussex/Bromley, Kent, 1978.

WILLIS, Avery T, Jr. *Indonesian Revival: Why Two Million Came to Christ*, William Carey Library, South Pasadena, California, 1977.

Notes

1 GOLDSMITH, Martin. *Islam and Christian Witness*, Hodder & Stoughton, London, 1982, p144.
2 Ibid, p145.
3 COOLEY, Frank L. 'Indonesia' section of 'The Comparative Status of Christianity and Islam in Southeast Asia', pp321–327 in *The Gos-

pel and Islam: A 1978 Compendium, Don M McCurry ed, MARC, Monrovia, California, 1979.

4 PARSHALL, Phil. *New Paths in Muslim Evangelism*, Baker Book House, Grand Rapids, Michigan, 1980, p31.

5 Ibid, p223.

6 Ibid, p229.

7 LAUSANNE OCCASIONAL PAPER NO 13, *Christian Witness to Muslims*, LCWE, Wheaton, Illinois, 1980, p18.

8 MURPHY, Dervla. *Full Tilt: From Ireland to India with a Bicycle*, Pan Books, London, 1965, p167.

9 CHAPMAN, Colin. *You Go and Do the Same*, CMS, BMMF Int, IFES, London, 1983, p55.

10 Ibid, p67.

CONCLUSION

Well friends, that's it! We hope we are friends, and that the course has been both helpful and interesting. Only time will tell how successful we have been in preparing you, or how successful you have been in assimilating the material. In one sense this is not the end but the beginning. We hope that, if you have not yet obtained the educational pack 'Committed to Action' and some or all of the recommended books, you may want to do so now. You may also want to get a small discussion group together in your church.

If you are now able to distinguish between the Abbasids and the Umayyads, that is good; if you are able to explain the difference between *ijma* and *qias*, even better; if you can see the significance of the ministries of Ramon Lull and Temple Gairdner, better still. Best of all, however, will be your lifetime of meeting Muslim friends and sharing with them what Christ means to you.

In Chapter 1 it was suggested that a basic principle of studying another religion is that our own faith should be deepened. We trust that this will be so with you and that through this strengthening of your own faith will come a greater understanding of that of your Muslim brother and sister.

In the April 1984 edition of *Evangelical Missions Quarterly*, H M Dard writes of his 'Reflections at a Muslim Grave'. He says:

> Our dogmatic proclamation, our western methodology, and our development projects must be permeated with the incarnate Christ. Let us draw near to share their grief and speak to them. We are not Christians preaching to Muslims; we are not westerners trying to communicate with easterners; we are not the developed seeking to lift the undeveloped. We are

fallen men embracing fallen men. We share their grief
so they will share the joy of his presence.[1]

It is in this spirit of our common humanity with its joys and its suf-
ferings that we have wanted to prepare you to go out, to meet
Muslims, and to share your faith with them.

> O God, to whom the Muslim world bows in homage
> five times daily, look in mercy upon its peoples and
> reveal to them thy Christ.

(Zwemer, *Call to Prayer*).

Note

1 DARD, H M. 'Reflections at a Muslim Grave', *Evangelical Missions
Quarterly*, April 1984.

BIBLIOGRAPHY

ABDUL-HAQQ, Abdiyah Akbar. *Sharing Your Faith with a Muslim,* Bethany Fellowship, Minneapolis, Minnesota, 1980.

ADDISON, J T. *The Christian Approach to the Moslem,* Columbia University Press, New York, 1942. Available in FFM Library.

AL-AZUZY, Muhammad. *Topical Concordance to Qur'an,* BCV Press, Lilydale, Australia, 2nd ed, 1981. Translated by Aubrey Whitehouse.

ANDERSON, Sir Norman. *Christianity and World Religions,* IVP, Leicester, 1984.

—. *God's Law and God's Love,* Collins, Glasgow, 1981.

—. *The Mystery of the Incarnation,* IVP, Madison, Wisconsin, 1978, Hodder and Stoughton, London, 1978.

ANGLICAN INTER-FAITH CONSULTATIVE GROUP OF THE BOARD OF MISSION AND UNITY. *Towards a Theology for Inter-Faith Dialogue,* Church Information Office, London, 1984.

ARBERRY, Arthur J. *The Koran Interpreted,* OUP, 1983.

—. *Religion in the Middle East,* CUP, 1969. Vol. 2.

BELL, Richard, and WATT, W Montgomery. *Introduction to the Qur'an,* Edinburgh University Press, Edinburgh, 1970. Bell's 1953 work revised and enlarged by Watt.

BENTLEY-TAYLOR, David. *Java Saga: Christian Progress in Muslim Java,* OMF Books, London, 1975. Originally published in 1967 under the title *Weathercock's Reward.*

—. *My Love Must Wait.* IVP, Leicester, 1975. Biography of Henry Martyn.

BOER, Harry. *A Brief History of Islam,* Daystar Press, Ibadan, 1968. Available in FFM Library.

BREWSTER, E Thomas, and BREWSTER, Elizabeth S. *Language Acquisition Made Practical,* Lingua House, Toronto, 1976.

BROCKELMANN, Carl. *History of the Islamic People,* Routledge & Kegan Paul, London, 1982.

BROWNE, L E. *Eclipse of Christianity in Asia,* CUP, 1933.

BURNETT, David. 'The Culture Factor', *Third Way,* June 15th, 1978.

CHAPMAN, Colin. *You Go and Do the Same,* CMS, BMMF Int, IFES, London, 1983.

CHRISTENSON, Jens. *The Practical Approach to Muslims,* NAM, Marseilles, 1977.

COOLEY, Frank. 'Indonesia' section of 'The Comparative Status of Christianity and Islam in Southeast Asia', pp321–327, in *The Gospel and Islam: A 1978 Compendium,* Don M McCurry, ed, MARC, Monrovia, California, 1979.

COULSON, N J. *A History of Islamic Law,* Edinburgh University Press, 1964.

CRAGG, Kenneth. *The Call of the Minaret,* OUP, 1956. New edition shortly.

—. *Muhammad and the Christian,* Darton, Longman & Todd, London, 1984.

—. *Sandals at the Mosque,* SCM Press, London, 1959.

DARD, H M. 'Reflections at a Muslim Grave', *Evangelical Missions Quarterly,* April 1984.

DAWOOD, N J. *The Koran Translated with Notes,* Penguin, Harmondsworth, Middlesex, 4th ed, 1974.

DI GANGI, Mariano, ed. *Perspectives on Mission,* BMMF International, Toronto, 1985.

DOI, Abdur Rahman. *Shari'ah: The Islamic Law,* Ta Ha Publishers, London, 1984.

DOUGLAS, J D, ed. *Let the Earth Hear His Voice,* World Wide Publications, Minneapolis, Minnesota, 1975.

EVANGELICAL ALLIANCE. *Christianity and Other Faiths,* Paternoster Press, Exeter, 1983.

EVERY, G. *Understanding Eastern Christianity,* SCM Press, London, 1980.

FAKHOURI, Hani. *Kafr el Elow: An Egyptian Village in Transition,* Holt, Rinehart and Winston, New York, 1972.

FYZEE, Asaf A A. *A Modern Approach to Islam,* OUP, Delhi, 1981.

GIBB, H A R, and KRAMERS, J H. *Shorter Encyclopedia of Islam,* E J Brill, Leiden, 1974.

GLUBB, John Bagot. *A Short History of the Arab Peoples,* Quartet Books, London, 1973.

GOLDSMITH, Martin. *Islam and Christian Witness,* Hodder & Stoughton, London, and STL Books, Bromley, 1982.

GUILLAUME, Alfred. *The Traditions of Islam,* Khayats, Beirut, 1966.

GULICK, John. *The Middle East: An Anthropological Perspective,* Goodyear Publishers, Pacific Palisades, California, 1976.

Have You Ever Read the Seven Muslim Christian Principles? Pamphlet.

HESSELGRAVE, David J. *Communicating Christ Cross-Culturally* Zondervan Publishing House, Grand Rapids, Michigan, 1978.

History of Christianity, Lion Publishing, Tring, Hertfordshire, 1977.

HUGHES, T P. *The Dictionary of Islam,* Premier Book House, Lahore, 1964.

JEFFERY, Patricia. *Frogs in a Well: Indian Women in Purdah,* Zed Press, London, 1979.

JONES, Violet Rhoda, and JONES, L Bevan. *Women in Islam,* Lucknow Publishing House, India, 1941.

KATEREGGA, Badru, and SHENK, David. *Islam and Christianity: A Dialogue,* Eerdmans, Grand Rapids, Michigan, 1980.

KHAIR-ULLAH, Frank. 'Evangelism among Muslims', pp823–824, in *Let the Earth Hear His Voice,* World Wide Publications, Minneapolis, Minnesota, 1975.

KRAFT, Charles H. *Christianity in Culture,* Orbis, Maryknoll, New York, 1979.

Lausanne Covenant, World Wide Publications, Minneapolis, Minnesota, 1975.

LAUSANNE OCCASIONAL PAPER NO 13. *Christian Witness to Muslims.* LCWE, Wheaton, Illinois, 1980.

LEWIS, Bernard. *The Arabs in History,* Hutchinson, London, 1970.

LINGS, Martin. *Muhammad,* Islamic Texts Society and George Allen & Unwin, London, 1983.

LUZBETAK, Louis J. *The Church and Cultures,* Divine Word Publications, Techny, Illinois, 1970.

MARSH, Charles R. *Too Hard for God,* Echoes of Service, Bath, 1970. Republished by Scripture Union in 1980 under the title *The Challenge of Islam.*

MAWDUDI, Abul A'la. *Towards Understanding Islam,* Islamic Foundation, Leicester, 1981.

McCURRY, Don M, ed. *The Gospel and Islam: A 1978 Compendium,* MARC, Monrovia, California, 1979.

McDOWELL, Josh. *Evidence that Demands a Verdict,* Here's Life Publishers, San Bernardino, California, 1979.

—, and GILCHRIST, John. *The Islam Debate,* Here's Life Publishers, San Bernardino, California, 1983.

MILLER, William. *A Christian Response to Islam,* STL Books, Bromley, Kent, 1981.

MUHAMMAD ALI, Maulana. *A Manual of Hadith,* Curzon Press, 1944, 3rd ed, 1978.

MURPHY, Dervla. *Full Tilt: From Ireland to India with a Bicycle,* Pan Books, London, 1965.

MUSK, Bill A. *Popular Islam: An Investigation into the Phenomenology and Ethnotheological Bases of Popular Islamic Belief and Practice,* The University of Pretoria, South Afirca, 1984.

—. 'Popular Islam: The Hunger of the Heart', pp208–221, in *The Gospel and Islam: A 1978 Compendium,* Don M McCurry, ed, MARC, Monrovia, California, 1979.

NAIPAUL, V S. *Among the Believers: An Islamic Journey,* Andre Deutsch, London, 1981.

NAZIR-ALI, Michael. *Islam: A Christian Perspective,* Paternoster Press, Exeter, 1983.

NEHLS, Gerhard. *Christians Answer Muslims,* 'Life Challenge', Capetown, 1980.

—. *Christians Ask Muslims,* 'Life Challenge', Capetown, 1980?

NEILL, Stephen. *Crises of Belief,* Hodder and Stoughton, London, 1984.

—. *History of Christian Mission,* Pelican, Penguin Books, Harmondsworth, 1964.

NIDA, Eugene. *Customs and Cultures,* William Carey Library, South Pasadena, California, 2nd ed, 1975.

—. *Religion Across Cultures,* William Carey Library, South Pasadena, California, 1979.

PADWICK, Constance. *Temple Gairdner of Cairo,* SPCK, London, 1929. Available from FFM Library.

PARRINDER, Geoffrey. *Jesus in the Qur'an,* Sheldon Press, London, 1965.

PARSHALL, Phil. *Bridges to Islam,* Baker Book House, Grand Rapids, Michigan, 1983.

—. *New Paths in Muslim Evangelism,* Baker Book House, Grand Rapids, Michigan, 1980.

PEARL, David. *A Textbook of Muslim Law,* Croom Helm, London, 1979.

PEERS, E Allison. *Fool of Love,* SCM Press, London, 1946. Biography of Ramon Lull. Available in FFM Library.

PICKTHALL, Marmaduke. *The Meaning of the Glorious Koran,* Mentor Books, New York, 1953.

PIPPERT, Rebecca Manley. *Out of the Saltshaker,* IVP, Leicester, 1979.

RHOTON, Dale. *The Logic of Faith,* STL, Bromley, Kent, 1978.

RICHARDSON, Don. *Peace Child,* Regal Books, Ventura, California, 1974.

RUNCIMAN, S. *History of the Crusades,* Penguin Books, Harmondsworth, Middlesex, 1971. 3 vols.

RUTHVEN, Malise. *Islam in the World,* Pelican, Penguin Books, Harmondsworth, Middlesex, 1984.

SARWAR, Ghulam. *Islam: Beliefs and Teachings,* Muslim Educational Trust, London, 3rd ed, 1984.

SAUNDERS, J J. *History of Medieval Islam,* Routledge & Kegan Paul, London, 1965.

SCHOOL OF ORIENTAL AND AFRICAN STUDIES. *The World of Islam: A Teacher's Handbook,* SOAS, 1977.

SHABAN, M A. *The Abbasid Revolution,* Cambridge University Press, Cambridge, 1970.

SHEIKH, Bilquis. *I Dared to Call Him Father,* Kingsway Publications/ STL Books, Eastbourne, Sussex/Bromley, Kent, 1978.

SMALLEY, William A, ed. *Readings in Missionary Anthropology,* William Carey Library, South Pasadena, California, 1974.

STACEY, Vivienne. *Henry Martyn,* Henry Martyn Institute of Islamic Studies, Hyderabad, India, 1980.

—. In *Perspectives on Mission,* Mariano Di Gangi, ed, BMMF International, Toronto, 1985.

—. *Practical Lessons for Evangelism among Muslims,* Orientdienst eV. Wiesbaden.

STOTT, John R W. *Understanding the Bible,* Scripture Union, London, 1972.

TAMES, Richard. *Approaches to Islam,* John Murray, London, 1982.

VAN DER WERFF, Lyle L. *Christian Mission to Muslims: The Record,* William Carey Library, South Pasadena, California, 1977.

VERHOEVEN, F R J. *Islam: Its Origins and Spread in Words, Maps and Pictures,* Routledge & Kegan Paul, London, 1962.

WATT, W Montgomery. *Mohammed and Mecca,* OUP, 1953.

WILLIS, Avery T, Jr. *Indonesian Revival: Why Two Million Came to Christ,* William Carey Library, South Pasadena, California, 1977.

Willowbank Report, Scripture Union, London, 1978.

WILSON, Christy. *Apostle to Islam,* Baker Book House, Grand Rapids, Michigan, 1952. Biography of Samuel Zwemer. Available in FFM Library.

WOOTTON, R W F. *Understanding Muslim Sects,* FFM, 1983.

ZWEMER, Samuel M. *Call to Prayer.*

—. *Studies in Popular Islam.*

LIST OF RELEVANT CASSETTES

ALL SOULS TAPE LIBRARY, 2 All Souls Place, London W1N 3DB.
'The Muslim and the Christian', Bishop Kenneth Cragg, J11. Series of seven.

ANCHOR RECORDINGS, 72 The Street, Kennington, Ashford, Kent TN24 9HS.
'What about Other Religions?', David Pawson, DP 210.
'From Darkness to Light', Bilquis Sheikh, AG 097.

GAIRDNER MINISTRIES, P O Box 26, Tunbridge Wells, Kent TN1 1AA.
'Josh McDowell-Ahmad Deedut Debate'. Two tapes.

JESUS TO THE MUSLIMS, 4b Bright Street, Benoni, 1500, Republic of South Africa.
Tapes, John Gilchrist. Series 4. Four tapes.

MINISTRY AMONG ASIANS IN BRITAIN. 12 Woodsley Road, Bolton BL1 5QL.
'Muslims in Britain: A Christian Response', Colin Chapman.

RED SEA MISSION TEAM, 33/35 The Grove, Finchley, London N3 1QU
Tapes, Jack Budd, set of ten, set of four, single tapes on witnessing to Muslims, Islam in Britain, Islam in this modern world.

GLOSSARY OF ARABIC WORDS

The Arabic words are transcribed approximately, as there are not exact English equivalents of each Arabic sound. As a guide to pronunciation, the (') is a glottal stop. The letter 't' is often the plural ending, but many Arabic words are now frequently used in English, and often with the English plural ending 's', e.g. Sufi, Sufis. The Arabic language is constructed from roots, which consist of three consonants. Vowels are added in different ways to make different parts of speech (adjectives, nouns, etc.).

Words are listed under the first letter of the word, but a few times the definite article 'al' appears in front of them. There is often an alternative English spelling for Arabic words ending in the 'a' sound, e.g. *surah* or *sura*. Both spellings are acceptable.

A

Abbasids	second dynasty after the Umayyads; 750–1258.
Abdullah	Muhammad's father.
Abu Bakr	First Caliph; Muhammad's successor; his uncle.
Abu Talib	Muhammad's uncle.
adda	perform a religious ritual.
adl	just, of good character. See *udul*.
Ahmad, Mirza Ghulam	founder of the Ahmadiyya sect in nineteenth century India.
Ahmadiyya	religious sect founded in the nineteenth century by Mirza Ghulam Ahmad, from Punjab, who was considered a final prophet.
akhirah	life after death.

Ali	Fourth Caliph, 656–661; married Muhammad's youngest daughter Fatima.
Allah	God.
ana	I, eg, *ana* al haqq, I (am) the truth.
al ana'an	the cattle.
ansar	helpers; plural form of *nasir*.
awliya	holy men; saints; plural form of *wali*.
ayat	verses in the Qur'an.
ayatallah	Shiite doctors of Islamic law.

B

baraka	blessing.
batil	void, not legal.
Bektashiya	a Sufi group in Turkey.
Beth Darazi	house of Darazi.
bismallah	see *bismillah*.
bismillah	in the name of God.

C

caliph	a ruler, a deputy.
caliphate	the rule of the caliph.
Chistiyya	a Sufi order in India.

D

Darazi	founder of Druze. See Beth Darazi.
Dawud	David.
Deobandi	an order of Sufis.
dervish	a Sufi miracle worker.
dhikr	repeating the names of God many times until in a trance.
dhimmi	a person of another religion, eg, a Jew or Christian.
din	religion, from the word for debt.
din al fitrah	natural religion.
diwan	under Umar, a system of registering the soldiers.
'dj'	see words at 'j'. 'dj' can be used for the Arabic sound 'j', but here all words are

210

	under 'j' only.
Druze	a Muslim sect in Lebanon.
du'a	a personal prayer.

F

faqirs	holy men; Sufis.
fassid	irregular.
Fatima	youngest daughter of Muhammad.

H

hadd	punishable offences.
hadith	traditions; the sayings of Muhammad.
hafiz	one who has memorised and is able to recite the whole Qur'an.
hajj	pilgrimage.
hajji	a person who has gone on the Pilgrimage to Mecca.
halal	lawful, legal. Opposite of *haram*.
Hanafi	the largest Sunni religious school of theology; involves India, Pakistan, Afghanistan, Iraq, Turkey, Syria, Jordan, and Lebanon; founded by Abu Hanifah.
Hanafiyya	an older Sunni religious school of theology; small, it revived in the twentieth century; takes a fundamentalist, purist view; followers are in Saudi Arabia, Libya, and Qatar, and include members of the Muslim Brotherhood; founded by Ahmad ibn Hanbal.
Hanbaliyya	followers of the Hanbali School.
hanif	a former Jewish community in Mecca.
haram	forbidden, unlawful. Opposite of *halal*.
hijra	emigration to Medina. See *muhajirun*.
hiyal	legal. See *halal*.

I

ibadat	worship.
Iblis	the devil.

ibn	son, eg, *ibn al Maryan*, son of Mary.
idda	the period of time a woman must wait between divorce and remarriage.
ijma	the consensus of the religious authorities or scholars of religious law.
Ikhwan al Muslimun	Muslim Brotherhood.
Ikhwan al Safa	Brethren of Purity; mystic poets in Basrah.
ilhamiyya	a Sufi sect; inspired of God.
imam	leader of the mosque; leader of the Shiite community.
iman	faith.
Injil	the Gospels or New Testament; the book brought by Jesus.
al insan	the man, e.g. *al insan al kamil*, the perfect man.
iqra	recite.
Isa	Jesus.
ishtirakiyya	those who share; socialism.
islah	to reform; a modernist school of reform; rationalist.
Islam	to submit; submission; surrender to the will of God or to the law of God. See Muslim.
Ismail	the seventh Shiite *imam*.
Ismailiyyah	a Shiite sect who follow Ismail, the seventh *imam*, and are thus called Seveners.
isnad	people who passed on the traditions; the chain of authority of the *hadith*.
Israfil	the name of an angel.
Ithna Ashariyyah	the major Shiite group who have 12 *imams* and thus are called the Twelvers; *ithna*, two; *ashar*, ten.
ittihadiyyah	a Sufi sect; believed to have, or to achieve, union with God.
Izra'il	the name of an angel.

J

Note: 'dj' is often seen as the transcription of the 'j' sound but is not used here.

jamaat	political party, group, class.

jamaat-i-Islam	the community of Muslims; the modern reformers, founded by *Mawlana* A A Mawdudi; a kind of 'theocracy' rather than a secular rule. See *ajma* which is from the same root word.
jamia tawhid	the ecclesiastical body of those who are believers in one God; monotheism.
jamshids	Persian rulers.
janissaries	guards of the Ottoman rulers.
Jibra'il	the angel Gabriel.
jihad	a holy war; to struggle to the best of one's ability to accomplish a job.
jinn	devils, evil spirits.
juhhal	ignorant, used of pagans.

K

al Ka'ba	the black stone at Mecca.
kafir	unbeliever, infidel.
kalima	the primary creed; the word of Islam.
kamil	perfect. See *al insan al kamil*.
karama	miracle worker.
Khadijah	Muhammad's first wife.
Kharidjite	member of the oldest religious sect; very aggressive.
khatib	court clerk.
Khatm Awliya	the seal of the saints; expression used by the Tijaniyya, Sufis of West Africa.
kufr	to cover up, conceal; to deny God.

M

madhab	a school, eg, Hanafi is one of the *madhab* of Islamic theology.
mahdi	a conqueror; a saviour who comes to rescue, to conquer, to guide.
majdhub	a holy man who has ecstatic, spontaneous illumination.
makruh	disapproved, hateful but permitted.
Maliki	the second largest school of Islamic theology; Sunni; practised in North Africa, West Africa, Kuwait, and Egypt; founded by Malik.
Malikite	a follower of the Maliki School.

Mamluks	white slave army who stopped the invading Mongols in 1260.
mandub	recommended, meritable law.
matn	the text, the body of the document.
mawlana	teacher.
Mecca	city in Saudi Arabia, Muhammad's home.
Medina	city in Saudi Arabia to which Muhammad and his followers emigrated; 200 miles north of Mecca.
Meveleviyya	Sufi order in Turkey.
Mikha'il	the angel Michael.
milla	sect; there are 72 or 73 *milla* of which 72 will go to hell and one to heaven.
monvir	announcer.
mubah	open to individual choice in following the law.
muezzin	the one who calls to prayer.
mufti	an Islamic leader; a leader of religious affairs; a legal consultant of Islamic law.
muhajirun	migrants. See *hijra*.
Muhammad	a prophet of Islam.
Munkar	the name of an angel.
Murdjites	those who hold a doctrinal position that a Muslim does not lose his faith because of sin.
murshid	leader, guide; the title of the grand master of the Sufi Brotherhood.
Musa	Moses.
Muslim	a follower of Islam. See Islam.
muta	temporary marriage.
Mutazila	a theological school that asserts that the grave sinner is neither a believer nor an unbeliever but is in an intermediate position.

N

nabi	prophet.
nadhir	warner.
Nakir	the name of an angel who visits the grave.
Nawruz	Persian New Year, 21st March.

| Nayshbandi | a Sufi order. |

Q

Note: pronounced as if a hard 'k'.

qadhf	slander.
qadi	judge, religious judge.
qadr	doctrine of predestination.
qalb	heart.
qarina	demon who appears at childbirth.
qias	measuring; reasoning by analogy to decide new issues, questions of doctrine, and practice.
qiblah	direction of the Ka'ba in Mecca.
Qur'an	the book of the revelations to Muhammad. Sometimes spelled Koran.
qurana	plural form of *qarina*.
Quraysh	Muhammad's tribe.
Qutb al Aqtab	pole of Poles; Ahmad al Tijani, an early nineteenth century Sufi.

R

raka'hs	bowing up and down in praying; prostrations.
Ramadan	the fast month; ninth month of the Muslim calendar.
rasail	letters, collection of letters.
rasul	apostle, messenger.
riba	usury.
ruh	spirit.

S

sadaqah	charity, alms.
sahih	valid, legal, true.
Salafiyyah	followers of *islah*, a rationalist, modernist group to reform and update Islam.
salat	prayer.
sawm	fasting.
Seljuks	a Turkish dynasty.

Shaban	eighth month of the Islamic year.
Shafi	the third largest school of Islamic theology; Sunni; practised in the Middle East, East Africa, lower Egypt, and Malaysia.
shahada	the creed; the confession: there is no God (or deity) but Allah and Muhammad is Allah's messenger, *La ilaha illallah wa Muhammad rasul allah.*
shariah	Islamic law based upon the Qur'an, *hadith, ijma,* and *qias.*
Shi'a	a sect; opposing Sunni; begun by Ali I.
Shiites	the followers of the Shi'a sect.
shirk	associating others with God, particularly Jesus to God; to be a polytheist, an idolater.
shurta	religious police.
sira	secret, mystery; biography of Muhammad.
suf	wool.
Sufi	Islamic mysticism legitimised by al Ghazali who died 1111 AD.
Sufiya	Sufism; internalisation of law.
sunnah	habits, customs, and sayings practised by Muhammad and his disciples; next in importance after the Qur'an.
Sunni	the major group wihtin Islam; opposite of Shi'a; the majority of Muslims are Sunni; for them the *sunnah* is a source of law with the Qur'an; schools are Hanafi, Maliki, Shafi, and Hanbali.
surah	a chapter in the Qur'an.
Surat-al-Ikhlas	*surah* 112; expresses the idea of *tawhid.*

T

tahrif	corruption, e.g. *tahrif-i-lafzi*, corruption of words, and *tahrif-i-manawi*, corruption of meaning.
Tanzimat	period of reform in Turkey, 1839.
tarikas	orders of Sufi disciples.
tawhid	monotheism, unity, doctrine of one God.
Tawrat	Torah, Books of Moses.

| Tijaniyyat | West African Sufi group who follow the Sufi teachings of Ahmad al Tijani. |

U

udul	notaries. See *adl.*
uhamiyya	protectors.
ukkal	see *uqqal.*
ulema	scholars of law.
Umar	Second Caliph.
Umayyads	the first Arab kingdom; rulers from 661–750 AD in Damascus.
ummah	the nation; the community of believers.
uqqal	the learned.
Uthman	Third Caliph, 644–656.

W

Wahabi	an eighteenth century reform movement which dominates Saudi Arabia; no saints, no tombs.
wahy	inspiration; revelation.
wajib	compulsory; binding.
wali	holy man. Singular form of *awliya.*
wudu	ritual washing; cleansing before prayer.

Z

Zabur	Psalms.
Zaidiyyah	a religious sect founded by Zaid.
zakat	alms; two-and-one-half per cent of one's income to be used to help the poor, build mosques, care for travelling guests.